Staging Reform, Reforming the Stage

Staging Reform, Reforming the Stage

PROTESTANTISM AND POPULAR THEATER

IN EARLY MODERN ENGLAND

HUSTON DIEHL

Cornell University Press

ITHACA AND LONDON

Cornell University Press gratefully acknowledges a
subvention from the University of Iowa,
which aided in the publication of this book.

First published 1997 by Cornell University Press.

Printed in the United States of America

This book is printed on Lyons Falls Turin Book, a paper that is
totally chlorine-free and acid-free.

Library of Congress Cataloging-in-Publication Data

Diehl, Huston, b. 1948
   Staging reform, reforming the stage : Protestantism and popular theater in
Early Modern England / Huston Diehl.
      p.   cm.
   Includes bibliographical references and index.
   ISBN 0-8014-3303-7 (alk. paper)
   1. English drama—Early modern and Elizabethan, 1500–1600—History and
criticism.   2. Protestantism and literature—History—16th century.
3. Protestantism and literature—History—17th century.   4. English drama—
17th century—History and criticism.   5. English drama (Tragedy)—History and
criticism.   6. Theater—Religious aspects—Christianity.   7. Theater—England—
History—16th century.   8. Theater—England—History—17th century.
9. Renaissance—England.   10. Aesthetics, British.   I. Title.
PR658.P724D54   1997
822'.051209382—DC20   94-41169

Cloth printing   10 9 8 7 6 5 4 3 2 1

For Jerry

Contents

List of Illustrations   ix

Acknowledgments   xi

A Note on Editorial Practice   xv

Introduction   1

1   The Drama of Iconoclasm   9

2   The Rhetoric of Reform   40

3   Censoring the Imaginary: The Wittenberg Tragedies   67

4   Rehearsing the Eucharistic Controversies:
The Revenge Tragedies   94

5   Ocular Proof in the Age of Reform: *Othello*   125

6   Iconophobia and Gynophobia: The Stuart Love Tragedies   156

7   The Rhetoric of Witnessing: *The Duchess of Malfi*   182

Epilogue   213

Bibliography   219

Index   231

Illustrations

1. *Pilgrimage to the New Church at Regensburg.* Michael Ostendorfer (c. 1519).　　10

2. "The ninth booke containyng the Actes and thynges done in the reigne of kyng Edward the 6." John Foxe, *Actes and Monuments.*　　12

3. "The Martyrdome of John Cardmaker Preacher, and John Warne Upholster. An. 1555. May. 30." John Foxe, *Actes and Monuments.*　　47

4. "Three Martyrs hangeth for takyng downe the Roode of Dovercourt. An. 1532." John Foxe, *Actes and Monuments.*　　48

5. "The order and maner of burnyng M. Martin Bucers and Paulus Phagius bones, and also of their Bookes, with a solemne generall procession, at Cambridge. Anno. 1557. February. 6." John Foxe, *Actes and Monuments.*　　50

6. Frontispiece to the second volume. John Foxe, *Actes and Monuments.*　　51

7. *Dance Round the Golden Calf.* Lucas van Leyden (c. 1530).　　55

8. *The Four Apostles.* Albrecht Dürer (1526).　　56

9. *Lucretia* and *Judith.* Lucas Cranach (c. 1537).　　60

10. "The foolishnes of Transubstantiation." Thomas Jenner, *The Soules Solace.*　　116

11. "A Table describyng the burning of Byshop Ridley and Father Latymer at Oxford, Doct. Smith there preachyng at

the tyme of theyr Martyrdome." John Foxe, *Actes and Monuments.*   187

12. "The burnyng of John Frith, and Andrew Hewet." John Foxe, *Actes and Monuments.*   188

13. "The burnyng of Maister John Hoper Byshop at Gloucester. Anno. 1555. February. 9." John Foxe, *Actes and Monuments.*   189

14. "Martyrs burned in various ways." Antonio Gallonio, *De S.S. Martyrum Cruciatibus.*   190

15. "The burning of the Archbishop of Cant. D. Tho. Cranmer, in the Towndich at Oxford, with his hand first thrust into the fire, wherewith he subscribed before." John Foxe, *Actes and Monuments.*   192

16. "The order and manner of the burning of Anne Askew, John Lacelles, and others, with certayne of the Counsell sitting in Smithfield." John Foxe, *Actes and Monuments.*   194

Acknowledgments

I have incurred many debts in the process of writing this book. Kathleen Ashley, Gail Gibson, and Sarah Stanbury expressed an early interest in my project and encouraged me to pursue it. Their perspective as medievalists interested in early English religious drama was invaluable to me as I began to think about religion and the secular drama of early modern England. Mary Lou Emery and Dee Morris also provided invaluable support, giving insightful critiques of work in progress and meeting regularly with me to discuss readings in symbolic anthropology and cultural theory. I trust each knows how much I gained from the many long walks we took together while I was writing this book. Miriam Gilbert, Dennis Moore, and Alvin Snider read portions of this manuscript and offered valuable suggestions. I am especially grateful to Alan Nagel, who read the entire manuscript with extraordinary care, deftly offering incisive criticism. I am also indebted to my readers at Cornell University Press, Frances Dolan and Donna Hamilton, for their astute and very helpful suggestions for revision.

For their advice and support over many years, I thank David Bevington, Ernest Gilman, and Dale B. J. Randall. For sharing their understanding of early modern drama and culture with me, I thank Karen Cunningham, Anthony Dawson, Robert Knapp, Debora Shuger, and Gary Taylor. For their feedback on my reading of Calvin and Reformation theology, I thank Brian Armstrong, Catherine Coats, Diane Mowrey, Kees van der Kooi, and James Weiss. I appreciate as well the many thoughtful responses to my work that I received from seminar participants, fellow panelists, and audience members at the annual conferences of the Shakespeare Association of America (1991, 1992, 1993, 1994, 1995), the Sixteenth-Century Studies Society (1992, 1993), the

Renaissance Society of America (1991), the Renaissance Society of America of Southern California (1988) and of the Southeast (1990), the Sister Arts Conference (1990), the International Congress of Medieval Studies (1990), and Loyola College of Baltimore (1994).

My work on religion and the drama of early modern England grew out of a number of graduate seminars I taught at the University of Iowa, and I am grateful for the critical insights and probing questions of my students. As participants in an evolving Renaissance Reading Group, many of them—including Bryan Crockett (whose recent book on sermons and plays I proudly cite in this book), Elizabeth Dietz, Eric Griffin, Nancy Hayes, Mary Lindroth, Mary Metzger, Kate Moncrief, Robert Morey, Pat Ryan, Kim Smith, and Katie Stavreva—read and responded to portions of my manuscript. I also wish to thank my research assistants, William Dix, John Hoppe, and Lera Smith, who approached their task of reading obscure, sixteenth-century theological tracts with unflagging energy; Larry McCauley, who devoted a summer to updating my computer files and bibliography; Jessica Renaud, who carefully checked my citations and proofs; and Kazuko Shimuzu, who helped with the index.

Much of this book was written with the support of a University of Iowa Faculty Scholar Award. From 1987 to 1990, I was fortunate to be part of a community of scholars housed at the University of Iowa Center for Advanced Studies. Thanks to its director, Jay Semel, and his assistant, Lorna Olson, for all they did to make my sojourn there pleasant and productive. I also thank John Raeburn and Ed Folsom, who, as chairs of the English Department at the University of Iowa, allocated funds for numerous research trips to the Folger Shakespeare Library. I am grateful to the staff members of the Folger for their friendly assistance.

An earlier version of Chapter 3 originally appeared in *The Journal of Medieval and Renaissance Studies* (now *The Journal of Medieval and Early Modern Studies*); of Chapter 4 in *Renaissance Drama*; of Chapter 6, in *English Literary Renaissance*. In addition, small portions of Chapters 2 and 6 appeared in *Renaissance Papers*. I thank the editors of these journals for permission to use revised forms of my essays.

Finally, I could not have written this book without the support of my family. Thanks to my daughter, Susannah, and my stepdaughter, Jamian, for helping out in many small ways, as well as for tolerating with such good humor a mother sometimes more attentive to early modern culture than to their own postmodern one. My greatest debt is to my husband, Jerry Wetlaufer. I don't know whether to marvel more at his ability to solve every imaginable computer glitch or his sustained enthusiasm for a project its author sometimes doubted. This book is dedicated to him.

H. D.

A Note on Editorial Practice

Original orthography has been retained in all quotations from early modern texts and facsimile editions, except that I have modernized *i, j, u,* and *v.*

For the reader's convenience I refer as much as possible to the modern edition of John Foxe's *Actes and Monuments,* ed. Stephen Reed Cattley (London, 1837–41). All references to *A&M* are to this edition. When I do cite sixteenth-century editions of Foxe, I add the date to my abbreviation: *A&M* (1563), *A&M* (1570). In general, I use the modern edition and translation of John Calvin's *Institutes of the Christian Religion,* trans. Ford Lewis Battles, ed. John T. McNeill, 2 vols. (Philadelphia: Westminster, 1960). I abbreviate this edition as *Institutes.* On the few occasions when I cite the 1562 English edition of the *Institutes* translated by Thomas Norton, I include this date.

When quoting from the dramatic texts, I have omitted full citations of passages of less than a line of blank verse to avoid excessive editorial interruptions that might impede the flow of my argument.

Staging Reform, Reforming the Stage

Introduction

In this book I argue that Elizabethan and Jacobean drama is both a product of the Protestant Reformation—a reformed drama—and a producer of Protestant habits of thought—a reforming drama. Drawing on the insights of symbolic anthropologists who believe that religious practices help shape both individual consciousness and cultural forms,[1] I show how the popular London theater that flourished in the years after Elizabeth reestablished Protestantism in England rehearses the religious crisis that disrupted, divided, energized, and in many ways revolutionized English society.

In the city of London, where the Edwardian reformers had attracted a significant number of Protestant sympathizers and the conditions of urban life predisposed citizens to embrace the new Protestant ideology, Elizabeth's ascension opened the way for intense and highly visible reform activity. Much of this activity was iconoclastic in the broadest sense, attacking the religious practices, as well as the sacred images, of the old religion and declaring many forms of popular piety idolatrous. Learned treatises argued that the doctrine of transubstantiation turned the eucharistic bread and wine into idols. Popular ballads satirized the Roman Mass, mocking its spectacle as trumpery and condemning its theatricality as trickery. Protestant sermons and catechisms taught that the relics, processions, and ceremonies of the old religion were superstitious, their efficacy fraudulent and illusory. Calvinist polemics denounced the human imagination and all its products as corrupt and untrustworthy. Commissioners responsible for carrying out the 1559

---

[1] See, for example, Clifford Geertz, *The Interpretation of Cultures* (1973); Victor Turner, *The Ritual Process* (1969) and *Dramas, Fields, and Metaphors* (1974).

Injunctions officially removed and systematically destroyed the sacred images of the traditional Church. And iconoclasts, sometimes in mob riots, smashed, burned, and defaced holy images, often mocking their supposed power.[2] Early Protestantism thus nurtured a deep distrust of the visible, the theatrical, and the imaginary.

Elizabethan and Jacobean tragedy emerged as a cultural form around the time that the reformers succeeded in suppressing the popular religious cycle drama. It flourished during a period when the English Church substituted new forms of religious rituals and practices in place of the forbidden Mass, the outlawed ceremonies, and the discredited images of the medieval Church. And it was produced at a time when a form of state censorship forbade the dramatization of explicitly religious material in the public playhouses.[3] Furthermore, its playwrights were among the first Englishmen to live their entire lives in a predominantly Protestant culture. And its audiences, comprising a wide spectrum of society, were required by law to practice the new religion.[4] Many of them must have also actively embraced Protestantism, for the citizens of London were among the first and most ardent English Protestants.[5]

It would therefore be surprising if the drama were not shaped in part by Reformation controversies—and if it did not participate in shaping its audience's understanding of religious reform. How are we to understand the extraordinary popularity of the theater in a city where Calvinist teaching and Protestant preaching also flourish? What might be the relation between the suppression of late medieval religious culture, with its well-established forms of popular piety, its rituals, symbols,

---

[2] For discussions of Protestant iconoclasm in England, see Margaret Aston, *England's Iconoclasts*, vol. 1: *Laws against Images* (1988); Eamon Duffy, *The Stripping of the Altars* (1992); and John Phillips, *The Reformation of Images* (1973).

[3] See, for example, Harold C. Gardiner, *Mysteries' End* (1946), and Annabel Patterson, *Censorship and Interpretation* (1984).

[4] According to Patrick Collinson, *The Religion of Protestants* (1982), p. 207, "The Act of Uniformity required attendance on Sundays and holy days, morning and evening, of 'all and every person and persons inhabiting within this realm,' not having lawful or reasonable excuse to be absent."

[5] For discussions of the local reception of the Reformation, see Christopher Haigh, ed., *The English Reformation Revised* (1987). Other important historical studies on the reception of Protestantism in England include Patrick Collinson, *The Birthpangs of Protestant England* (1988); Maria Dowling and Peter Lake, eds., *Protestantism and the National Church in Sixteenth-Century England* (1987); Peter Lake, *Moderate Puritans and the Elizabethan Church* (1982); and J. J. Scarisbrick, *The Reformation and the English People* (1984).

plays, processions, and devotional practices, and the emergence of a popular theater under the Protestant monarchs Elizabeth and James? In what ways might the tragedies of the English Renaissance stage rehearse the drama—and the trauma—of reform? And in what ways might they be agents of reform, destabilizing their audiences' relation to images and nurturing new, Protestant ways of seeing?

Using as my central texts the tragedies of Kyd, Marlowe, Shakespeare, Middleton, and Webster, I demonstrate that Elizabethan and Jacobean dramatists represent, reflect on, and sometimes seek to redress the ruptures caused by the English Reformation.[6] My focus is on what Clifford Geertz identifies as "the disruptive, disintegrative, and psychologically disturbing" aspects of religion, for in the period of English history I consider, religion was neither a stable nor a unifying influence, but rather the very "center and source of stress" in English society.[7] Contending that Renaissance tragedies employ a Protestant rhetoric that is both destabilizing and transformative, I treat the drama of Elizabethan and Jacobean London as one arena in which the disruptions, conflicts, and radical changes wrought by the Protestant Reformation are pub-

---

[6] Victor Turner provides a paradigm for understanding the relation between the English Reformation—a social drama of enormous magnitude—and the tragedies of the commercial London stage—understood to be cultural performances—that were produced in Elizabethan and Jacobean England. Using the term *social drama* to refer to any discrete "sequence of social interactions of a conflictive, competitive or agonistic type," he believes that social dramas "provide the 'raw stuff' " out of which theater and other cultural genres emerge, and he argues that cultural performances of various types—judicial, religious, aesthetic—function during the redressive phase of a social drama to symbolically replicate and mediate the events of the breach and crisis phases. Far from being transparent reflections of reality, they thus interpret social conflicts and shape their audiences' understanding of them. See *The Anthropology of Performance* (1987), pp. 33, 42; see also *Drama, Fields, and Metaphors*, pp. 32–43.

[7] Geertz, *Interpretation of Cultures*, pp. 143, 164. Even though revisionist historians emphasize the divisiveness of the Reformation, literary scholars have to a remarkable extent disregarded the contested nature of sixteenth-century Christianity. Many who examine the Christian elements of Renaissance drama ignore Reformation controversies altogether, instead choosing to treat Christianity as a single, unified religion and to focus on archetypes, myths, and biblical narratives that are shared by all Christian faiths. Roy W. Battenhouse cites Aquinas fifty-four times, but Calvin only six times in *Shakespearean Tragedy: Its Art and Its Christian Premises* (1969); in *Christian Ritual and the World of Shakespeare's Tragedies* (1976), Herbert R. Coursen Jr. mentions the Reformation once, and—inexplicably, given the heightened attention to different interpretations of the sacraments during the Reformation—deliberately focuses on the aspects of the eucharist that Roman Catholics and Protestants of all persuasions share; and in *Shakespeare's Religious Background* (1973) Peter Milward concentrates on biblical echoes in Shakespeare without regard to sixteenth- and seventeenth-century controversies about the Bible and its interpretation.

licly explored. I am particularly interested in the religious controversies surrounding the images and rituals of the medieval Church because the issues they raise—about representation, art, theatricality, spectacle, interpretation, and imagination—so clearly pertain to the drama.[8]

An intense interest in images and acts of seeing manifests itself in the tragedies of the Elizabethan and Jacobean stage, an interest that I wish to locate in the reformers' struggle to suppress a persistent iconophilia among the English people. Characters in these plays treat skulls, corpses, and bloodied tokens of the dead as religious relics, displaying, cherishing, and holding onto them (*The Spanish Tragedy* and *The Revenger's Tragedy*). They gaze devoutly on and even kiss paintings, paintings that are eventually poisoned in order to kill the person who adores them (*Arden of Feversham* and *The White Devil*). They trust in the magical efficacy of artifacts such as handkerchiefs (*Othello*). They find themselves unable to distinguish between the dramatic representation of a killing and literal killing (*The Spanish Tragedy* and *Women Beware Women*). And, with the spectators in the theater, they gaze upon supernatural and man-made images that are, variously, seductive, haunting, illusory, meaningful, ambiguous, deceptive, dangerous, and even fatal (e.g., *Doctor Faustus, Hamlet, Macbeth, The Duchess of Malfi*).

In attending so closely to the nature and function of images, including their own theatrical images, the English Renaissance tragedies thus engage a cluster of issues that arise from specific religious controversies raging in the sixteenth century and have broad cultural implications. The English reformers' systematic campaigns to rid the churches of all taint of idolatry and superstition directly challenged the complex system of symbols by which people in the late Middle Ages understood their world. By instituting radical changes in the religious practices of the English people and destroying almost all the sacred symbols on which late medieval lay piety was centered, the Reformation disrupted and transformed established modes of perception and knowledge as well, affecting the way the English people viewed images, engaged in ritual practices, interpreted the physical world, and experienced theater.[9]

[8] For a provocative discussion of the way these issues inform epic poetry, see Linda Gregerson, *The Reformation of the Subject: Spenser, Milton, and the English Protestant Epic* (1995).

[9] In his critique of anthropologists who treat religion as static and ahistorical, Clifford Geertz shows how religion is sometimes the source of social conflict, and he argues that

Elizabethan and Jacobean tragedies articulate the anxieties created by Protestant assaults on late medieval piety, but I do not believe that they are hostile to Protestantism or particularly sympathetic to the old religion. Although they sometimes stage the forbidden rituals and spectacles of the traditional Church, they typically do so in order to demystify and contain them. They sometimes celebrate the magic of the theater, but they are much more likely to expose both magic and older forms of theatricality as fraudulent. And although they sometimes mourn the loss of beloved images and familiar rituals, many also endorse and even engage in acts of iconoclasm.

Nor do I think that the reformed religion is inherently antitheatrical. Even though the reformers condemn the theatricality of the Roman Church, a theatricality they associate with externals, hypocrisy, and seduction, they rely heavily on dramatic genres and theatrical modes of presentation, and they develop their own dramatic forms to replace the "idolatrous" spectacle and theatricality of the Roman Church.[10] The reformed ritual of the Lord's Supper, public acts of iconoclasm, polemical narratives of Protestant martyrdom, and the internal drama of conscience, all are highly theatrical and all are appropriated by the playwrights of the secular stage. By inspiring new kinds of rituals, spectacles, and dramas, the reformed religion, I argue, contributes to the formation of a uniquely Protestant theater in early modern England.

A number of scholars have recently called into question the widely held assumption that Protestant reformers are universally opposed to the stage. Their work provides substantial evidence that Calvinists, puritans, and militant Protestants were playwrights, playgoers, and patrons of theater, as well as antitheatricalists. In *Theatre and Reformation* Paul

---

it has the capacity to tear apart a society and even to transform it. He is particularly attentive to the way religious crises disrupt what he calls "the complex of received cultural patterns . . . one has for mapping the empirical world." Arguing that the concrete symbols of a religious system "induce dispositions in human beings and formulate . . . general ideas of order," as well as relate a culture's metaphysics to its ethics and aesthetics, he sees any threat to their integrity as traumatic. Because he believes that humans are utterly dependent upon symbols, he argues that any sustained challenge to a symbol system such as religion arouses "the gravest sort of anxiety" and "tends to lead to a deep disquiet." If, as Geertz theorizes, religion both explains the world to its practitioners and shapes their experience of it, then the reformation of religion in the sixteenth century necessarily altered the way the English people interpreted and experienced the physical world, transforming their fundamental "sense of the reasonable, the practical, the humane, and the moral." See Geertz, *Interpretation of Cultures*, pp. 100, 98, 99, 100, 124.

[10] See, for instance, Ritchie Kendall, *The Drama of Dissent* (1986).

White convincingly demonstrates that there was a well-established tradition of Protestant playwriting, patronage, performance, and play-
going in mid-sixteenth-century England. Although he does not address
the impact of this didactic, polemical, Calvinist, and vehemently anti-
Catholic dramatic tradition on the development of the drama written
for the commercial Elizabethan and Jacobean theaters, he lays the
groundwork for just such a study.[11]

Other scholars have established significant ties between the dramatists of the commercial London stage and the reformed religion. In her
book *Puritanism and Theater: Thomas Middleton and Opposition Drama under the Early Stuarts,* Margot Heinemann argues that Thomas Middleton
had strong ties to parliamentary puritanism, as did many patrons of the
stage, and she points out that the best-known *defenses* of the stage were
written by men with puritan sympathies.[12] Her argument that Middleton was a moderate puritan or Calvinist has since been developed by
John Strachniewski, Gary Taylor, and Albert H. Tricomi.[13] In her book
on Thomas Dekker, Julia Gasper asserts that Marlowe, Chapman, Heywood, Webster, Fletcher, and Massinger, as well as Dekker, "were all
involved with the cause [of militant Protestantism] from time to time,"
and she shows how Dekker's plays, especially, "participate energeti-
cally in religious-political affairs, attacking, defending, or satirizing, and
always stirring up support for the protestant cause at home and
abroad."[14] And Donna Hamilton argues in *Shakespeare and the Politics of
Protestant England* that many patrons of Shakespeare's theater were
"sympathetic to Puritanism" and even leaders in "Calvinist protestant
politics."[15]

Although since the early 1980s students of early modern drama have
tended to focus either on the politics of monarchy and state or on
issues of race, class, gender, and sexuality, there has been a growing

---

[11] Paul White, *Theatre and Reformation* (1993). For additional studies of early Tudor
drama and the reformed religion, see also Mark Brietenberg, "Reading Elizabethan Iconicity" (1988); James C. Bryant, *Tudor Drama and Religious Controversy* (1984); John N. King,
English Reformation Literature (1982); and Robert S. Knapp, *Shakespeare—The Theater and the
Book* (1989).

[12] Margot Heinemann, *Puritanism and Theater* (1980), pp. 18–52.

[13] John Stachniewski, "Calvinist Psychology in Middleton's Tragedies" (1990); Gary
Taylor, "Forms of Opposition: Shakespeare and Middleton" (1994); and Albert H. Tricomi, *Anticourt Drama in England 1603–1642* (1989).

[14] Julia Gasper, *The Dragon and the Dove* (1990), pp. 9–10.

[15] Donna Hamilton, *Shakespeare and the Politics of Protestant England* (1992), pp. 20–23.

awareness that the religious beliefs and practices, as well as the religious institutions, of Elizabethan and Jacobean England inform all these concerns. Building on studies of sixteenth- and seventeenth-century religious literature by Barbara Lewalski, Ernest Gilman, and Debora Shuger, among others, scholars have begun to explore in earnest the impact of religion on the secular stage.[16] Some, including Bryan Crockett, Stephen Greenblatt, Jeffrey Knapp, Martha Tuck Rozett, and James Siemon, specifically seek to illuminate the relation between the theology of early Protestantism and the aesthetics of Renaissance drama, a project I take up here.[17]

My book has seven chapters. The first two are introductory. Chapter 1 gives a historical account of the Protestant reformers' responses to a pronounced iconophilia in Reformation England. Focusing on narratives of iconoclasm from John Foxe's influential *Actes and Monuments,* I show how Foxe's inherently dramatic historiography engages the central dialectics of Reformation culture. Chapter 2 demonstrates that early Protestant artists, as well as Protestant polemicists like Foxe, employ a revolutionary rhetoric that reinterprets the sacred genres and images of the traditional Church and depicts scenes of martyrdom and iconoclasm as powerful and even spectacular theater. In both chapters I identify specific rhetorical strategies Protestant writers and artists use to stage reform, strategies that I believe are appropriated by Renaissance playwrights.

In the remaining five chapters, I turn to the tragedies themselves in order to explore some of the ways the Reformation, with its radical critique of late medieval popular piety, its iconoclastic violence against

---

[16] Barbara Lewalski, *Protestant Poetics and the Seventeenth-Century Religious Lyric* (1979); Ernest Gilman, *Iconoclasm and Poetry in the English Renaissance* (1986); Debora Shuger, *Habits of Thought in the English Renaissance* (1990).

[17] In *The Play of Paradox* (1996), Crockett discusses the relation between the rhetoric of Protestant sermons and Renaissance plays; Greenblatt, who is currently writing about the eucharist and cultural memory, treats the Catholic ritual of exorcism in his essay on *King Lear* in *Shakespearean Negotiations* (1988); arguing that the "Elizabethans were capable of regarding the theater as a spiritually valuable institution," Knapp analyzes the Protestant aesthetics of Shakespeare's history plays in "Preachers and Players in Shakespeare's England" (1993), p. 33; Rozett, *The Doctrine of Election and the Emergence of Elizabethan Tragedy* (1984), finds a "rhetoric of the elect" operating in Elizabethan moralities and tragedies, and she argues that the Calvinist doctrine of election influences the development of the tragic protagonist; Siemon, *Shakespearean Iconoclasm* (1985), shows how Shakespeare employs an iconoclastic rhetoric that complicates and problematizes the iconic elements of his plays and destabilizes his audiences.

the devotional images of the Roman Church, and its suppression of the Roman Mass and popular religious drama, stimulates theatrical production. In Chapter 3 I show that Elizabethan and Jacobean drama reflexively addresses the reformers' inquiry into the legitimacy of the theater, exploring Protestant-induced fears that plays seduce and corrupt their audiences. I then examine some of the ways Marlowe in *Doctor Faustus* and Shakespeare in *Hamlet* reconcile their own theatrical art with the reformers' efforts to censor the theatrical, spectacular, and imaginary. In Chapter 4 I analyze the distinctive habits of mind that the Roman Mass, on the one hand, and the reformed Lord's Supper, on the other, induce in their worshipers, and I show how Elizabethan and Jacobean revenge tragedies—with their intense exploration of mystery and representation—rehearse the crucial differences between these competing ritual experiences. Chapter 5 argues that early modern tragedies represent a world filled with false and demonic as well as divine signs, engaging their spectators directly in the problem of interpretation. By confronting their own audiences with visible signs of indeterminate meaning, these plays arouse a troubling anxiety about how to interpret both the theater and the theater of the world. Chapter 6 focuses on representations of erotic love and marriage in Stuart love tragedies, showing how they interrogate the fatal identification of images and women in early Protestant culture. Contending that stage violence against the female beloved rehearses the trauma of iconoclasm, I show how these tragedies reflexively examine their own erotic power, employing an antitheatrical rhetoric that is profoundly disturbing. Finally, in Chapter 7, I analyze the way Webster appropriates a Protestant rhetoric of witnessing in *The Duchess of Malfi*, nurturing in his own spectators a self-reflexivity that can best be understood in terms of Calvinist theories of the conscience. In all five chapters I argue that Shakespeare and his fellow dramatists, in their struggle against the antitheatricalists to legitimize the theater, develop a Protestant aesthetics, thereby reforming the stage.

CHAPTER ONE

The Drama of Iconoclasm

But now may we see,
What gods they be,
　　Even puppets, maumats and elfes:
Throw them downe thryse,
They can not aryse,
　　Not onse, to helpe them selves.
　　　　　　　　　　—William Gray, "The Fantasy of Idolatry"

Roman and Reformed Spectacles

A remarkable print by Michael Ostendorfer, made sometime between 1519 and 1521, records the intensely emotional veneration of the *Schöne Maria* of Regensburg, a
painting of the Madonna declared in 1519 to have miraculous power
(Figure 1). In Ostendorfer's print, throngs of pilgrims push through
the door of the New Church of Regensburg, where the marvelous painting can be seen on the back wall. Others surround a statue of the virgin
placed on a column at the front of the church, their adoration of it
frenzied and passionate. A woman kneels in prayer. Some men crowd
the base of the column, embracing it as they look up at the image in
awe. Dazed pilgrims lift their arms to the statue in supplication. Others
fall prostrate before it as if in a trance or overcome by religious rapture.
Ostendorfer is not exaggerating the fervor of the pilgrims who came
to Regensburg to worship the *Schöne Maria* in the early part of the
sixteenth century. According to Michael Baxandall, who discusses the
outpouring of emotion elicited by this particular image, "the pilgrims
came in thousands, often whole villages together; some elected to come
naked, others on their knees; visions and wonders increased . . . crowds
danced howling around the statue."[1] So many people wished to see the
wonderful image and hoped to benefit from its miraculous power that

---

[1] Michael Baxandall, *The Limewood Sculptors of Renaissance Germany* (1980), p. 84.

FIGURE 1. *Pilgrimage to the New Church at Regensburg.* Michael Ostendorfer (c. 1519). By permission of the Graphische Sammlung Albertina, Vienna.

more than one hundred thousand clay pilgrimage badges, and almost ten thousand silver ones, were manufactured in 1520 to meet the demand of pilgrims eager to possess a replica of it.[2]

A. L. Meyer identifies such devotion, typical of late medieval lay culture, with a "purely bodily seeing," a mode of vision based on the belief that the sight of certain images "made present the holy, and by looking, one received both spiritual healing and salvation." Elaborating on Meyer's discussion of medieval modes of vision, R. W. Scribner describes such "bodily seeing" as "a superstitious seeing close to magic, entailing a belief in the efficacy and power of the viewing itself."[3] For many laypeople, Scribner and Meyer emphasize, a sacred image like the *Schöne Maria* provided access to divine power and the very act of gazing upon it was curative and salvific.

An illustration in John Foxe's 1570 edition of *Actes and Monuments*, depicting "Actes and thynges done in the reigne of kyng Edward the 6," only a quarter of a century after Ostendorfer's pilgrims flocked to Regensburg, gives a startlingly different version of sixteenth-century popular piety (Figure 2). In it, sacred images are being hauled out of a church and loaded onto a boat identified as "the ship of the Romish Church." An inscription explains that the men and women who board the ship, their holy images in tow, are "the Papistes packing away their paultrye." Another inscription refers to the images as "trinkets." In the background one man pulls down a statue decorating the exterior of the church while others gather around a huge bonfire, burning images. Beneath this iconoclastic scene is the interior of a church, labeled "The Temple well purged." There, King Edward reaches out for a copy of the Bible being offered by one of his counselors while Protestant worshipers listen to a preacher in a church utterly devoid of images. Only a plain, unadorned "Communion Table" and a baptismal font stand where the altar, altarpiece, rood screens, statues, and other images of the medieval Church once stood.

Foxe's illustration records—and seeks to inculcate—a strikingly different mode of seeing than that practiced by the Regensburg pilgrims. Privileging the word of God over the man-made images of the Roman Church, it declares devotional images like the *Schöne Maria* to be idols,

[2] See David Freedberg's discussion of the cult of the *Schöne Maria* in *The Power of Images* (1989), pp. 100–104.

[3] R. W. Scribner, *For the Sake of Simple Folk* (1981), p. 4. Meyer is quoted in Scribner.

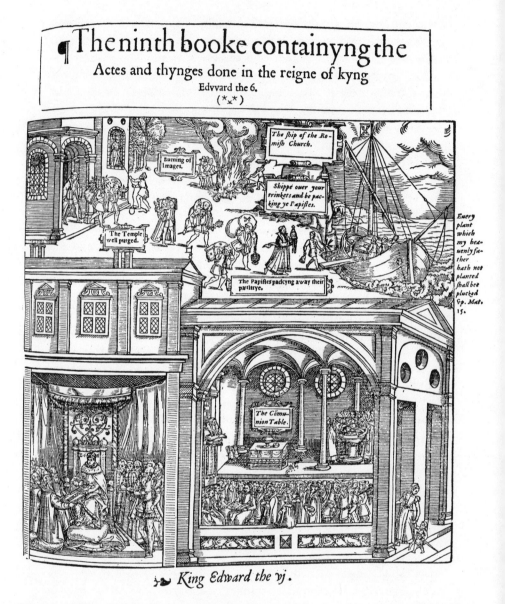

¶ The ninth booke containyng the
Actes and thynges done in the reigne of kyng
Edvvard the 6.
(*ₓ*)

King Edward the vj.

FIGURE 2. "The ninth booke containyng the Actes and thynges done in the reigne of kyng Edward the 6." John Foxe, *Actes and Monuments* (London, 1570), p. 1483. By permission of the University of Iowa Libraries (Iowa City).

nothing more than trivial diversions and worthless trash, and it presents their systematic removal from the churches as a purgation, a welcome and beneficial cleansing of polluted objects. It depicts a sanctuary purified of images, save two simple objects, the baptismal font and communion table. Rather than functioning as miraculous images that inspire awe or provide access to divine power, they serve in the newly reformed church as representational signs, reminding worshipers of spiritual rebirth and Christian redemption. Celebrating iconoclasm, Foxe's illustration encourages a meditative or transcendent kind of seeing. Its images elicit spiritual reflection by calling to mind what is absent, promised, or invisible and pointing to a world beyond the physical.

Because of the ultimate success of the English Reformation, there is a tendency among students of early modern England to think of the kind of popular piety represented in Ostendorfer's print as a fifteenth-century phenomenon, a defining characteristic of late medieval spirituality that was—as Foxe's illustration implies—completely eradicated at a relatively early stage of reform, replaced by preaching and Bible reading. Christopher Haigh, J. J. Scarisbrick, Eamon Duffy, and other revisionist historians, however, have recently questioned this premise. Haigh and Scarisbrick document popular resistance to religious reform, showing that it was often intense and persistent, continuing in some parts of England during Elizabeth's reign.[4] Duffy rejects the work of earlier Reformation historians who assume that by the beginning of the sixteenth century "medieval religion was decadent, unpopular, or exhausted." He argues instead that well into the sixteenth century the traditional religion was "vigorous, adaptable, widely understood, and popular." He thus views the Reformation as "a violent disruption, not the natural fulfillment of most of what was vigorous in late medieval piety and religious practice," and he examines the complex process by which the English people, often reluctantly, came to accept the new faith.[5]

If Duffy is correct, then the iconophilia so characteristic of the traditional religion in the fifteenth century continues to manifest itself in the sixteenth century. Rather than view the expressions of piety rep-

---

[4] Christopher Haigh, ed., *The English Reformation Revised* (1987); Scarisbrick, *The Reformation and the English People* (1984).

[5] Eamon Duffy, *The Stripping of the Altars* (1992), pp. 4, 5.

resented in Ostendorfer's print as irrelevant to the age of Reformation, I therefore see them as existing in a dynamic relation with the iconoclastic sentiments represented in Foxe's illustration of "The Temple Well Purged." The pronounced iconophobia manifested in so much of the writings of the early reformers can best be understood in the context of the widespread appeal of images in the sixteenth century. Indeed, popular belief in the power of images drives the iconoclastic impulses of the reformers, generating a fear of images that is at least as intense as the image-centered devotion of the old religion.

In their efforts to remove the offending images from the hearts and imaginations of the English people, as well as from the churches, English reformers like Foxe invoke antitheatrical sentiments, denouncing the images, spectacles, rituals, and ceremonies of the Roman Church as fraudulent theater. Nevertheless, they imagine their struggle to wrest the English Church from Rome as a grand heroic drama, staging their defiant acts of iconoclasm in highly theatrical ways and constructing Protestant martyrdoms as powerful theater. Their tendency to rely on theatrical forms to achieve their iconoclastic goals leads Ritchie D. Kendall to conclude in his study of nonconformist writing that "the radical reformer reveals himself not as a single-minded enemy of the drama but as its troubled lover."[6] Focusing in this chapter on four narratives about image worship and iconoclasm in John Foxe's *Actes and Monuments,* I introduce some of the central conflicts in the drama of reform and identify some of the conventions of the stage that the reformers used to counter the power traditionally invested in images.

Iconophilia and Iconophobia in Early Modern England

Traces of the iconoclastic violence that swept through England during the years of religious reform are still visible today. A mutilated stone statue of the Virgin Mary—eyes gauged out, nose broken, arms torn off—stands forlornly in a parish church. The desolate ruins of an ancient abbey, its roof gone, lie exposed to the elements. The original images painted on a medieval rood screen show faintly through the biblical texts that were painted over it by Protestant reformers in the sixteenth century. Defaced, ruined, and whitewashed images all remind

---

[6] Ritchie D. Kendall, *The Drama of Dissent* (1986), p. 8.

the contemporary viewer of the systematic Protestant campaign to rid the church of the sacred images of the old religion.

Heirs in many ways to the iconoclastic impulses of the Protestant Reformation, many of us raised in the dominant culture of twentieth-century America are apt to misunderstand the widespread destruction of sacred images in northern Europe during the sixteenth and seventeenth centuries precisely because the reformers were so successful in suppressing popular belief in the efficacy of images. If we adopt the modernist perspective of, say, the Dadaist and equate the act of beheading a statue of the Virgin Mary with Duchamp's act of painting a mustache on the Mona Lisa, our assumption that iconoclasm is a heroic liberation from a tyrannizing past is a legacy of the Reformation. In their attacks on the images and ceremonies of the Roman Catholic Church, the Protestant reformers conceive of iconoclasm as a liberating act, a defiant challenge of a dominant ideology that they believe has enslaved the unwary.[7]

If, on the other hand, we adopt the materialist perspective of the art collector and denounce the ruin of so many valuable objects, so many potential possessions, or the aesthetic perspective of the art historian and lament the loss of so many finely wrought artifacts, so much exquisite beauty, even our disapproval is based on assumptions fostered by the reformers in their assault on images. In a concerted attempt to counter the magical power popularly invested in the sacred image, the Protestant reformers repeatedly insist that images are material objects, made of wood or marble, "stocks and stones," created objects, the work of "men's hands."[8] Although we may mystify the material and aesthetic in ways unimaginable to the reformers, who try to undermine images by insisting they are merely physical, nothing more than human artifacts, we nevertheless share with the early Protestants an understanding that images are material objects, handcrafted products of the human imagination.[9] To many people in early modern England, however, sacred images were neither objects to be possessed for their material value nor things of beauty to be admired for their aesthetic value; they

---

[7] See, for example, Carlos Eire, *War against the Idols* (1986), pp. 6, 62, 111.

[8] John Foxe, *A&M*, 8:143, 500.

[9] See, for example, Carl C. Christensen, *Art and the Reformation in Germany* (1979), p. 107: "To what degree has the cultural legacy of modern man been permanently impoverished in terms of actual physical artifacts irrevocably lost to later aesthetic enjoyment and scholarly study?"

were mysterious, marvelous, and efficacious objects which they held in awe.

Despite Roman Catholic doctrine that never officially condoned image worship, and early Protestant teachings that condemned it as superstitious and idolatrous, popular belief in the supernatural power of images was widespread in sixteenth-century Europe, so much so that the reformers seem compelled to prove that sacred images are mere objects.[10] In their detailed descriptions and impassioned critiques of image worship, the continental reformers condemn what they believe are rampant abuses of sacred images. Leo Jud, for example, complains in Zurich in 1523 that images are held in such esteem that people "entreat them with ornaments, silver, gold, precious stones, with sacrifices and with reverence, that is by taking off their hats, bowing, and kneeling before them."[11] John Calvin denounces images because people treat them as if they were gods. Citing as an example the purported "head of Mary Magdiline" in Marseilles, he laments that "Men do make a treasure of her, as it were a god descended from heaven."[12]

English reformers express similar concerns. During the reign of Edward VI, the Lord Protector acknowledges that he himself has participated in the veneration of images, admitting that "We cannot but see that images may be counted marvelous books, to whom we have kneeled, whom we have kissed, upon whom we have rubbed our beads and handkerchiefs, unto whom we have lighted candles, of whom we have asked pardon and help." But he goes on to renounce such adoration, pointedly comparing the adoration of images—defended by traditionalists as layman's "books"—with reverence to the Bible: "which thing hath seldom been seen done to the gospel of God, or the very true Bible," he notes wryly, "for who kisseth that . . . or who kneeleth unto it, or setteth a candle before it?"[13] Images, he fears, have supplanted the very word of God.

As late as 1624, an English reformer attacks the "idolatry of these

---

[10] See, for example, Keith Thomas, *Religion and the Decline of Magic* (1971), pp. 27–36, 75–77; Margaret Miles, *Image as Insight* (1985), pp. 95–99; Christensen, *Art and Reformation*, p. 21; Eire, *War Against the Idols*, pp. 191–92; Foxe, *A&M* 6:60. For a detailed discussion of the widespread belief in the power of images in early modern England, see Duffy, *Stripping of the Altars*.

[11] Qtd. in Charles Garside, *Zwingli and the Arts* (1966), p. 134.

[12] Calvin, *A very profitable Treatise* (1561), sig. B1^r.

[13] Foxe, *A&M*, 6:29.

times" by countering the assumption, still apparently viable, that sacred images are efficacious and powerful. "For Idols are called Ælilim, that is, things of naught," Henry Ainsworth finds it necessary to insist, "because they have nothing of that which fools think they have, that is, of the divine power and Godhead, or of true Religion: and so, can neither help those that honour them, nor hurt those that abhor them; neither sanctifie any creature, nor pollute the same."[14] Sixty-two years earlier, John Veron makes the same point, explaining in a sermon against idolatry that Paul called images "nothing" because "they be of no value, force, or strength."[15] Both Veron and Ainsworth seek to persuade people who presumably do believe images have just such value, force, and strength. The enduring appeal of images is evident in their frustration at the persistence of devotional practices they believe to be idolatrous.

It is also evident in the way devout adherents of the old faith respond to acts of iconoclasm. Traditionalists declare iconoclasm a blasphemous and inhuman act that violates the very core of religion. Expressing outrage at the destruction of sacred images, one conservative theologian denounces the iconoclasts as "hogs and worse than hogs (if there be any grosser beasts than hogs be)."[16] Complaining that their churches "looked like stables," witnesses to the widespread iconoclasm of Basel in 1529 "could have wept blood,"[17] this in sharp contrast to the celebratory joy Foxe reports among the people in Basel in 1523 "for turning their images to ashes."[18] Others lament that the physical church "seemeth naked and ruinous" after the images were removed, a charge that the Hungarian preacher Scultetus, in a sermon translated into English in 1620, finds compelling enough to address in his sermon against images. Concerned about the deep attachment many people have for images, Scultetus complains that were they to "see, that a Crucifix should bee hewed in pieces, or burned into ashes, oh! how would even their very heart[s] then bleed for griefe?"[19]

The anguished response of one traditionalist, Stephen Gardiner,

---

[14] Henry Ainsworth, *An Arrow against Idolatrie* (1624), pp. 13. The first edition was published in 1610.

[15] John Veron, *A stronge battery against the idolatrous invocation of the dead Saintes* (1562), fol. 89^r.

[16] Qtd. in Foxe, *A&M*, 6:26–27.

[17] Qtd. in Christensen, *Art and Reformation*, p. 102.

[18] Foxe, *A&M*, 4:341–42.

[19] Scultetus, *A Short Information, but agreeable unto Scripture: of Idol-Images* (1620), sig. B4^r.

bishop of Winchester, to the iconoclastic reforms sweeping England during the reign of Edward IV is recorded by John Foxe in *Actes and Monuments*. Quoting in full seven letters Gardiner wrote to the Lord Protector on the subject of religious reform, along with the Lord Protector's replies, Foxe casts the bishop as an archenemy of the Protestant cause and urges his readers to "perceive and understand the proud and glorious spirit of that man, his stubborn contumacy against the king, and malicious rebellion against God and true religion with sleight and craft enough to defend his peevish purposes." But the Gardiner letters Foxe prints—letters written between 1547 and 1550—seem far less the writing of a proud and malicious man than the misgivings of a deeply conservative thinker, anxious about "these inward disorders" and desperate to preserve "quiet, tranquillity, unity, and concord." He denounces Protestant agitators as "chief stirrers" of social unrest, accuses them of causing "confusion and disorder," and expresses his own disquiet about religious reform. "I see . . . religion assaulted, the realm troubled, and peaceable men disquieted," he laments.[20]

For Gardiner, iconoclasm is "detestable." It is also dangerous. He believes that the very order of society is threatened when the reformers break, burn, and desecrate the images of the medieval church, and he predicts that iconoclasm will bring "a dissolution and dissipation of all estates." Fearful of the "trouble and disquiet" he believes will follow in the wake of iconoclasm, he warns that both the aristocracy and the monarchy are at risk. "The destruction of images," he declares, "containeth an enterprise to subvert religion, and the state of the world with it, and especially the nobility, who, by images, set forth and spread abroad, to be read of all people, their lineage and parentage, with remembrance of their state and acts." Furthermore, he continues, iconoclasm calls into question the very means by which the king commands the awe and devotion of the people, for "the poursuivant carrieth not on his breast the king's name" but "images of three lions, and three fleurs-de-lis, and other beasts holding those arms" so that everyone "be they never so rude" recognizes the royal images and knows to show proper respect and "put off his cap."[21] For Gardiner and other traditionalists, Protestant iconoclasm is a dangerous enterprise that under-

20 Qtd. in Foxe, *A&M*, 6:24–32.
21 Qtd. in Foxe, *A&M*, 6:26–32.

mines religious, political, and social order by calling into question the central symbols of that order. His fears suggest how threatening iconoclasm was to a powerful elite who depended on sacred and political images to assert and maintain their privileged positions in the social hierarchy.

The question of how people who are not themselves theologians or active reformers understand and process the iconoclastic activities of the reformers is especially vexed in England, where the succession of Tudor monarchs results in sudden and radical shifts in official doctrine: iconoclasts are encouraged, indeed, stirred to action, under Edward VI, put to death under Mary, and tolerated under Elizabeth; images are publicly burned and privately hidden under Edward, officially restored and defiantly violated in acts of rebellion under Mary, and ordered removed once again under Elizabeth.

When John Machyn lists the considerable expenses for the Marian restoration of the Roman Catholic worship at one chapel, describing in detail the reinstated ornaments, and then cites the payments made under Elizabeth for the destruction of these very same ornaments, does he feel torn by a divided loyalty to his monarchs or an inability to trust either? Do the abrupt changes in policy offend, bemuse, or unmoor him? What is his motive for listing, with such detailed attention to costs, and with no apparent emotion, the scores of images that, in a few years' time, are destroyed, restored, and then destroyed again?[22] And how does Charles Wriothesley experience the iconoclasm he documents when "coapes, vestments, aulter clothes, bookes, banners, sepulchers, and other ornaments of the churches were burned" only four years after he records the restoration of "the old [Roman Catholic] service" on Palm Sunday, 1554? Having witnessed the reinstatement of such Roman rituals as the "bearing of Palmes, and creepinge to the Crosse on Good Fridaye, with the Sepulcher lights and the Resurrection on Easter daye," how does Wriothesley feel when these rituals are once again abolished?[23] Does the man who labels an earlier iconoclastic act under Mary as "a villanouse fact" accept and approve the official burning of "the roodes and images that stoode in the parishe churches"

---

[22] Henry Machyn, *The Diary of Henry Machyn* (1848), pp. 208–9.

[23] Charles Wriothesley, *A Chronicle of England during the Reigns of the Tudors* (1877), 2: 113–14, 2:146.

under Elizabeth or does his oddly dispassionate list of destroyed objects mask outrage, loss, anxiety, or a sense of impotency?[24]

We can only speculate from such fragmentary evidence how the general populace experiences iconoclasm or responds to the reformers' call to "destroy & brake downe out of the publique Houses of God Service, all kind of Idol- Imagery" so that "not one churche wyndowe should bee lefte hole theroughoute all England, there should bee neyther crosse nor crucifixe lefte."[25] We know that some people mutilate sacred images and tear apart church ornaments in mob riots while others salvage the condemned images and hide them in their homes, where these stand, according to one disapproving Protestant, "like a Dianaes shrine for a future hope and daily comforte of old popish beldames and young perking papists."[26] We know that some dance for joy before the bonfires that burn wooden images they have ripped out of choir stalls and altars, while others, unable to tolerate the absence of the burned and destroyed images, replace them with their own amateur drawings, "sketch[ing] in a cross," for instance, "with chalk or paint."[27] We know that some Protestant preachers seek to suppress popular belief in images by declaring them "dead, blind, mute, and dumb," while some Roman Catholic prelates continue to assert their divine power and status, attributing a fatal accident that occurred during one act of iconoclasm, for instance, to "the will of God for the pulling downe of the said idolls."[28]

Although many historians and art historians find iconoclastic acts incomprehensible and irrational, declaring them "mindless" or "premised in hatred," the evidence suggests that iconoclasts and traditionalists alike are motivated by the widespread perception that images are magical, powerful, and sacred.[29] The traditionalists hold tenaciously to this view; the iconoclasts deliberately set out to disprove

[24] Ibid., 2:114, 2:146.

[25] Scultetus, *Short Information*, sig. D3ᵛ; Veron, *Stronge battery*, sigs. 93ᵛ–94ʳ.

[26] Qtd. in John Phillips, *The Reformation of Images* (1973), p. 134; see also p. 95.

[27] Ibid., p. 133.

[28] John Hooper, "A Declaration of Christ and his Office, 1547," qtd. in Phillips, *Reformation of Images*, p. 86; for additional references to "dead" images, see Foxe, *A&M*, 4: 175, 8:143, 340–41; Wriothesley, *Chronicle*, 2:1.

[29] John Rowlands, *Holbein* (1985), p. 63 laments that "unfortunately, the iconoclasts attacked and damaged the Last Supper, badly, hacking out the head of Christ," and he calls this attack "a mindless act" attributable to "fanatics"; Margaret Aston, *England's Iconoclasts* (1988), 1:17.

it. Nevertheless, both groups experience iconoclasm as a fundamental challenge to a late medieval belief in the divinity and potency of images.

Iconoclastic riots frequently break out after preachers expose devotional images as fraudulent, thereby arousing the anger of people who had fervently believed in their efficacy. When, for example, the Rood of Grace is taken from the Cistercian Abbey of Boxley in 1538 and exhibited to a gathered crowd to show that its "miraculous" ability to move its limbs was caused by nothing more than some hidden wires, the spectators riot. They obliterate the image in a wild mass frenzy, their fury surely an expression of how deeply and completely they had formerly believed in its miraculous nature: "Then when the Preacher began to wax warm, and the Word of God to work secretly in the hearts of his hearers, the wooden trunk was hurled neck over heels among the most crowded of the audience. And now was heard a tremendous clamour of all sorts of people; —he is snatched, torn, broken in pieces bit by bit, split up into a thousand fragments, and at last thrown into the fire; and there was an end of him."[30] For the angry mob, the reliability of the Rood of Grace—and, perhaps, all images—is shattered by the revelation of a hidden mechanism, its earlier assumptions about the visible world challenged by the exposure of a man-made illusion. Mystery is exposed as trickery.

Iconoclastic activity has an equally profound effect on people who neither engage in nor condone the violence. An eyewitness to the 1566 outbursts of iconoclasm in the Netherlands records the terror felt by many who observe the destruction of images they hold sacred. "These changes," he writes, "so radical and so sudden, terrified many people, to the point where they cried out, 'And the air doesn't change!' finding it unbearable that God had not seen fit to show signs of His anger. . . . Others became sick; men and women passed the nights sighing and weeping, wringing their hands."[31] Nonparticipants in the iconoclastic acts, the bystanders nevertheless cannot escape the meaning of the event: images they have loved and adored are violated, smashed to pieces, "and the air doesn't change!" Piety gives way to anxiety.

We oversimplify the meaning of such iconoclastic acts if we merely

---

[30] Qtd. in Phillips, *Reformation of Images*, p. 74.

[31] Qtd. in Phyllis Mack Crew, *Calvinist Preaching and Iconoclasm in the Netherlands, 1544–1569* (1978), pp. 26–27.

lament the material destruction or celebrate the impending "enlight-enment," for the iconophobia that characterizes so much of Refor-mation culture is, in a very real sense, the function of the iconophilia that pervades Western culture at the dawning of the modern age. The intensity of the rage vented against images by rioting iconoclasts has the same source as the intensity of the horror felt by disapproving by-standers who witnessed the iconoclastic acts: a deeply held belief, how-ever threatened, in the power of images.[32] Whether that belief is tested by willing participation in iconoclastic events or challenged by unwill-ing observation of them, the implicit relation between visible images and God is suddenly disrupted and forever changed. The intimate bond late medieval culture had established between the visible and the divine is irrevocably severed.

John Foxe's *Book of Martyrs* and the Dialectics of Reform

One reformer intent on achieving the permanent rupture of the bond between the visible and the divine is John Foxe. His *Actes and Monuments*, popularly referred to as *The Book of Martyrs*, is generally held to be one of the most widely known and most profoundly influential works in sixteenth- and seventeenth-century England. Described by He-len White as "second only to the Bible and *Pilgrim's Progress* for its influ-ence upon Protestant England," by Richard Helgerson as "enormously influential" in "shaping England's religious self-understanding," and by Tessa Watt as having "achieved a status close to that of a second Bi-ble," *Actes and Monuments* occupied a central place in the cathedrals, parish churches, rectories, and homes—and even in the offices of the court of Elizabeth and the Companies of London—in the late sixteenth and early seventeenth centuries.[33] Watt provides evidence of its wide-

[32] Steven Ozment, *The Reformation in the Cities* (1975), p. 44, makes a similar argument when he disagrees with historians who conclude that iconoclasm indicates "that inner religious commitment could not have run very deep." He speculates instead that Refor-mation iconoclasm "may rather indicate the reaction of people who felt themselves fooled by something that they had not taken lightly at all but had in fact believed all too deeply. . . . It is a reaction that might have been expected from those whose piety had been sincere and 'appetite for the divine' immense." See also Miles, *Image as Insight*, pp. 107–8.

[33] Helen C. White, *Tudor Books of Saints and Martyrs* (1963), pp. 168; Richard Helger-son, *Forms of Nationhood* (1992), pp. 249, 253; Tessa Watt, *Cheap Print and Popular Piety*,

spread influence on popular culture. In her book, *Cheap Print and Popular Piety, 1550–1640*, she shows how sixteenth- and seventeenth-century popular ballads, broadside pictures, and chapbooks used and popularized textual narratives and illustrations from *The Book of Martyrs*.[34] Helgerson points out the extraordinary impact Foxe's book had on England's uneducated and poor. In *Forms of Nationhood* he cites the historian J. H. Plumb's comment that along with the Bible and Bunyan's *The Pilgrim's Progress, Actes and Monuments* was perhaps the only book "which the illiterate, the semiliterate, and the literate poor ever knew in any detail," and he quotes Plumb's assertion that these three books "burned a 'sense of progress and destiny into the unconscious mind of the British people.' "[35]

Because its influence on the sixteenth- and seventeenth-century popular imagination is undisputed, *The Book of Martyrs* is a particularly valuable text for anyone who wishes to understand how the religious conflicts of the mid-sixteenth century—and the social disruptions that accompanied them—were remembered and interpreted during the Elizabethan and Jacobean age, especially by people who were not themselves theologians or active reformers. Written in the vernacular and incorporated into the popular culture of early modern England, it appealed to the same broad spectrum of people as the drama of the commercial London stage. Like the drama, too, it helped to forge a sense of national identity among a diverse people. I thus read Foxe's history of the Reformation as narrative literature that, through repeated readings and tellings, helped to shape the English people's understanding not only of the Reformation but of the world they inhabited as well.[36]

1550–1640 (1991), p. 90; see also, John N. King, *English Reformation Literature* (1982), p. 435. White notes that "the upper house of convocation of Canterbury did in 1571 order that a copy of the Bishop's Bible of 1568 and a copy of Foxe's book should be installed in every cathedral church, and every member of the hierarchy from archbishop down to resident canon should have a copy of the latter in the hall or dining room of his house for the use of all who came there. There is plenty of evidence, too, that it was chained beside the great Bible in many parish churches," pp. 167–68. Watt points out that *The Book of Martyrs* was a "prized possession in seventeenth-century rural wills," p. 158.

[34] Watt, *Cheap Print*, pp. 90–91, 158–159, 318.

[35] Qtd. in Helgerson, *Forms of Nationhood*, p. 287.

[36] For an excellent discussion of the way Foxe forges a Protestant community among his readers, see Mark Breitenberg, "The Flesh Made Word: Foxe's *Actes and Monuments*" (1989).

Because *The Book of Martyrs* articulates so forcefully the iconoclastic and antitheatrical sentiments of early Protestantism, sentiments that are later appropriated by antitheatricalists like Rankins, Gosson, Rainolds, and Stubbes in their attacks on the London stage, I am particularly interested in the way Foxe constructs the history of the Reformation as a riveting and dynamic drama. Although he condemns the theatricality of the Roman Church, declaring its rituals fraudulent, its spectacles empty, and its sacred symbols impotent, Foxe champions another kind of theater, substituting the theatrics of martyrdom for traditional pomp and pageantry. He attends to the gestures, moods, emotions, personalities, and eccentricities of both those destined to become Protestant heroes and those cast as the enemies of reform, thus capturing the inherent drama of rebellions and persecutions, inquisitions and executions. And he constructs acts of iconoclasm, too, as powerful—and even spectacular—theater. Depicting the violent destruction of sacred images as a liberating act, at once radical and welcome, he conveys the dramatic suspense in the moment when iconoclasts dare to violate an image widely believed to be efficacious.

In striving to write the definitive history of the Reformation, Foxe compiles an enormous amount of primary material—including letters, sermons, dreams, legal documents, oral histories, and theological tracts. Because he includes letters written by conservatives like Gardiner alongside the letters and testimonies of the reformers, Foxe foregrounds opposing positions even as he champions the Protestant side. He thus sets the beliefs and assumptions of the old religion up against those of the new in a dialectical manner, aligning his history to the drama by calling attention to the differences, the divisions, and the conflicts between the Roman and reformed churches. Indeed, Anthony Kemp, finding in *Actes and Monuments* "a delineation of difference almost shocking in its intensity," describes Foxe's concept of history as "a history against," one that is "dynamic, fissured, full of 'diversities and alterations.' "[37]

As a compendium of competing voices—immediate, eloquent, and passionate in their responses to religious crisis—*The Book of Martyrs* engages its readers directly in the conflicts between the reformers and the traditionalists. It records in full transcripts of the Marian inquisitions, using emotionally charged exchanges between Roman Catholic

[37] Anthony Kemp, *The Estrangement of the Past* (1991), pp. 84, 90; Kemp quotes Foxe's *Actes and Monuments*, 1:4–5.

ecclesiastical authorities and individual Protestants to clarify and elaborate the theological issues at stake. Printed as dialogue—like the scripts of plays—these examinations lay out the arguments of both the martyrs and their persecutors in a way that highlights the dramatic conflict between them. By thus adopting the techniques of a playwright, Foxe renders the theological controversies of the Reformation immediate, accessible, and relevant to his audiences. Explaining sophisticated church doctrine in idiomatic speech and simple, direct language, he puts theology and Scripture into the mouths of poor people and servants, craftsmen and merchants, women and the dispossessed. His dramatic narratives typically focus on a struggle between powerful men and individuals who are empowered by God's word. Constructing ordinary citizens as Protestant heroes, he shows how they courageously fight the oppression, tyranny, cruelty, arrogance, and fraud of authorities he associates with the pope, Rome, Spain, and other "un-English" influences. His book thus helps to shape a national and religious identity among a diverse people by imagining the Reformation as a dramatic struggle for the soul of England.

In arguing that Foxe's historiography is dramatic, I wish to question the widely held assumption that the reformed religion is essentially antitheatrical and thus necessarily hostile to the London theater that flourishes under Elizabeth and James. Although it is true, as John Knott points out, that Foxe uses words like "play," "players," and "pageants" pejoratively, disparaging priests by identifying them with actors and mocking the Roman Mass by calling it theater, it is a mistake to assume that Foxe rejects all kinds of theater when he condemns the theatricality of the Roman Church and churchmen. In fact, as I show more fully in Chapter 7, he portrays the struggle between the Protestant martyrs and their adversaries as cosmic theater, witnessed by God as well as human spectators. And although Foxe identifies Protestant martyrs with plainness and authenticity, the traits he so effectively naturalizes are themselves theatrical postures, dramatic roles. As Knott himself admits, the Protestant martyrs cannot escape theatricality, engaging in a kind of role playing when they go to the stake consciously imitating Christ.[38]

In order to illustrate how Foxe uses anecdotal history to convey the

---

[38] For a discussion of plainness in John Foxe's *Acts and Monuments*, see John R. Knott, *Discourses of Martyrdom in English Literature, 1563–1694* (1993), pp. 69–74; I discuss the aesthetic of plainness in the Epilogue.

drama of reform in all its particularity and immediacy, I quote at length from four intriguing narratives in *Actes and Monuments*. In all four anecdotes Foxe addresses central cultural issues that are pertinent to early modern English drama, including, for example, the status of art, the nature of visible signs, the legitimacy of magic, and the limits of the human imagination. All four engage the dialectic between iconophilia and iconophobia that I believe is operating in both early Protestant culture and the drama of Elizabethan and Jacobean England. And all four employ a number of rhetorical strategies to disrupt the devotional gaze, demystify sacred images, and nurture Protestant habits of thought, strategies I believe were appropriated by English playwrights and used to address religious controversies in the playhouses of Elizabethan and Jacobean London.

Robert King, Robert Debnam, Nicholas Marsh, and Robert Garner:
Testing the Power of the Image

In the same year of our Lord 1532, there was an idol named the Rood of Dover-court, whereunto was much and great resort of people: for at that time there was great rumour blown abroad amongst the ignorant sort, that the power of the idol of Dover-court was so great, that no man had power to shut the church-door where he stood; and therefore they let the church-door, both night and day, continually stand open, for the more credit unto their blind rumour. This once being conceived in the heads of the vulgar sort, seemed a great marvel unto many men; but to many again, whom God had blessed with his Spirit, it was greatly suspected, especially unto these, whose names here follow: as Robert King of Dedham, Robert Debnam of Eastbergholt, Nicholas Marsh of Dedham, and Robert Gardner of Dedham, whose consciences were sore burdened to see the honour and power of the Almighty living God so to be blasphemed by such an idol. Wherefore they were moved by the Spirit of God, to travel out of Dedham in a wondrous goodly night, both hard frost and fair moonshine, although the night before, and the night after, were exceeding foul and rainy. It was from the town of Dedham, to the place where the filthy Rood stood, ten miles. Notwithstanding, they were so willing in that their enterprise, that they went these ten miles without pain, and found the church-door open, according to the blind talk of the ignorant people: for there durst no unfaithful body shut it. This happened well for their purpose, for they found the idol, which had as much power to keep the door shut, as to keep it open; and for proof thereof, they took the idol from his shrine, and carried him a quarter of a mile from the place where he stood, without any resistance of the said idol. Whereupon they struck fire with a flint-stone, and suddenly set him on fire, who burned out so brim, that he lighted them homeward one good mile of the ten.[39]

Foxe portrays the iconoclasts King, Debnam, Marsh, and Garner as heroic men who, moved by the Holy Spirit and presumably aided by a divine gesture of clear skies and bright moonlight, bravely defy the magical power popularly believed to reside in an image called the Rood of Dovercourt. Celebrating their daring capture of the sacred image, considered a "marvel" so extraordinary it rendered men powerless to shut the church door where it stood, Foxe uses their story to demystify images by exposing them as impotent: the iconoclasts steal, carry away, and burn the marvelous image, and nothing happens. They accomplish their feat "without any resistance of the said idol." When the four men test the legendary power of the image, what had "seemed a great marvel" is thus proven to be, in reality, a mere thing which "had as much power to keep the door shut as to keep it open." Wrested from its sacred place, deprived of its divine status, the rood of Dovercourt burns like any other ordinary, wooden object.

Foxe acknowledges the awesome powers believed to reside in the sacred image, but he does so only to discredit it. Calling the image-worshipers "ignorant people," he identifies their belief in the supernatural power of the Rood with "blind" rumor and superstition and declares it to be a fantasy "conceived in the heads of the vulgar sort" by their own runaway imaginations. By distancing his readers from the image lovers and constructing iconoclastic violence as a form of enlightenment, Foxe requires them to identify not with the believers but with the skeptics, not with the acts of devotion but with the acts of desecration. Driving a wedge between the pious practitioners of the old faith and his own readers, Foxe links the beloved image to impurity, referring to it as a "filthy" idol. In his narrative, it is the iconoclasts, not the Roman Catholic devout, who are "moved by the Spirit of God." The godly heroes are those who defy the authorities and not those who obey them, those who suspect the power of the image—men "whom God had blest with his Spirit"—and not those who hold it in awe.

[39] Foxe, *A&M*, 4:706–7.

Although the authorities treat the burning of the Rood of Dovercourt as a crime, a sacrilegious and subversive act that demands the severest possible penalty, death by hanging, Foxe disputes their judgment. He insists that the iconoclasts did not act out of greed or a desire for material gain, and he vigorously denies reports that they profited from their act. Far from acquiring "great riches," he assures his readers "they had neither penny, halfpenny, gold, groat, nor jewel." Instead of being motivated by money, he depicts King, Debnam, Marsh, and Gardner as being motivated by their own consciences: "their consciences were sore burdened to see the honour and power of the Almighty living God so to be blasphemed by such an idol." Protestant heroes, they risk their lives to defend their God from the true sacrilege, idolatry. Traveling ten miles in the dark to challenge the power of the Rood of Dovercourt, they prove that claims about its extraordinary powers are false simply by carrying it away.

According to Foxe, their deaths, which he constructs as martyrdoms, served to "edify the people in godly learning, than all the sermons that had been preached there a long time before," and his own retelling of their defiant iconoclastic act and their capital punishment also seeks to edify. Arousing suspicion of the marvelous and fostering a skepticism about received beliefs, his narrative encourages readers to trust in "the Spirit of God" rather than in images. It privileges the individual conscience, making obedience to one's own internal conviction preferable to obedience to external authority. And it nurtures an empiricism that questions and tests the validity of magical beliefs. In so doing, the narrative of the Rood of Dovercourt transfers power from the image that arouses devotion to the spectator who doubts what he sees.

Edmund Allin: Empowering the Skeptic

Then they reviled him, and laid him in the stocks all the night; wherewith certain that were better minded, being offended with such extremity, willed Allin to keep his conscience to himself, and to follow Baruch's counsel in the sixth chapter: "Wherefore when ye see the multitude of people worshipping them behind and before, say ye in your hearts, O Lord, it is thou that ought only to be worshipped." Wherewith he was persuaded to go to hear mass the next day; and suddenly, before the sacring, went out; and considered in the church-yard with himself, that such a little cake between the priest's fingers could not be Christ, nor a material body, neither to have soul, life, sinews, bones, flesh, legs, head, arms, nor breast; and lamented that he was seduced by the place of Baruch, which his conscience gave him to be no Scripture, or else to have another meaning. And after this he was brought again before sir John Baker [and Baker's chaplain, a man named Collins], who asked why he did refuse to worship the blessed sacrament of the altar.

Allin:—"It is an idol."

Collins:—"It is God's body."

Allin:—"It is not."

Collins:—"By the mass it is."

Allin:—"It is bread."

Collins:—"How provest thou that?"

Allin:—"When Christ sat at his supper, and gave them bread to eat."

Collins:—"Bread, knave?"

Allin:—"Yea bread, which you call Christ's body. Sat he still at the table, or was he both in their mouths, and at the table? If he were in their mouths, and at the table, then had he two bodies, or else had a phantastical body; which is an absurdity to say it."[40]

In "The Story of Edmund Allin" Foxe describes the spiritual development of a Protestant who is ultimately martyred because he rejects the Roman Catholic interpretation of the sacrament of the Eucharist and insists on his right to interpret for himself Christ's words instituting that sacrament. A miller by trade, Allin begins what Foxe presents as an interior journey to enlightenment with a charitable act: "in a dear year, when many poor people were like to starve, he fed them, and sold his corn better cheap by half than others did." But Foxe immediately turns the miller's gift of food into a metaphor, praising Allin for an even greater act of charity. He explains that Allin not only fed the poor corn "but also fed them with the food of life, reading to them the Scriptures, and interpreting them." For this, Allin is identified as a subversive.

Throughout his narrative of persecution, Foxe asserts the individual's right to interpret Scripture, showing how this right is central to Allin's struggle with the authorities. When Allin is apprehended after returning from exile, the Catholic authorities ransacked his home and "found there certain books, as Psalters, Bibles, and other writings." In response

---

[40] Ibid., 8:324; see 8:321–25 for the complete anecdote.

to this discovery, the justice, John Baker, "taunting and reviling him without all mercy and pity, asked him if those were the fruits of the gospel, to have conventicles to gather people together, to make conspiracies to sow sedition and rebellion." To both the ecclesiastical and secular authorities, the miller's attempts to read the Bible to others, interpret the Scriptures, and preach are highly threatening acts of sedition, which undermine their power to control what the people believe.

The record of Allin's examination begins with Baker's question, "Who gave thee authority to preach and interpret?" Taking a position that infuriates his examiners, the miller answers, "I am persuaded that God hath given this authority, as he hath given to all other Christians." He then quotes the Bible, asserting that "we are all kings to rule our affections, priests to preach out the virtues and word of God . . . and lively stones to give light to others." As is typical in Foxe's narratives about the Marian martyrs, an ordinary person challenges the learned authorities of the church by quoting scriptural passages that, when applied to the contemporary religious crisis, are radical, indeed, revolutionary in their import. Adopting the notion of a priesthood of all believers, Allin asserts his right to interpret the Bible for himself, his duty to challenge church doctrine that has no foundation in Scripture, and his belief that his interpretations are as valid as a priest's.

At the center of his struggle with the authorities is the contested interpretation of the sacrament of communion. Foxe tells how Allin, wavering somewhat under the stress of his imprisonment and inquisition, agrees to attend Mass. Before the Mass is completed, he is struck by what he identifies as the "absurdity" of the doctrine of transubstantiation, reasoning the sacramental bread could not be Christ himself. Foxe encourages his readers to identify with the lone individual who has withdrawn from the public celebration of the Roman Mass to ponder by himself the logic of a complex, theological doctrine. Questioning a central tenet of the old faith with what Foxe portrays as a healthy skepticism, Allin concludes that the host cannot be Christ, as the Roman Church teaches, because "such a little cake" could not also be "a material body" or have "a soul, life, sinews, bones, flesh, legs, head, arms, [nor] breast." Rejecting the doctrine of transubstantiation, Allin insists on interpreting the eucharistic bread figuratively. It is, he argues, a material thing that represents Christ's body, and not the very body of God.

In his report of the debate between Allin and Collins, Foxe captures the tense drama that unfolds when Allin—defiant, confident, and unwavering—challenges the priest by refusing "to worship the blessed sacrament." The miller relies on an empirical form of reasoning, pointing out that at the Last Supper, the disciples did not eat of Christ's body, but rather sat in Christ's presence and ate bread.[41] In constructing men like Allin as Protestant heroes—men of conscience and conviction who manifest great courage in the face of cruelty and torture—Foxe thus attempts to undermine the doctrine of transubstantiation by appealing to common sense, nurturing skepticism, and inculcating a rationalized, empirical method of interpretation. He celebrates individuals who raise questions, express doubts, refuse to accept unexamined doctrines, insist on their own authority to interpret texts, apply empirical criteria, and resist coercion. In short, he empowers the skeptic.

Prest's Wife: Estranging the Image

In the mean time . . . it happened that she [Prest's wife], entering into St. Peter's Church beheld there a cunning Dutchman, how he made noses to certain fine images which were disfigured in King Edward's time: "What a mad man art thou," said she, "to make them new noses, which within a few days shall all lose their heads!" The Dutchman accused her, and laid it hard to her charge. And she said unto him, "Thou art accursed, and so are thy images." He called her "whore." "Nay," said she, "thy images are whores, and thou art a whore-hunter; for doth not God say 'You go a whoring after strange gods, figures of your own making?' And thou art one of them." Then was she sent for, and clapped fast; and from that time she had no more liberty.[42]

In this confrontation between a Dutch artist and a poor, illiterate old woman, Foxe depicts a marginalized female challenging the authority of an artist who labors to restore sacred images broken by Protestant iconoclasts. An outsider by choice—she left her husband and children

---

[41] The dialogue he records between the Protestant martyr Allin and his Roman Catholic inquisitors, documenting his view of the fundamental differences between the reformed and the Roman interpretations of the eucharistic sacrament, is repeated, in slightly different versions, throughout *The Book of Martyrs*. See, for example, the stories of Thomas Moor and John Newman in Foxe, *A&M*, 8:242, 244.

[42] Ibid., 8:500; see 8:497–503 for the complete anecdote.

when they tried to force her to worship the Roman Catholic Mass she has renounced as idolatrous—this unnamed woman, "the wife of one called Prest," threatens the established church and state so much that she is eventually silenced, burned at the stake outside the walls of Exeter in 1558.

As in so many of Foxe's narratives, a powerless figure turns the words of Scripture against the powerful, achieving extraordinary attention and influence through her command of the Bible. Although Prest's wife is a plain woman—"as simple a woman to see to, as any man might behold; of a very little and short stature, somewhat thick, about fifty-four years of age"—she possesses a remarkable power to move others with her godly speech. A gentlewoman "of noble wit," who "declared . . . that in her life she never heard a woman (of such simplicity to see to) talk so godly, so perfectly, so sincerely, and so earnestly," converts after listening to her; a former preacher afraid of persecution recommits himself to preaching the gospel after speaking with her; fellow Protestants who have heard her speak demonstrate their support by being "present with her, both in the hall and in the prison." Indeed, her defiant speaking (persecuted and homeless, "she never ceased to utter her mind") is, in Foxe's narrative, both the reason she is martyred and the single most important characteristic that defines her heroism.

Foxe uses the exchange between Prest's wife and the Dutch artist to highlight the ideological struggle between the Roman and the Protestant faiths. Attempting to control this rebellious woman, the Roman Catholic authorities construct her as a mad, eccentric, ignorant whore, calling her "an Anabaptist, a mad woman, a drunkard, a whore, a runagate" in order to marginalize and contain her. Instead of allowing herself to be so constructed, however, Prest's wife throws the offensive epithets back against the authorities, calling the artist a madman and whoremonger, his images strange and whorish. Thus invoking scriptural passages that proclaim the spiritual power of the dispossessed and highlight the alienation of image worshipers from God, Foxe undermines the legitimacy of the artist and the Roman Church he serves. Denying their attempts to define Prest's wife as other, he recasts the established artist and the powerful churchmen who persecute her as spiritual outcasts, strangers in the eyes of God.

For example, Foxe reports that the Roman Catholic authorities attempt to undermine Prest's wife by declaring her "a mazed creature,

and not in her right wit." Allowing that her defiant challenge of the
Roman Church is a kind of madness or folly, Foxe transforms her folly
in the eyes of the world into spiritual wisdom, noting that it "is no new
thing for the wisdom of God to appear foolishness to carnal men of
this world." In marked contrast to the Pauline ideal of spiritual folly
that Prest's wife epitomizes, the Dutch artist is portrayed as exhibiting
a very different kind of madness. When Prest's wife ridicules him as "a
mad man," he appears crazy in her eyes for restoring sacred images
that she believes are forbidden by God and thus destined to be destroyed. If her spirituality seems a madness to the artist, that is because
he is a worldly—a "carnal"—man, and that, Foxe implies, is the true
madness.

Foxe also reinterprets the marginality of Prest's wife by declaring her
"the very servant and handmaid of Christ," and he undermines the
legitimacy and authority of the Dutch artist by invoking biblical passages that denounce images as "strange gods." Although he admits that
Prest's wife is impoverished, nameless, and without any social status—
a "poor woman, and a silly creature . . . whose name I have not yet
learned," he casts her in the role of the courageous Protestant heroine
who endures "hard imprisonment, threatenings, taunts, and scorns"
with "her heart fixed"; she thus serves as "a rare ensample of constancy
to all professors of Christ's gospel." In contrast, he portrays the Dutch
artist, presumably a respected craftsman whose work is supported by
the established church and perhaps by Queen Mary, as a foreigner who
serves a foreign—Roman, "popish"—church. The Roman Church, he
implies, misleads the faithful by teaching them to worship idolatrous
images, the "strange gods" that seduce men, alienating them from an
invisible God.

When, during the exchange in the church, the artist calls Prest's wife
a whore and she retorts by calling his images whores and him a "whore-
hunter," Foxe also interrogates the notion of a whore, once again relying on Scripture to legitimize Prest's wife (and her Protestant beliefs)
and to marginalize the artist and his Roman images. When the authorities accuse her of whoredom, telling her, "If thou wert an honest
woman, thou wouldest not have left thy husband and children, and run
about the country like a fugitive," she denies their accusation, insisting
that "I fled not for whoredom." Indeed, she defines herself as the
faithful bride of Christ, explains that she left her husband for "my

heavenly spouse," and asserts with confidence that "I have but one husband, which is here already in this city and in prison with me, from whom I will never depart."

Fighting her examiners' attempts to marginalize her, Prest's wife asserts that they, not she, are the ones that practice whoredom. Denouncing them as "the chaplains of that whore of Babylon," the Roman Church, she accuses them of partaking "of that foul idol the mass" and of practicing idolatry. And idolatry, she reminds them, is a spiritual form of whoredom because it involves the worship of forbidden images in place of God. Rejecting her examiners' attempts to brand her a whore, Prest's wife associates the very religion they seek to impose on her with a metaphoric whoredom of the heart, linking Roman Catholicism with seduction, uncleanness, promiscuity, and unfaithfulness. Foxe develops the link between the Roman Church and whoredom by revealing that one of the inquisitors, Blackstone, "being the treasurer of the church, had a concubine." Foxe recounts how this inquisitor had Prest's wife "called forth to his house, there to make his minion with the rest of the company some mirth," and then examined her "with such mocking and grinning, deriding the truth, that it would have vexed any christian heart to have seen it." Foxe's female martyr must thus endure the humiliation of a man who, quick to denigrate her as whore, himself openly and hypocritically practices a literal, as well as a spiritual, whoredom.

Foxe also uses the narrative of Prest's wife to arouse in his readers a suspicion of the imagination and all its products. Grounding his contempt for sacred art in the Calvinist belief that all human creation is corrupt, he emphasizes the way Prest's wife ridicules the artists' images as "figures of your own making"; he endorses her rejection of the doctrine of transubstantiation, which she believes rests on a human construction, "a false god of your own making." Insisting that God does not "dwell in temples made with hands," she dismisses as idolatrous the belief that "a piece of bread should be turned by a man into the natural body of Christ." Declaring that "there was never such an idol," she accuses the priests of teaching people to worship the Eucharist "with many fond fantasies; whereas Christ did command it to be eaten and drunken in remembrance of his most blessed passion for our redemption." She ridicules the belief that the eucharistic bread is literally the body of God by pointing out that the sacramental bread grows musty and "mice oftentimes do eat it, and it doth mould, and is burned," and she insists that God cannot be "kept in prison, or boxes, or aumbries." For similar reasons she denounces pardons, accusing Roman priests of teaching people to "trust in the foolish inventions of your own imagination." At the heart of her opposition to the Roman Church is her judgment that it substitutes "idols, stocks, and stones, the works of men's hands" for the one true God, and thereby seduces people into believing in the man-made rather than the divine.

In recording her examination, imprisonment, and martyrdom, Foxe articulates the contradictions he believes are inherent in late medieval Roman Catholicism, a religion he sees as foolishly encouraging the production of images to celebrate and affirm a God who has expressly forbidden graven images. He seeks to alienate his readers from sacred images by likening them to whores and strangers, and he questions the legitimacy of art by opposing the crafted object of a "cunning" artist to the "Spirit of God" which speaks through a simple, plain woman. Although Prest's wife is ridiculed as a madwoman and a whore by the Roman Catholic authorities, Foxe invokes the Biblical tropes of madness and whoredom to construct the Roman Church and its images, not the rebellious woman, as the alien "other."

Rochus: Making Signs and Commodifying Art

Rochus was born in Brabant, his father dwelling in Antwerp. By his science he was a carver or graver of images; who, as soon as he began first to taste the gospel, fell from making such images as use to serve for idolatry in temples, and occupied himself in making seals, save only that he kept standing on his stall an image of the Virgin Mary artificially graven, for a sign of his occupation. It happened unhappily, that a certain inquisitor passing by in the street, and beholding the carved image, asked of Rochus what was the price thereof? which when Rochus had set (not willing belike to sell it), the inquisitor bade him scarce half the money. The other answered again, that he could not so live by that bargain. But still the inquisitor urged him to take his offer; to whom Rochus again: "It shall be yours," said he, "if you will give me that which my labour and charges stand me in, but for that price I cannot afford it: yea I had rather break it in pieces." "Yea" said the inquisitor, "break it? let me see thee;" Rochus with that took up a chisel, and dashed it upon the face of the image, wherewith the nose, or some part of the face was blemished. The inquisitor, seeing that, cried out that he were mad, and commanded Rochus forthwith to prison: to whom Rochus cried again, that he might do to his own works what he listed; and if the workmanship of the image were not after his fantasy, what was that to them? But all this could not help Rochus, but within 3 days after [he was sentenced to burn].[43]

In the story of Rochus, a convert to Protestantism who was martyred in Spain in 1545, Foxe presents what seems to be a paradox: an iconoclastic artist. But if Rochus is "a carver" who deliberately defaces his own work rather than relinquish it to the Roman Catholic authorities, he is not a man who, when he embraces the new religion, stops carving images. Rather than renouncing his profession, he ceases "making such images as use to serve for idolatry in temples" and instead applies his artistic skill to "making seals." In other words, he turns from creating sacred objects to creating images that are, by definition, man-made signs or representations. As a maker of seals he creates "artificially graven" images that explicitly stand for something invisible and absent. The direction his art takes after his conversion enables him to continue practicing his craft without participating in the production of sacred images his new faith declares to be idolatrous.

Rochus even turns a sacred image that he had carved before his conversion into a secular sign. He keeps "an image of the Virgin Mary" displayed on his stall as "a sign of his occupation" so that potential customers will be able to find his wares. No longer occupying a sacred place or inviting adoration, Rochus's image of the Virgin Mary serves a commercial rather than a religious purpose. The artist thus transforms one of the most precious and revered images of medieval spirituality—an image the reformers find especially offensive because it elicits such intense awe—into a mere sign simply by altering his rhetorical presentation of it. His statue of the Virgin Mary, which sits on his stall to call attention to his merchandise, is a thoroughly demystified image.

But Rochus cannot completely control the way his viewers see his images, and he eventually falls victim to the authorities who seek to enforce the practice of the Roman faith. In recounting his run-in with the Spanish inquisitor, Foxe helps to construct the ideological battle over images that he and his fellow reformers wage against their Roman Catholic opponents. What Rochus has declared a sign, the inquisitor

[43] Ibid., 4:450–51.

insists on treating as a sacred object. What Rochus declares to be his personal "workmanship," the product of his own imagination and therefore his to mar if "the image were not after his fantasy," the inquisitor claims for the church. What Rochus views as a legitimate act—breaking an artifact that he himself has made—the inquisitor judges to be a capital offense—the willful defacement of a holy object.

Their struggle centers on the issue of who owns, and has the right to control, the artist's production. As an agent of the Church, the inquisitor asserts his right, first to set his own price for the statue of the Virgin Mary, and then to confiscate it. Rochus, however, denies the inquisitor this power. He asserts ownership over his own creation and, in so doing, refuses the Church the right to determine how his image is valued, used, and, ultimately, interpreted. Because Rochus has so thoroughly demystified this image of the Virgin Mary, disassociating it from the sacred, claiming for it no magical properties, and openly acknowledging its artifice, he feels free to do with it what he would—set its price, determine how it is used, define what it signifies, alter it, and even destroy it. He asserts that his statue, divested of all mystery, ceases to fall under the control of the Church, and he claims that as its creator, he can use it for whatever purposes—personal or commercial—he wishes. When he refuses to sell it and then smashes it to pieces in order to prevent its confiscation, Rochus sees himself as exercising his right of ownership.

Although the Protestant artist asserts his liberation from the authoritative control of the Roman Church, his independence comes at a cost. Foxe implies that Protestantism empowers the artist, paradoxically, by disempowering—desacralizing—his images. In removing his images from sacred spaces where they elicit wonder and awe and displaying them as commercial signs and commodities in the marketplace, Rochus not only secularizes his art, he decenters it as well. Displaced from their privileged position in the church, where they were a central focus of devotion, and stripped of the extraordinary powers that had earlier been invested in them, his images are understood to be merely material objects, human artifacts that have no power to comfort, heal, or save the spectator who gazes upon them. Instead of giving access to the divine, they function as secular signs, deflecting attention away from themselves, pointing toward the absent and invisible.

Indeed, the Protestant artist seems compelled to mark his images as signs in order to prevent viewers from believing they are magical or powerful. Rochus does so when he chooses to make seals instead of religious icons and, again, when he uses the statue of the Virgin Mary as a sign of his enterprise. Nevertheless, his strategy fails to prevent the inquisitor from treating the statue of the Virgin as a religious totem. Since he cannot keep his image from being abused, Rochus destroys it. For Foxe, even the artist who explicitly defines his images as artificial signs or who deliberately evacuates his art work of all divinity and magic must be willing to play the iconoclast, breaking his own images if he cannot prevent their abuse.

In memorializing Rochus and his martyrdom, Foxe asserts the artist's right to control the images he produces, privileges image breaking over image making, and nurtures in his readers an awareness of art as representation. By featuring the artist's struggle to produce acceptable images in a culture deeply divided over the status of images, Foxe also explores the boundary between abused and unabused images.[44] Rather than condemn the profession of the artist, as some of the more radical reformers do, his narrative approves of the production of certain kinds of secular images while it condemns the creation of sacred images. Foxe thus uses the story of Rochus to develop for his readers the distinction between images that elicit reverence or devotion and images that are used for nonreligious purposes, a distinction reinforced as well in a reformed English catechism: "The artes of paynting, ingraveing, imbroydering, carving, casting metall, etc., are not to be simply forbidden: but [what is forbidden is] that anything so devised should be used for any holinesse, or that any affection of holinesse, should bee attributed thereunto."[45]

In documenting how Rochus, upon his conversion to Protestantism, switched from making religious icons to making seals, Foxe defines an emerging Protestant aesthetics, one that restrains the power of the image to elicit awe and wonder by forcing the spectator to become conscious about how it signifies. After Rochus ceases to make sacred images and turns to making signs, which have no essential value and no fixed meaning, he feels free to determine both the price of his art and what his images signify. Thus, his conversion to Protestantism does not shut down his creative energies, despite Protestant hostilities toward sacred

[44] Phillips discusses the reformers' distinction between abused and unabused images in *Reformation of Images*, pp. 55–77, 88–91, 147–50.

[45] John Calvin, *The Catechisme* (1582), sigs. C4^v–C4^r.

images, but rather authorizes him to enter into and attempt to manipulate a new symbol system, one that is characterized by self-reflexivity, arbitrariness, and the free-floating play of signifiers.

Although they can only suggest the narrative power and thematic richness of *Actes and Monuments*, the four anecdotes I discuss here illustrate how Foxe dramatizes the clash of two competing and irreconcilable theologies to convey both the unsettling and the exhilarating effects of religious crisis. Each anecdote foregrounds key terms in the debate between the traditionalists and the reformers, using individuals to give voice to the opposing principles of the Roman and the reformed religions. Edmund Allin and the martyrs who carry away the Rood of Dovercourt interrogate the truth claims of the old religion, expose its marvels as superstitions, and reinterpret its mysteries as fictions. Prest's Wife and Rochus insist on divorcing the sacred from the aesthetic; they declare art to be the invention of man and deny that images possess divine power. All four anecdotes show how a conversion to Protestantism alters, often profoundly, the way individuals perceive and understand the physical world. Foxe's protagonists look upon miraculous images with skepticism, demystify mysterious rites with empirical reasoning, resist the appeal of the imaginative with appeals to faith and the word of God, and desacralize images by calling attention to their artifice and identifying them as representations.

Foxe uses their stories to undermine traditional beliefs about images, driving a wedge between the medieval past and a present he helps to define. But if Eamon Duffy is right in arguing that "the wholesale removal of the images, vestments, and vessels which had been the wonder of foreign visitors to the country, and in which the collective memory of the parishes were, quite literally, enshrined" was a "sacrament of forgetfulness" and an "act of oblivion," surely Foxe seeks to substitute his own narrative history in England's collective memory, replacing dramatic anecdotes celebrating Protestant iconoclasm and skepticism for the shattered and discredited images of the Roman Church.[46] The degree to which he succeeds will, I think, become evident in the following chapters, as I show how Renaissance dramatists replicate his plots of demystification, appropriate his metaphors of stranger and whore, rehearse the eucharistic controversy he explores, and grapple with the questions he raises about the nature and function of their art.

[46] Duffy, *Stripping of the Altars*, pp. 480, 494.

CHAPTER TWO

The Rhetoric of Reform

On the third day, which was Ash Wednesday (as the pope's ceremonial
church doth call it), . . . it was agreed that the said images should be
burnt altogether; so that in nine great heaps all the stocks and idols
there the same day were burnt to ashes before the great church door.
And thus, by God's ordinance it came to pass, that the same day
wherein the pope's priests are wont to show forth all their mourning,
and do mark men's foreheads with ashes, in remembrance that they
be but ashes, was to the whole city festival and joyful, for turning their
images to ashes; and so is observed and celebrated every year still, unto
this present day, with all mirth, plays, and pastimes, in remembrance
of the same ashes; which day may there be called a right Ash Wednesday of God's own making.

—John Foxe, *Actes and Monuments*

A Revolutionary Rhetoric

In the above description of an iconoclastic event that occurred
in Basel in 1523, John Foxe substitutes the ashes of burned
images for the ashes which the "the pope's priests" use on
Ash Wednesday to "mark men's foreheads with ashes, in remembrance
that they be but ashes." In doing so, he subverts a traditional image of
the Roman Church. Rather than affirm the image of ashes as a sacred
sign conferred by priests, a sign that symbolizes mortality and penitence, Foxe uses it to celebrate the deliberate destruction of "stocks
and idols," an iconoclastic act that reduces all the beautiful images of
the Roman Church to an insignificant, charred rubble. And yet, of
course, Foxe does not obliterate the image of ashes in his iconoclastic
narrative but instead employs it in a powerful, new way. His ash pile—
all that remains of the beloved images gathered from the magnificent
churches of Basel—serves as a memorable sign of the people's repudiation of the Roman Church, its images and ceremonies, its priests
and pope. Foxe thus appropriates a sacred symbol of the traditional
church, wresting it from its original context and reinterpreting it. Ashes

still signify mortality, but now they stand for the death of the traditional church, its images and iconic practices, including the practice of marking the forehead of penitents with ashes.

By juxtaposing the ceremonial ashes and the iconoclastic ashes, Foxe calls into question the Roman Catholic ritual observation of Ash Wednesday, exposing it as theatrical and artificial—and thus deserving of repudiation. By pointedly contrasting the priests' celebration of Ash Wednesday to the people's celebration of the iconoclasts' bonfires, however, Foxe not only denies the legitimacy of the Roman ritual but also lays claim to an "authentic" new ritual, asserting that the Protestant commemoration of the burning of the sacred images, with its "mirth, plays, and pastimes," is "a right Ash Wednesday of God's own making." Although he attempts to discredit the traditional observation of Ash Wednesday, refusing its emotionally charged drama of penance, he thus champions another kind of theatricality, one that features the spectacular destruction of images rather than the visual display of the penitent. Foxe imagines here a new, Protestant theater, one that he defines as God's own theater. It is a theater capable of liberating its spectators from the false "idols" and ceremonies of the traditional church, understood to be mere human inventions.

That the people enthusiastically participated in their liberation and joyfully commemorated it in the years that followed this particular iconoclastic event is a central assertion of Foxe's narrative, an assertion that is contradicted by traditionalists who report profound emotional distress among the eyewitnesses to the iconoclasm that swept Basel in the early years of the Reformation.[1] Foxe's rhetoric seems calculated to appeal to the common people and is illustrative of the way the English reformers—mostly members of an educated elite—sought to convert the masses by writing them into their narratives as proponents, and sometimes even as heroes, of the Reformation. Throughout *Actes and Monuments* Foxe casts common folk as central players in the Reformation, courageous Protestant protagonists in the struggle against the Roman Church. He repeatedly puts his reformed beliefs into the mouths of craftsmen, artists, millers, and runaway wives who speak the collo-

---

[1] Describing the reaction of Roman Catholic believers to the iconoclasm in Basel, Carlos Eire writes, "The Catholics, griefstricken at the sight of the iconoclastic ravages, shed 'tears of blood' over this 'saddest of all spectacles of superstition' " (*War against the Idols* [1986], pp. 118–19). See also Carl Christensen, *Art and the Reformation in Germany* (1979), p. 102.

quial language of the common person. At the same time, he puts traditional religious beliefs into the mouths of powerful men—archbishops, inquisitors, and officers of the crown—who speak the language of a learned elite. Nurturing identifications between the radical reformers and the masses he seeks to persuade, Foxe distances his readers from the familiar and destabilizes their relation to the past. He aligns the theology of the medieval church with men of privilege who abuse their authority, intimidate their social inferiors, and flaunt their power. He is consequently able to examine in some depth the theological issues at stake in this religious conflict without alienating the very people who might be expected to cling most vigorously to the old religious practices. The success of his rhetorical strategy can be measured by the persistent assumption, only recently discredited by revisionist historians, that the common people eagerly and quickly embraced Protestantism, when in fact many were highly resistant to the reforms of the church.

Clearly, Foxe is not interested merely in recording the pronounced changes that occurred in the way the English people worshiped, believed, and interpreted the world during the Reformation era. He aggressively seeks to bring them about. He attempts to achieve rhetorically the same kind of transformation his protagonists—Protestant reformers and martyrs—experience when they embrace the reformed religion and challenge the old one. That transformation, Anthony Kemp reminds us, was sudden and profound: "The reversal of historical vision, from union to difference, must have taken place in a decade at most for Foxe, and his experience must have been replicated by almost all who followed the movement for reform; the past changed its shape, revealed the beliefs held universally by the Western world for fifteen-hundred years to have been falsehood, in a single generation." Noting the enormity of Foxe's rhetorical task, Kemp goes on to observe that "Foxe must declare the world to be the opposite of its appearances, must prove the great majority of those who profess Christianity to be no Christians and to have no connection whatsoever to the Church of Christ." Foxe must, in effect, devise a "rhetoric against the declared and obvious in the world."[2] His challenge is to convince his readers that their most fundamental and cherished beliefs are false without alienating them. How does he accomplish this daunting task?

[2] Anthony Kemp, *The Estrangement of the Past* (1991), pp. 85, 96.

In the brief anecdote about iconoclastic activity in Basel that I quote above, I have identified a number of rhetorical strategies that Foxe uses to transform, or reform, his own readers: he appropriates and reinterprets a traditional image of the Roman Church; he displays an older form of theatricality in order to critique and contain it; he invents a new, Protestant form—an iconoclastic drama—which he naturalizes and identifies as God's creation; he denies the legitimacy of the traditional church by naming it "the pope's ceremonial church" (by inference, an institution corrupted by externals and serving men rather than God) while legitimating the burning of images as an act done "by God's ordinance"; and he aligns the people with the new, Protestant theology, portraying their loss as liberation and imagining them embracing the new, reformed rituals with joyful enthusiasm.

Foxe's rhetoric, here and in his larger work, is a striking example of what Kenneth Burke identifies as a "revolutionary" or "transitional" rhetoric, a rhetoric he defines as "propaganda by inclusion." Burke believes that an effective revolutionary rhetoric creates the conditions for change not by absolute negation or complete rupture but by appropriating and conserving the rhetoric of the very ideology it seeks to unmask and replace. In order to create "a collective will for change," Burke argues that the revolutionary must "plead with the unconvinced, which requires him to use *their* vocabulary, *their* values, *their* symbols, insofar as this is possible." Thus, Burke insists that effective propaganda is dialectical, not oppositional. By including the terms of the old as well as the new, even as it repositions and reevaluates those terms, the dialectical rhetoric Burke advocates, according to Frank Lentricchia, "establishes—forges—its historicity, its continuity as the inevitable, emergent language" and thus convinces the people to embrace the new ideology.[3]

The extraordinary success of *The Book of Martyrs* is surely due in part to its author's adoption of just such a revolutionary rhetoric. For example, Foxe appropriates a popular late medieval genre, the medieval saint's tale, preserving its conventions while reshaping its religious import. By so doing, he links the new, reformed theology with the historical past and appeals to his readers' desire for continuity and tradition

---

[3] Frank Lentricchia, "An Analysis of Burke's Speech" (1989), pp. 292–95; Kenneth Burke, "Revolutionary Symbolism in America" (1989), pp. 271–72; Lentricchia, "Analysis," p. 296.

even as he advocates profound change. Fitting the medieval genre to his own reformist ends, he recasts its martyrs as Protestants and its villains as papists. In his construction of Reformation history, Protestant sympathizers resemble the beloved saints of the old religion in their faithfulness to God, their perseverance in the face of torture and persecution, their courage, and their simple piety. However, they are persecuted not by pagan tyrants, but by the Roman Catholic clergy—the very men who, in an earlier era, authorized the saints' tales. And, like the pagan tyrants, the priests and archbishops in Foxe's narratives are arrogant, merciless, and cruel.

Furthermore, Foxe omits from his narratives of martyrdom any references to wondrous miracles or efficacious relics. In place of the conventional "proof" of God's favor toward the suffering martyr—awesome and spectacular manifestations of the divine—Foxe quotes the Scriptures, substituting the word of God for the efficacious image of the saint, faith in what cannot be seen for the visible miracle. Although he patterns his tales on medieval stories of persecution and martyrdom, he thus pointedly departs from generic expectations, eliciting a different set of responses from his readers.

By adopting a medieval genre that had great popular appeal and using it in the service of a reformed religion explicitly opposed to the ideological assumptions of the original genre, Foxe thus reinterprets a familiar narrative of persecution. He identifies the old religion with the tyranny, oppression, and superstition of pagan monarchs and religions and associates the reformed religion with the true faith. He attempts to cut his readers off from the immediate past by rendering it alien and anti-Christian, and he encourages them to identify his revolutionary reforms with the primitive church and the original Christian evangelists. His narratives are revolutionary, in Burke's sense of the term, because they appropriate an older genre, only to turn it against the very institution—the Roman Church—that had, in an earlier age, created and sustained it. His use of the popular, medieval genre protects his readers from fully confronting the radical break with the past that the choice of Protestantism actually represents.

In his study of Reformation historiography, Kemp makes a similar observation. Interested in the way Foxe uses "medieval forms of historiography" paradoxically to repudiate medieval assumptions about historical continuity, he observes that "Foxe's devotion to his models is deceptive. Within the traditional structure he proposes radical ideas that often negate and reverse the intentions of his originals. Foxe inhabits the old forms in order to take account of them, to discount them." Kemp argues that Foxe subverts the traditional forms, using them to refute the past and legitimize a radical, new ideology while obscuring the revolutionary nature of his project. "The elegance of the scheme," he notes, "is that it justifies revolution while denying innovation."[4] Foxe, in other words, appeals to a medieval fiction of continuity in order to achieve a radical break with the past.

Foxe's revolutionary rhetoric thus works in part by destabilizing "the declared and obvious." Although Foxe challenges his readers' fundamental assumptions about the world, he does so by manipulating familiar forms and appropriating well-known images. Rather than openly reject or attack the past, he appeals to his readers' desire for continuity, but he does so by presenting a radically revised version of the past, thus further disrupting his readers' sense of the familiar and the known. If the popularity of *Actes and Monuments* or the remarkable endurance of its historical constructions is any indication, the rhetorical strategies Foxe uses to reform the English people were extraordinarily effective. They are typical of Reformation discourse and widely adopted not only by other polemical writers but also by artists and writers who, deeply affected by sixteenth-century religious reforms, responded by forging a new, Protestant aesthetics. In the remaining part of this chapter, I show how visual artists who embrace the new faith employ a revolutionary rhetoric similar to Foxe's, appropriating the images and forms of the medieval past only to subvert and reinterpret them. Their art, I argue, is both destabilizing and transformative, for it alters, in fundamental ways, the spectator's relation to its images.

By extending my analysis of the rhetoric of reform to the work of visual artists, I want to consider how the theology of the reformers, and in particular the iconoclastic fervor of early Protestantism, informs the aesthetics of Protestant art. I begin with a discussion of polemical, or propagandistic, art, then turn to major paintings that feature religious subject matter, and, finally, look at a painting with a secular subject. Through an examination of a range of visual art produced during the Reformation, I hope to identify the elements of an emerging Protestant aesthetics that I find operating as well in the tragedies of the London commercial stage.

[4] Kemp, *Estrangement of the Past*, pp. 88, 87.

The Reformation of the Gaze

Far from suppressing the visual, sixteenth-century religious reform provides a stimulus for the production of images. The breaking of familiar and well-loved images necessitates the making of new ones. Because the iconoclasts raise questions about the relative powers of the visual image and the spectator's gaze, they draw attention to the act of seeing. Looking becomes a problematic activity, at once dangerous and meaningful, an activity to be examined and tested. Many of the visual artists in the sixteenth century who embrace Protestantism respond to the iconoclastic fervor of the reformers by disrupting traditional modes of sight and deliberately nurturing new ways of seeing—more skeptical, more self-reflexive, and more attentive to what lies beyond visual representations. In so doing, they embark on an ambitious project to reform vision.

Although they are hostile to the images of the Roman Church, the English reformers use images to serve their own polemical purposes, deploying them to attack the Roman Church, its rituals, its ceremonies, and especially its sacred images. Foxe, for instance, illustrates *Actes and Monuments* with scores of pictures, adding even more woodcuts in later editions of his work. In prefatory and editorial comments, he shows no ambivalence about his use of illustrations. Indeed, one of his stated objectives is to make visible the "persecuted church" which he declares "hath been . . . almost scarce visible or known to worldly eyes," in striking contrast to the Church of Rome which, he believes, is "so visible and glorious in the eyes of all the world, so shining in outward beauty" that the people mistake it for the true church.[5]

Catherine Coats believes that Foxe's use of illustrations marks him as a transitional figure "between Catholics and Calvinists." She suggests that Foxe "would prefer to eliminate imagery, but fears an inability to fully communicate without it."[6] I disagree. Although the images of martyrs engulfed in flames, which appear again and again in *Actes and Monuments*, might seem to replicate the familiar medieval images of persecuted saints and martyrs and thus identify Foxe as an author who has not yet achieved a total break with the medieval past, Foxe's illus-

[5] Foxe, *A&M*, 1:515.
[6] Catherine Coats, *(Em)bodying the Word* (1992), pp. 50–51.

❧The Martyrdome of Iohn Cardmaker Preacher,and Iohn Warne Vpholſter,An.1555.May.30.

Cardmaker talkng with the Shꝛieffe.

The Mar=tyꝛdome of M.Iohn Cardmaker Pꝛeacher, and Iohn VVarne Upholſter, in Smith=field, An.1555. May.30.

FIGURE 3. "The Martyrdome of John Cardmaker Preacher, and John Warne Upholster. An. 1555. May. 30." John Foxe, *Actes and Monuments* (London, 1570), p. 1752. By permission of the University of Iowa Libraries (Iowa City).

trators use a range of rhetorical strategies—revolutionary in their impact—to disrupt the devotional gaze.

An illustration of the martyrdom of John Cardmaker and John
Warne, for instance, includes a verbal inscription, citing Warne's last
words, that prevents its viewers from venerating its central image of the
two martyrs. Tied to the stake and preparing to burn, Warne addresses
the spectators in the crowd gathered to watch his execution, warning
them (and Foxe's readers) to "Beware of idolatry" (Figure 3). Here
the illustrator uses a familiar medieval image of the suffering martyr,
but he does so to call attention to the danger of the traditional practice
of adoring images (including images of martyred saints). Throughout
Actes and Monuments, similar illustrations appropriate the visual conventions of medieval depictions of martyrdom, but in fact they seem cal-

Three Marshals hanged for takyng downe the Roode of Dousrcowrt. An.1532.

FIGURE 4. "Three Martyrs hangeth for takyng downe the Roode of Dovercourt. An. 1532." John Foxe, *Actes and Monuments* (London, 1570), p. 1173. By permission of the University of Iowa Libraries (Iowa City).

culated to undermine traditional forms of piety. For Foxe, the spectacle of martyrdom is not an idolatrous but rather a reforming image, capable even of turning the spectators' eyes away from images.

Another Foxe illustration, depicting the execution of the three men condemned to death for stealing and burning the Rood of Dovercourt, features an impressive state spectacle—the hanging of three criminals—yet it deliberately subverts the awesome spectacle of the scaffold by juxtaposing it to the familiar religious image of the crucified Christ (Figure 4). Even though the main scene presents the official hangings as powerful political theater that would seem to reinforce the authority of the crown—the monarch's soldiers, spears in hand, look on as the lifeless bodies of the rebels dangle from nooses—the secondary scene of Christ on the cross that appears as a vision in the left-hand corner undermines the official meaning of the event and denies the Roman Catholic monarch the power such a spectacle would ordinarily affirm. The dreaded power of the crown is linked to the enemies of God and thus contained, and the rebellious men are celebrated as Christian martyrs who, embracing the paradigm of Christ's martyrdom, spiritually triumph over their oppressors.

Since this picture illustrates the execution of the three iconoclasts responsible for destroying an image believed to have marvelous powers, the visual depiction of their martyrdom is especially intriguing, for it employs an image of the crucified Christ to demystify a legendary image of Christ on the cross, one that was widely believed to have efficacious powers. In his narrative about the destruction of the Rood of Dovercourt, discussed in Chapter 1, Foxe celebrates these iconoclasts for their courage in testing the validity of the image's purported magic. But in his illustration he aligns an image of the martyred iconoclasts with an image of Christ. In contrast to the discredited Rood of Dovercourt, however, his image—fragmentary, visionary, marginal, pointing beyond itself—seems calculated to prevent its viewers from adoring it. It is not offered as a salvific or curative image but rather as a reminder of the historical crucifixion, and thus it redefines the established church's heretics as Christian heroes and the state's criminals as martyrs willing to die for the truth.

Some of the illustrations in Foxe's *Actes and Monuments* feature the rituals and ceremonies of the Roman Church, but in doing so they expose them as idolatrous. Although they display Roman Catholic mysteries, they thus demystify them and attempt to estrange the viewer from them. One such illustration depicts a particular Roman Catholic procession that occurred in Cambridge in 1557 (Figure 5). It presents the ceremonial event in all its theatrical and spectacular detail: clerics, altar boys, and laypeople march in a huge procession through the streets, carrying banners, torches, bells, candles, books, and canopies. They circle a bonfire. A few onlookers kneel in reverence as the procession passes while others turn towards the fire. There, Foxe's caption explains, the Catholic authorities burn the newly disinterred bones of Martin Bucer and Paulus Phagius as they throw the two reformers' books into the fire. The activity at the center of this picture—the spectacular burning of dead men's bones and books—calls into question the validity of the Church. Foxe seeks to undercut the ornate and impressive pageantry of the circling procession by linking it to injustice, persecution, and the Inquisition. Roman Catholic ceremony, with its attention to visual magnificence and theatrical splendor, here becomes associated with an excessive—and perverted—attention to the body

FIGURE 5. "The order and maner of burnyng M. Martin Bucers and Paulus Phagius bones, and also of their Bookes, with a solemne generall procession, at Cambridge. Anno. 1557. February. 6." John Foxe, *Actes and Monuments* (London, 1570), p. 2151. By permission of the University of Iowa Libraries (Iowa City).

(dead men's bones), and Roman Catholic rituals are identified with an antagonism toward the word. In illustrations like this one, Protestant artists display traditional images in an effort to destabilize their viewers' relation to them.

Perhaps the most striking example of the way the illustrators of *Actes and Monuments* employ a revolutionary rhetoric, appropriating and re-interpreting traditional forms to advance a radical new ideology, is the elaborate frontispiece of the 1570 edition (Figure 6). It presents what at first appears to be a very conventional image of the Last Judgment. In it, Christ sits in judgment in the heavens, presiding over the final, absolute division of souls into the saved and the damned. But in Foxe's version of the Last Judgment, the damned are not depicted as heathens or conventional sinners. Instead, they are identified as the Roman Catholic faithful, doomed to eternal punishment *because* they practice the traditional religion. In sharp contrast, the saved are the Protestant be-

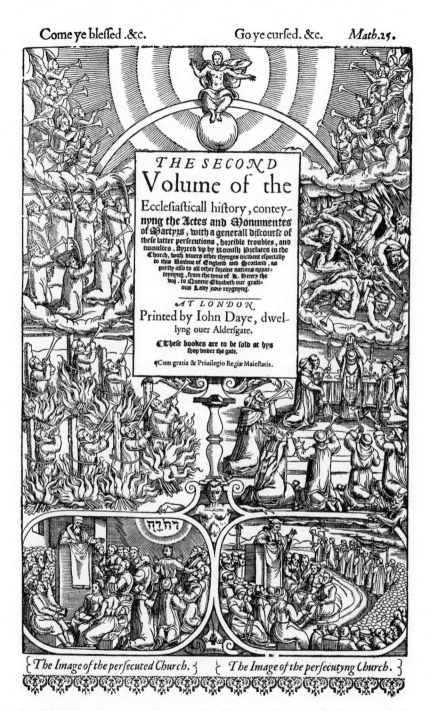

FIGURE 6. Frontispiece to the second volume. John Foxe, *Actes and Monuments* (London, 1570). By permission of the University of Iowa Libraries (Iowa City).

lievers and martyrs. Using the bipartite structure of Last Judgment paintings, the artist expresses the divisive nature of the religious conflict that splits the Christian church in the sixteenth century. He identifies the Roman Catholic Church with demons and damnation, Protestantism with Christ and eternal salvation.

Foxe's frontispiece also carefully distinguishes traditional and reformed practices, paying particular attention to the role of sight in each. The Roman Catholics engage in what the illustrator depicts as an idolatrous kind of looking: they kneel in adoration of the elevated Host, attend to their rosaries, and march in a holy procession towards a sacred shrine, their eyes fixed on the sacred images of the Roman Church. In striking contrast, the reformed worshipers are shown listening to the minister preach the word of God while they read their Bibles or gaze heavenward. Their looking—what we might call a transcendent gaze—constructs them as saved souls. Foxe's frontispiece thus depicts Roman Catholics as damned because they practice idolatry while it celebrates Protestants as saved because, inspired by the word, they sustain faith in an invisible God. Nevertheless, it employs *images* to attack image worship and also to teach a new, reformed mode of seeing. Although Foxe's frontispiece ridicules traditional modes of sight that seek God in visible things, it uses pictorial representation to teach its readers to turn away from material images and to direct their eyes inward and heavenward.

The frontispiece might also be said to juxtapose two kinds of theater, the Roman Mass and the Protestant martyrdom. Depicting the Mass as a highly theatrical ceremony, it represents the dramatic moment when the priest elevates the host, displaying the transubstantiated body of Christ, the central mystery of the Mass. The elevation of the host is presented here as a wondrous and idolatrous spectacle, eliciting devotion and awe from the worshipers, who encircle it, kneel to it, and blow their trumpets in celebration of it. A very different drama unfolds in the parallel space devoted to the Protestant martyrs. Tied to burning stakes and undergoing unimaginable physical torture, they willingly relinquish their bodies while looking up to heaven and blowing their trumpets to the risen Christ. By juxtaposing two rival theaters, a demonic one featuring the carnal display of an image and a heavenly one showing the heroic surrender of the body through faith, the illustrator imagines a divinely sanctioned theater even as he declares the theatricality of the Roman Church dangerous and false.

John Bale employs a similar rhetorical technique in his play, *Thre laws*. Ritchie Kendall shows how Bale "resolves his own ambivalent attitude toward the rectitude of his vocation" as a dramatist by distinguishing between a demonic playacting—represented by the "singing, dancing, jesting, and plotting" of the Vice Infidelity—and a holy or godly playacting—"compyled" by Bale but ordained by God himself. Bale, in other words, demonizes one kind of theater—characterized by artifice, trickery, intrigue, and lavish spectacle and identified with the Roman Church—and naturalizes another kind—characterized by the reenactment of a "pattern of sanctification" and identified with the Protestant faith.[7] Whereas the demonic (Roman Catholic) theater is fraudulent and seductive, the godly (Protestant) theater is true and direct—not "theatrical" at all but, Bale would have us believe, natural and authentic. As Kendall sees it, "Bale's purified drama" surrounds and controls the "polluted drama of the Vices."[8] If he is correct, Bale's holy playacting functions much as the image of the Protestant martyrs in Foxe's frontispiece does, offering an alternative to the "polluted" spectacle and theater of the old religion. Although Bale condemns the cunning theatricality of the Vice and Foxe's illustrator repudiates the priest's idolatrous display of the host, both feature theatricality and spectacle to advance their reformist goals, and both appropriate traditional genres in an effort to forge new, Protestant art forms.

I have thus far examined images produced for explicitly polemical or propagandistic purposes, showing how they disrupt traditional modes of sight and undermine confidence in traditional images. But many other sixteenth- and early seventeenth-century works of art produced in countries where the Reformation flourished can also be understood to nurture habits of sight that are distinctly Protestant. In the early stages of the Reformation, as the controversy over images intensifies, artists like Albrecht Dürer, Lucas van Leyden, and Lucas Cranach begin to employ a revolutionary rhetoric similar to Foxe's, appropriating the sacred genres of late medieval and Italian Renaissance art in order to disrupt the devotional gaze and foster new ways of seeing. Instead of arousing awe or eliciting adoration, they make their viewers self-conscious about how they see and, in effect, reform vision.

In *Dance Round the Golden Calf* (c. 1530), for example, Lucas van

---

[7] Ritchie D. Kendall, *The Drama of Dissent* (1986), pp. 108–11.
[8] Ibid., *Drama of Dissent*, p. 109.

Leyden depicts the Israelites worshiping the idol of a golden calf, a
Biblical story repeatedly invoked by the Protestant reformers in their
attacks on the idolatry of the Roman Church (Figure 7).[9] Although
many reformers of the time condemn altarpieces as idols that arouse
the devotional gaze, van Leyden paints one calculated to disrupt that
gaze. Rather than feature a divine image in the central panel, as conventional altarpieces do, he depicts the very act of idolatry. The foreground of his painting is dominated by the Israelites at play—eating,
drinking, losing themselves in physical pleasures, as the Bible characterizes them after they have been "corrupted" by idolatry. Behind them
ecstatic worshipers dance joyfully around the golden calf they have
erected.

The image of the calf, far in the background, is dwarfed by the foreground scene of revelry and the looming mountains of the background
landscape. It could hardly inspire adoration from van Leyden's own
viewers, and, of course, it is not itself an image that would have elicited
veneration among Christians of any persuasion. Indeed, it is perhaps
the best known of the pagan idols denounced in the Bible, and by
displaying it in the central panel of an altarpiece, where the image of
the divine would ordinarily appear, van Leyden subtly links visual representations of God with pagan idols. Furthermore, the dark figure of
Moses emerges from the mountain directly behind the idol, followed
by an ominous black cloud, so that the viewer of the painting can have
no doubt that divine punishment of the idolaters is imminent. By using
the sacred altarpiece to stage idolatry in all its theatrical detail, van
Leyden subverts the medieval genre he appropriates. His painting depicts an idolatrous image and idolatrous acts for iconoclastic purposes.
Like Foxe when he appropriates the medieval genre of the saint's life
and uses it to further the Protestant cause, van Leyden uses a traditional
altarpiece to display an idolatrous spectacle in order to condemn and
contain it.

Albrecht Dürer constructs the two companion paintings of *The Four
Apostles* as the outer two panels of a triptych, a conventional form of
the late medieval altarpiece (Figure 8). Painted shortly after he had
embraced Lutheranism, he donated them to the city of Nuremberg in

---

[9] For a discussion of van Leyden's painting, see David Freedberg, *The Power of Images*
(1989), pp. 378–85.

FIGURE 7. *Dance Round the Golden Calf.* Lucas van Leyden (c. 1530). By permission of the Rijksmuseum-Stichting, Amsterdam.

FIGURE 8. *The Four Apostles.* Albrecht Dürer (1526). By permission of Alte Pinakothek, Munich.

1526, a year after the city had decided to "give leave to the Pope."[10] Some art historians believe the artist had originally intended to paint a third, central panel—typically the central and most significant devotional image of an altarpiece. Others insist that the two pictures were meant to be viewed as a single, unified work, without reference to the genre of the altarpiece. But I would argue that Dürer uses this older genre to call attention to what is not there—to assert the material absence of God and to insist on God's invisibility. The empty space where a representation of the sacred would have appeared in a medieval altarpiece is, I think, profoundly destabilizing. If Dürer's spectators find themselves searching for a representation of God in the place between these two panels where the central panel would conventionally be, they must confront their futile desire to see God and reorient their gaze —turning it inward or looking beyond the material world. By thwarting the devotional gaze, Dürer nurtures in his spectators a self-consciousness about their own seeing, reminding them, as they view his painting, that God cannot be perceived with the senses and inviting them to contemplate the spiritual. One of the earliest paintings inspired by the Reformation, *The Four Apostles* is thus characterized by a remarkable self-reflexivity.

Perhaps the most striking feature of *The Four Apostles* is Dürer's attention to the gaze of his four subjects, John, Peter, Paul, and Mark. In the left-hand panel, John looks down at an open book in his hands. Peter, nearly hidden by the taller and younger John, casts his eyes to the ground. In the right-hand panel Paul, holding a closed book and a sword, gives a stern, sideways glance and seems to look out toward the viewer of the painting. His gaze is penetrating, authoritative, knowing. Behind him, almost swallowed in darkness, is Mark. Holding a scroll, he stares intently past Paul, beyond the picture frame, as if he were looking at something in the dark space occupied by the viewers.

Beneath the painted images appear four scriptural passages in German, each a quotation from one of the four men admonishing the viewer to distrust externals and to value the spiritual above the worldly. If the viewers move between the image and the quoted words of each apostle, they will find themselves being instructed in how to look. The passage from John, for instance, asserts that "God is Spirit, and they that worship him, must worship him in spirit and in truth." This would

---

[10] Erwin Panofsky, *The Life and Art of Albrecht Dürer* (1943), p. 233.

seem to associate John's gaze upon the book with attention to God's word. The passage from Peter, in contrast, condemns "them that walke after the flesh . . . as brute beasts, led with sensualitie." Linked to the image of Peter, who casts his eyes to the ground, this quotation may serve to remind the viewer that all carnal things are but dust. Because Peter is the symbolic head of the Roman Church, Dürer may also be using Peter's words against the established Church, which Dürer, like so many Protestant polemicists, associates with carnality, sensuality, and the kind of "bodily seeing" typical of late medieval spirituality.

The words of Paul and Mark also contextualize the gazes of the apostles in Dürer's painting, for the quotation from Paul entreats the viewers to consider their own imperfections and the quotation from Mark warns of the "Scribes" who make a theatrical display of their piety while "devour[ing] widows' houses, even under a colour of long prayers." Dürer's extraordinary attention to the gaze of his subjects, I suggest, nurtures a Protestant mode of seeing. By directing Paul's scrutinizing gaze towards his own spectators and Mark's piercing eyes out into the world they inhabit, Dürer's painting elicits the kind of self-examination advocated by early Protestants, one that is interior, self-reflexive, and critical. In the play between written word and painted image, Dürer thus encourages his spectators to look beyond externals. Using the medium of paint, he provokes them to remember what cannot be rendered in paint or perceived with the eye.

The Four Apostles is an early example of the tendency among artists in Protestant countries to thematize sight. Dürer's intense interest in vision is typical of the way their work calls attention to the gazes of their subjects, whom they depict as spectators: awed idolaters, inquisitive voyeurs, empathetic witnesses, divinely illuminated blind men, inwardly focused readers. Many of their paintings, like van Leyden's *Dance Round the Golden Calf*, are drawn from the Bible, especially the Old Testament. They often explore biblical narratives, like the story of Lot's wife, that illustrate the danger of looking. Others, like Cranach's painting of Lucretia discussed below, use secular narratives. Whether religious or secular, they introduce a profoundly unsettling ambivalence towards the visual image, forcing their viewers to become self-conscious about their own looking.

Two companion paintings by Lucas Cranach, portraying the classical heroine Lucretia and the Jewish heroine Judith, illustrate how Protestant artists self-reflexively address the erotic power of their own images, simultaneously eliciting and disrupting the adoring (idolatrous) gaze (Figure 9). Both feature the isolated nude body of a well-known heroine, using a few narrative details that call attention to the violent climax of each woman's story. Judith holds the severed head of her people's enemy, Holofernes, and the sword she used to slay him. A lavish necklace reminds the viewer that the Jewish heroine lured Holofernes to his death by adorning her body with jewelry, seducing him with her ornamented beauty. Lucretia holds a dagger to her breast, preparing to kill herself after she has been raped by Tarquin, a man inflamed by reports of her beauty and chastity. In both paintings, then, Cranach explores the seductive power of female beauty and yet destabilizes the implied male gaze by linking the eroticized female body to violence and death.

Painted sometime after 1537, the two limewood panels are, I believe, the work of an artist highly sensitive to the Protestant reformers' intensely iconophobic attacks on late medieval iconophilia. An established artist before the Reformation, Cranach befriended Luther, converted to the Lutheran faith, and, like many other German artists during the religious conflicts of the sixteenth century, altered, often in striking ways, the style and content of his art in the years following his Lutheran conversion.[11] Shortly after embracing Luther, Cranach "became intensely interested in the naked human form"—an interest that Max Friedlander attributes to "the secular spirit of the Renaissance, with its bold eroticism."[12] But Cranach's interest in the nude female body is, I believe, far more conflicted, and far more attuned to the religious spirit of the Reformation, than Friedlander's "bold eroticism" implies. In his paintings of Venus, Eve, Salome, Delilah, Omphale (telling subjects, all) as well as Judith and Lucretia, Cranach expresses a deep ambivalence towards the images of beautiful women that he renders so beautifully. Critical discussions of the erotic dimension of Cranach's nudes have tended to ignore the tension in his paintings between

---

[11] Max J. Friedlander and Jakob Rosenberg, *The Paintings of Lucas Cranach* (1978). Arguing that no early sixteenth-century German artist "changed his temperament and his relationship to visible reality so completely as did Cranach," Friedlander laments that after Cranach embraced Luther, "the impassioned symphony of nature gives way before a cool, precise, rational exposition" in his work (p. 16).

[12] Friedlander and Rosenberg, *Cranach*, p. 23.

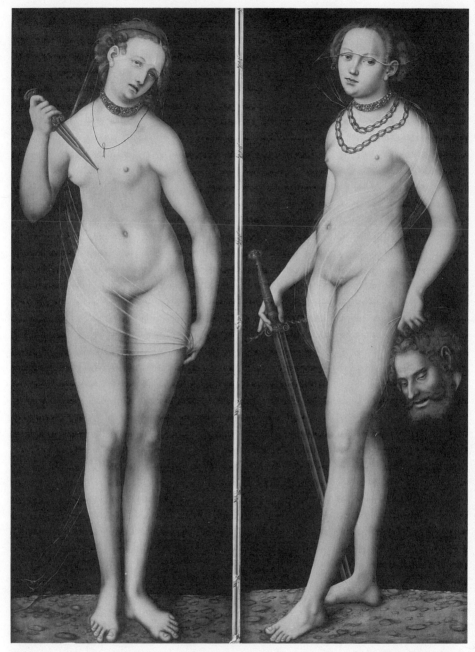

FIGURE 9. *Lucretia* and *Judith*. Lucas Cranach. (c.1537). Formerly in Gemaldegalerie, Staatliche Kunstsammlungen, Dresden, Germany. Destroyed during World War II. By permission of Alinari/Art Resource, New York.

the seductive allure of the female body and narrative details that problematize that allure.[13]

Judith and Lucretia are widely used subjects in sixteenth-century Italian and northern European art, and their stories often inspire erotic paintings that wholeheartedly celebrate the seductive power of images.[14] Cranach, however, interprets this narrative material in a startlingly different—a revolutionary—way. His depiction of Lucretia, for example, employs an iconoclastic rhetoric that disrupts the eye and destabilizes the viewer's pleasure in the erotic image. Naked except for a transparent veil draped around her torso, Cranach's Lucretia stands, uncomfortably exposed, holding a dagger between her breasts. Its hard metal point pierces her soft flesh, and blood trickles from the open wound. Her right hand grasps the knife with extraordinary intention; her left hand clutches the veil in a determined but futile attempt to cover herself. A thick, ornamental choker adorns her neck along with a thin, threadlike necklace, tied in a knot just above her breasts. A sorrowful figure, she stands alone in a fallen landscape, her bare feet resting on stony ground. She glances away from her self-inflicted wound, her eyes pained but resolute, her expression one of overwhelming sadness. Resigned to her suicidal act, Lucretia faces death with haunting dignity.

Cranach's painting simultaneously appeals to the male viewer, encouraging his eye to linger on the gentle contours of an alluring, sensual, nude female body, and repels his aroused gaze, shaming him for his voyeuristic desire to look upon the exposed woman. The viewer cannot help looking at Lucretia, and yet, by looking, he, like the rapist Tarquin, violates her: unlike the conventional female nude, she does not want to be seen.[15] Cranach's image makes the viewer self-conscious about his own looking, and his act of seeing, not the female image, becomes the subject of the painting.

[13] A number of art historians acknowledge a potential conflict between Cranach's eroticism and his Protestant beliefs, but they attempt to resolve it either by invalidating the Protestant dimension of Cranach's work or by asserting that Cranach and his contemporaries, in Rosenberg's words, "saw no inconsistency in such contradictory interests." See, for instance, Jakob Rosenberg, "Lucas Cranach the Elder" (1969); Werner Schade, *Cranach* (1980), p. 68; and Robert A. Koch, "Venus and Amor by Lucas Cranach the Elder" (1969).

[14] See, for example, Ian Donaldson, *The Rapes of Lucretia* (1982); I am also indebted to the insights of Mary Garrard, "Artemisia and Susanna" (1982), pp. 147–71.

[15] I am indebted to John Berger, *Ways of Seeing* (1972), for this distinction.

By making the viewer aware of his own impulse to gaze at images, take pleasure in them, and fantasize about them, Cranach's painting forges identifications not with the wronged woman but with the men of Rome who idealize and eroticize Lucretia. Cranach situates his viewer in the place of the men Lucretia summoned to witness her suicide: her husband, father, and Brutus, men who are compelled by the spectacle of Lucretia's death to act to purge Rome of corruption. Like her husband, whose too ardent and imaginative narratives idealized her, making her body a desired object, her reputation a seductive fantasy, and like Tarquin, whose aroused imagination drives him to see and violate her, the viewer finds the image alluring, his imagination stimulated. Although he is horrified at Lucretia's mutilation of her own lovely body, he thus feels himself uncomfortably implicated in it. Made self-conscious about his own looking, he is forced to relinquish the very image that fires his imagination and to accede to its destruction.

Cranach's painting of Lucretia may well anticipate and even help to construct a modern male gaze that takes a pornographic pleasure in the image of a woman who is both pure and violated, chaste and abused. Lucretia's shame may perversely heighten the pleasure some viewers experience in this image. But our own familiarity with a pornographic tradition that eroticizes shame and dwells on the sadomasochistic may prevent us from recognizing more local cultural influences on Cranach's work. In a career that spans the early years of the Reformation crisis, in a city—Wittenberg—closely identified with Luther and his theological reforms, in a country traumatized by outbursts of iconoclastic violence, Cranach paints at least thirty-five versions of Lucretia, a woman who chooses to destroy her beautiful body because others cannot resist its allure. Might Cranach find in Lucretia an ideal subject through which to enact a symbolic renunciation of his own seductive and beguiling images? Might his repeated representations of Lucretia's suicide be, at heart, iconoclastic?

The story of Lucretia may well have great personal significance to Cranach as he tries to reconcile his craft—his image making—with his faith. In his paintings of Lucretia he explores the "problem" of images in the age of reform. Because beautiful images are, for the reformers, always vulnerable to abuse, because artifice arouses in them fears of seduction and wantonness, because the imagined and man-made, in their thinking, lure people away from an invisible God, sixteenth-century artists who convert to Protestantism face a professional crisis, one that requires them either to repudiate their craft or to develop ways of preventing their viewers from misusing—that is, adoring, desiring, overvaluing—their images. Continuing to create images after his conversion to Lutheranism, Cranach employs an iconoclastic rhetoric that, because it both exemplifies and seeks to contain the erotic power of images, is profoundly disturbing. Lucretia's mournful intentionality as she plunges the dagger into her heart is, in a sense, the artist's own as he repels the viewer from the powerful image he so lovingly portrays, "killing" his own creation, perhaps so that another Rome can be purified.

An Iconoclastic Theater?

The paintings and printed illustrations I analyze above show how visual artists sympathetic to religious reform develop a range of rhetorical strategies to guard against the idolatrous gaze and inculcate a new, Protestant mode of seeing. Cranach, Dürer, van Leyden, and the illustrators of *Actes and Monuments* internalize the iconoclastic impulses of early Protestantism, revising images and redefining their art in accordance with Protestant concerns about idolatry. Although they produce images of great power, their pictures work in disruptive ways, often arousing a wariness and uneasiness about the very act of gazing upon them.

Acknowledging that early reformers like Foxe used visual and dramatic art forms to further the cause of reform in England, Patrick Collinson argues in *The Birthpangs of Protestant England* that beginning in the 1580s, English reformers "turned their backs on these same cultural media, which now became the enemy no less than popery itself." In what he sees as a second phase of reform, he finds an "absolute and irretrievable divorce" between Protestantism and the drama of the Elizabethan and Jacobean stage, a divorce that "emancipated the English theatre by completing its secularisation." For Collinson, the Reformation exerts a significant influence on the development of English drama, "but only in a negative sense. No one turns Shakespeare himself into a chapter of the English Reformation."[16] Collinson articulates the widely held assumptions that English Protestantism is an enemy of the

[16] Patrick Collinson, *The Birthpangs of Protestant England* (1988), pp. 98, 112, 114, 94.

stage and that the drama of early modern England is a wholly secularized art form, assumptions I wish to challenge.

Working in a Protestant country whose enemies vigorously seek to return it to the Roman religion, Shakespeare and his contemporary playwrights face increasingly hostile attacks from enemies of their own, Protestant antitheatricalists who seek to close the theaters. They could hardly ignore the religious controversies threatening both their country and their occupation. Far from being "emancipated" from religion by the Reformation or influenced by it only in so much as it freed them "to explore the moral and social complexities of the human condition on their own terms and in their own language,"[17] the dramatists I study use the theater to dramatize the divisive conflicts and explore the central religious controversies of the Reformation. The moral and social complexities they explore often originate in religious crisis and change; the language they use is not infrequently the language of Protestant discourse and the Protestant English Bible; "their own terms" are sometimes explicitly Calvinist.

In the chapters that follow I argue that Elizabethan and Jacobean dramatists do not so much write outside of or in opposition to a Protestantism that is, at heart, iconoclastic and antitheatrical, as create new forms of drama that are both energized and threatened by the antitheatricality of the new religion. Like the paintings of van Leyden, Dürer, and Cranach that I discuss above, their plays are disruptive, for they interrogate their own medium and sometimes even turn theatricality against itself. In fact, Kyd, Marlowe, Shakespeare, Webster, and Middleton all exhibit the same "unsettling ambivalence" about the theater that Jonas Barish attributes to Ben Jonson when he asserts that Jonson "does not shed his antitheatrical bias" when he writes for the stage, but rather "builds it in."[18]

Laura Levine makes a similar point, observing "that the playwright is as 'contaminated' by the anxieties of the attacks which we think of him as 'defending' against as the attackers are themselves."[19] I agree. However, whereas she locates early modern antitheatricality in "the fear that there is no masculinity except in the performance of mascu-

[17] Ibid., p. 114.
[18] James Barish, *The Antitheatrical Prejudice* (1981), pp. 132, 145.
[19] Laura Levine, *Men in Women's Clothing* (1994), pp. 2, 9.

linity," I locate it in a Protestant-induced fear of idolatry and Reformation controversies about the validity of the imagination, the function of signs, and the nature of art. And I believe the dramatists defend their plays against the charges of the antitheatricalists by employing a revolutionary rhetoric that subverts and reinterprets older forms of theater while fostering new—Protestant—ways of seeing.

Many scholars read the antitheatrical tracts of men like Stephen Gosson and Phillip Stubbes as representative of Protestant (and especially puritan) attitudes towards the stage. In doing so, they honor the antitheatricalists' sharply defined opposition between the reformed religion and the theater and between themselves and the dramatists they condemn, and they therefore assume that the dramatists are antagonistic to the Protestant Church. But I find some intriguing parallels between the projects of the antitheatricalists (some of whom were formerly playwrights) and the dramatists, parallels that suggest that playwrights and antitheatricalists alike are responding to issues raised by the religious reforms.[20]

Both, for instance, relentlessly interrogate a kind of theatricality associated in Protestant discourse with the Roman Church, and both appropriate the rhetorical strategies of the reformers in an effort to discredit certain kinds of spectacle and theater. One such strategy involves putting the offending spectacle and theater on display. However disgusted Stephen Gosson is by the "wanton" and "wicked" spectacles of the stage, for example, he describes them in great detail, staging them, it would seem, in order to master them. "For the eye beeside the beautie of the houses, and the Stages," he complains, the devil "sendeth in Gearish apparell maskes, vauting, tumbling, daunsing of gigges, galiardes, morisces, hobbi-horses; showing of judgeling castes, nothing forgot, that might serve to set out the matter, with pompe, or ravish the beholders with varietie of pleasure."[21] As I will argue in my next chapter, Christopher Marlowe employs a similar strategy, staging magnificent theatrical spectacles, even as he attributes them to the devil. Although his spectacles are so dazzling they threaten to enthrall his spectators, Marlowe displays them not just to demonstrate their

---

[20] Levine makes a related point when she argues that "attacks against the stage regularly seem to conceive of themselves *as* plays" (ibid., p. 2).

[21] Gosson, *Plays Confuted in Five Actions* (1582), sigs. E1^v, E2^r, E1^r.

power but also, like Gosson, to exhaust them. He rehearses the magic, mystery, and wonder of the traditional religion in order to master and contain them.

The real difference between the antitheatricalists and the dramatists of early modern England, I suggest, lies not in their religious orientations, as has often been assumed, but rather in how they interpret the iconoclastic agenda of the reformed religion. Whereas the antitheatricalists conclude that all forms of theater are polluted and should be forbidden, the dramatists seek to reform the stage, developing rhetorical strategies that disrupt older modes of sight and producing plays that conform to Protestant theories of art and representation. Even as they display discredited forms of theatricality and spectacle, exposing them as fraudulent and illusory, they also use the stage to advance new—reformed—modes of seeing and interpreting. In the chapters that follow, I argue that Shakespeare and his contemporary playwrights invent a new form of theater, one that is, in the broadest sense, Protestant.

CHAPTER THREE

Censoring the Imaginary:
The Wittenberg Tragedies

O, reform it altogether!
> —*Hamlet*

Antitheatricality and the Stage

Ioan P. Couliano defines the Renaissance as "a culture of the phantasmic" and attributes its demise to the Protestant Reformation. In his provocative study, *Eros and Magic in the Renaissance*, he asserts that the reformers, and especially Geneva's Calvinists and London's puritans, impose what amounts to a "*total censorship of the imaginary, since phantasms are* [for these Protestants] *none other than idols conceived by the inner senses.*"[1] By identifying the imaginary with the idolatrous, Protestantism, he argues, destroys Renaissance culture. Couliano reiterates here a familiar narrative, one that divides the early modern era into two distinct and antagonistic movements, the Renaissance and the Reformation. The reformed religion, according to him, forbids and discredits what Renaissance culture cultivates and celebrates: the disciplined mastery of the imagination.

Couliano identifies an important dimension of the Calvinism that characterizes early English Protestantism, its distrust of the imagination.[2] That distrust becomes more pronounced in late sixteenth-century

---

[1] Ioan P. Couliano, *Eros and Magic in the Renaissance* (1987), p. 193.

[2] For a discussion of Calvin's influence on the sixteenth-century English Church, see Patrick Collinson, *Godly People* (1983), pp. 213–44; A. G. Dickens, *The English Reformation* (1964), pp. 197–201, 252; William Haller, *The Rise of Puritanism* (1984), pp. 8, 19, 84–85; George Huntston Williams, *The Radical Reformation* (1962), p. 780; R. T. Kendall, *Calvin and English Calvinism to 1649* (1979). For a discussion of Calvin's distrust of the imagination and human inventions see William J. Bouwsma, *John Calvin* (1988), p. 80. For evidence of English reformers' attitudes towards the imagination, see William Perkins, *A Warning against the idolatrie of the last times* (1601), sig. F8ᵛ; W. A. Wood, *A Fourme of*

England when Protestant efforts to censor, control, and suppress the imagination and its products intensify. English historians document a heightened fear of the imaginary and the "inner idols" of the mind in the sermons and polemics of many Elizabethan and Jacobean Protestant divines. They show how the later reformers advocate an inner iconoclasm more far-reaching, more pervasive, and more devastating even than the physical violence that destroyed so much of the sacred art that ornamented medieval English churches.[3] Their attacks on the imaginary not only intensify at the end of the sixteenth century but also coincide with the emergence of the Elizabethan and Jacobean theater, a theater that explores the phantasmic realms of eros and magic, witchcraft and demonology, obsession and fascination, a theater conventionally celebrated as the achievement of Renaissance culture. This theater's capacity to flourish in that historical moment when Protestantism becomes the established state religion in England would seem to cast doubt on Couliano's thesis that "by asserting the idolatrous and impious nature of phantasms, the Reformation abolished at one stroke the culture of the Renaissance."[4]

In this chapter I explore the relation between Protestant hostility toward the imagination and the remarkable flowering of the theater in late Elizabethan London. Although the stage draws much of its material from what Couliano calls the phantasmic, I do not view Elizabethan and Jacobean drama as a late expression of a culture that is being destroyed by the Reformation, an art form that somehow escapes for a time the reformers' attempts to suppress it. Instead, I find the plays of the English Renaissance stage to be fully engaged in reform culture's efforts to test the power of phantasmic and man-made images. Through their dazzling spectacles and lavish shows, these plays explore Protestant-induced fears about the validity of the stage. Attentive to their status as representations, they reflexively address the Protestant inquiry into their own legitimacy. Even though the drama is attacked with increasing vehemence by Protestant polemicists, it is, I argue, never simply a target of fanatical zeal; it is also very much a product of Reformation culture.[5]

Cathechizing in true religion (1581), sig. P7ʳ; John Phillips, *The Reformation of Images* (1973), p. 87; Ernest B. Gilman, *Iconoclasm and Poetry in the English Reformation* (1986), pp. 45–46.
   [3] Patrick Collinson, *From Iconoclasm to Iconophobia* (1986); Margaret Aston, *England's Iconoclasts*, vol. 1 (1988).
   [4] Couliano, *Eros and Magic*, p. 194.
   [5] Jonathan V. Crewe proposes a similar thesis in "The Theater of the Idols: Marlowe,

Because the reformers fear that any act of the imagination is potentially idolatrous, seducing people from God, the theater cannot escape Protestant suspicions that it is dangerous even though it is a secular art form. If "a thing fained in the mind by imagination is an idol," theatrical art can be constructed as God's rival.[6] If "The blyndest betles and maddest bedlems in the worlde, account the woorde Creation, as a holie and sacred thing, and will say, that God is the very Creator or maker of all things," playwrights are vulnerable to charges they appropriate a creativity that properly belongs to God.[7] If people are by nature apt to become "so intangled in the delight of earthly things which of themselves are good" that they "place their chiefe felicitie" in the created thing rather than the Creator, the capacity of drama to dazzle and delight is dangerous.[8] If "Idolles are conceyved by fond fancye, and brought forth by the hande [and] therefore are they Idolaters, also, whose Idolle lurketh like a shapelesse conception in the woombe of their imagination," all idealizations and interior images called up by the stage are problematic and, perhaps, endanger the souls of the audience members.[9]

Although the imagination had traditionally been thought to function as a necessary intermediary between the body and the soul, converting sensory messages into phantasms—mental images—so they could be understood by the soul, the reformers thus seriously undermine its validity.[10] "Man's wit," laments Calvin, is "as a shop of Idolatrie and

---

Rankins, and Theatrical Images" (1984), suggesting that "it is also possible to see both dramatists and antitheatricalists as participants by 1587 in a cultural dialogue" (p. 321). Focusing on a single pamphlet by Rankins and on Marlovian drama, he argues that "the plays that reflect upon and defend theatre against an ostensible antitheatrical 'prejudice' must also embody and virtually become defenses against—or attempted transformations of—the suspicion of occult powers of theatre" (p. 322). See also Frances Yates, *The Art of Memory* (1966), p. 286, who asks the provocative question, "May not the urgency and the agony of this conflict [over images and the imagination] have helped to precipitate the emergence of Shakespeare?"

[6] Perkins, *Warning*, p. 94.

[7] John Calvin, *The sermons of M. John Calvin upon the Epistle of S. Paule too the Ephesians* (1577), fol. 78[r]; Bouwsma, *John Calvin*, p. 80.

[8] Wood, *Fourme of Cathechizing*, sig. C1[r].

[9] Theodore Beza, *A Book of Christian Questions and Answers* (1586), sig. D11[r].

[10] Couliano, *Eros and Magic*, p. 5. Couliano focuses on philosophical theories of the imagination, attending closely to the concept of the imagination in the Aristotelian and Galenic traditions that still dominated Renaissance thinking. These theories attribute to the phantasmic, or inner sense, the essential "role of translating" the language of the body into the language of the soul (p. 5). Calvin, in contrast, tends to devalue the imagination by equating it with the fanciful, erroneous, unreal, and illusionary. Rather than

superstition.''[11] Like Shakespeare's Theseus, Calvinist reformers suspect the "shaping fantasies" of the "strong imagination," dismissing them as "tricks," illusions that are "more strange than true."[12]

The antitheatrical polemics of the late sixteenth and early seventeenth centuries reiterate early Protestant arguments against art and reinforce a Calvinist distrust of the imagination. Plays are "filthy" not only because they portray erotic love or dress boys as women but because they are man-made.[13] Since "whatsoever proceedeth from the wicked nature of manne, is unperfect, pollute, and defiled," argues William Rankins, "such then are Playes, unperfect, pollute, and defiled."[14] In Stephen Gosson's view, "Stage plaies were suckt from the Devilles teate, to Nurce up Idolatrie"; they were "consecrated to idolatrie"; they are "the Sacrifices of the Devill, taught by himselfe to pull us from the service of our God."[15] Attacks on the stage accuse playwrights of arrogance and disrespect for God, claiming that the dramatists "as if in derision of nature to scoffe theyr maker" presume to be "more cunning then their Creator."[16]

Plays are thus not only agents of blasphemy, idleness, duplicity, and lechery; they are also idolatrous. They "so bleareth mens eyes, that they [the audience members] take playes to be profounde Scripture" and consequently "forgette God."[17] Like sacred images and ecclesiastical ceremonies, plays are considered dangerous because they dazzle, enchant, seduce. Attacks on the stage confer the power of magic and eros on plays: they "bewitcheth the myndes of menne"; they are "inchanted by charmes"; they "lead the people with intising shewes to the divell, to seduce them to sinne"; their "inchaunting Charmes" and "be-

---

granting the imagination a central role in intellectual understanding, he associates it with the fallen condition and opposes it to the truth. In an article that addresses the influence of the Reformation on the concept of the imagination, Patrick Grant describes "a strong English empirical tradition in philosophy" that developed "during the later Renaissance," and that "insisted so firmly on the exact description of things that it held imagination gravely in suspicion as a distorter of clear knowledge" ("Imagination in the Renaissance" [1986], p. 86).

[11] Calvin, *Sermons upon Ephesians*, fol. 86^r.

[12] *A Midsummer Night's Dream*, in Shakespeare, *The Complete Works*, ed. Alfred Harbage (1969), 5.1.1–22.

[13] Henry Crosse, *Vertues Common-wealth* (1603), sig. Q3^r.

[14] William Rankins, *A Mirrour of Monsters* (1587), sig. G4^r.

[15] Stephen Gosson, *Plays Confuted in Five Actes* (1582), sigs. B8^v, C3^r, B8^r, B4^v, C2^{r-v}.

[16] Rankins, *Mirrour*, sig. C3^r.

[17] Ibid., sigs. C2^r, C3^r.

witched wyles . . . alienate theyr [spectators'] mindes from vertue.''[18]
Theater thus takes on the qualities of the forbidden: openly denounced, it is also eroticized and highly charged with repressed appeal.

The powerful allure of plays in Elizabethan England is therefore exceedingly problematic, for the fantastic world of the theater draws to
it—in the tens of thousands—the very citizens required by law to
practice a religion that seeks to instill a deep distrust of the imaginary,
the spectacular, the theatrical, and the man-made. The obvious pleasure the citizens of London derive from plays is a pleasure that Protestant divines attempt to undermine as ''the pleasure that men take in
their own vain inventions.''[19] If their religion arouses and attempts to
sustain an unsettling anxiety that they are prone to desire the phantasmic images of their own seething imaginations and hence are apt ''to
fall away from God,''[20] the theaters they flock to are not shelters from
that anxiety but, as products of the human imagination, fully implicated
in it.

Apologists for the stage clearly understand how Protestant distrust of
artifice and imagination extends to the theater, calling into question
its spectacles and narratives, threatening its status and legitimacy. In
defending theater against the antitheatricalists, however, they emphatically align themselves with the reformed, not the traditional church.
Literary scholars have generally ignored the way in which those who
defend the stage, as well as those who attack it, appropriate the rhetoric
and arguments of the reformers, bolstering their defense of the stage
by invoking Protestant notions of art. Apologists and antitheatricalists
alike, in other words, situate their arguments within Protestant discourse, staking out their positions by laying claim to the reformed religion, while accusing their opponents of papistry.

In his defense of the stage, for instance, Thomas Heywood mocks
the grounds on which the antitheatricalists object to boy actors playing
women, comparing their citation of the Biblical injunction against sod-
omy to the papists' literal interpretation of Christ's words ''This is my
body.'' Both, he argues, misinterpret the Scriptures by taking them
literally.[21] He thus turns the Scriptures back against those who would

---

[18] Ibid., sigs. C4^r, B3^v, B2^v, E1^v.
[19] Henry Ainsworth, *An Arrow against Idolatrie* (1624), p. 60.
[20] Ibid.
[21] Thomas Heywood, *An Apology for Actors* (1612), sig. C3^r.

use them to suppress the stage and invokes a reformed interpretation of the sacraments to counter the antitheatricalists' opposition to cross-dressing. In doing so, he raises important questions about the nature of representation.

Even more startling, Thomas Nashe bases his defense of the stage on the very distrust of theatricality that the reformers seek to arouse. The theater, he asserts, is valuable because it deconstructs—"anatomizes"—theatricality. Instead of praising the artifice of the stage, he argues that drama reveals and holds up for examination a dangerous and duplicitous artfulness that pervades human affairs. "In plays," he observes, "all cozenages, all cunning drifts overgilded with outward holiness . . . are most lively anatomized."[22] Rather than celebrate the power of theatrical spectacle, Nashe argues that plays illuminate the ways in which hypocritical rulers, malicious villains, and clever con-artists trick people by manipulating images. Far from dazzling the eyes of its spectators, theater, he claims, *exposes* the very agents of bedazzlement. By using the language of Protestant polemics against idols, he reiterates and reinforces the reformers' fears of art, and he praises the theater because it uncovers fraud, reveals hypocrisy, unmasks artifice. For Nashe, theater is an agent of reform, not an idolatrous spectacle, and it functions in much the same way as the antitheatricalist tracts themselves, anatomizing cunning artifice in order to suppress it, displaying theatricality in order to demonstrate its fraudulent nature.

Nashe's remarks provide insight into the way Renaissance playwrights responded to Calvinist critiques of the imagination and antitheatrical attacks on the stage. How typical are they? To examine in more depth the way early modern English playwrights addressed Protestant fears of images, plays, and other products of the imagination, I turn to Marlowe's *Doctor Faustus* and Shakespeare's *Hamlet*, two plays that link their protagonists with Wittenberg, the city of Luther, Karlstadt, Melancthon, and, in the 1580s, a group of Calvinists who oppose Lutheran orthodoxy. *Doctor Faustus* both exploits and critiques its own power to dazzle its spectators. *Hamlet*, in contrast, articulates an alternative kind of theater, one that locates its power not in its capacity to dazzle but in its ability to mirror nature. Although Shakespeare distances his drama from the spectacular theatricality that Marlowe self-consciously displays, both playwrights call attention to the gaze of the spectator and both

[22] Thomas Nashe, *Pierce Penniless his Supplication to the Devil* (1964), p. 65.

conceive of the world they represent as a "dazzling theater" where "people, immersed in their own errors, are struck blind."[23] Here I am quoting Calvin, who paradoxically urges the faithful to look upon the created world as "an open stage whereon God will have his majestie seen" and warns them that they are vulnerable to being so "stunned" by this "most beautiful theater" of the world and its "dazzlement" that they will become "bound by intemperate love of it."[24] Calvin simultaneously praises a God who "shows his glory to us, whenever and wherever we cast our gaze," and warns that humans are constantly in danger of becoming "captivated" by the world's "many allurements" and "much show of pleasantness, grace, and sweetness."[25]

This Calvinist paradox complicates the idea of the theater in the English Renaissance. By celebrating the created world as a divine theater wherein God manifests himself while simultaneously arousing fears that its beauty dazzles and blinds its fallen spectators, early English Protestantism contributes to the formation of a new kind of theater, one that enacts Reformation culture's struggle to master and contain the seductive appeal of the visible, imagined, and created.

Doctor Faustus, Dazzling Theater, and the Rapt Spectator

Based on an English adaptation of the explicitly Protestant *Faustbuch* and dramatizing the conflict a creative individual experiences between a demonic magic that provides access to a rich, phantasmic world and a religion that requires faith in an invisible God, *Doctor Faustus* addresses its culture's profound anxiety about the human imagination. Yet, while the orthodox Lutheran ideology of the popular German *Faustbuch* has been well documented by Reformation historians, there is little agreement among literary scholars on how—if at all—the reformed religion informs Marlowe's play.[26] And no wonder. There is the

---

[23] John Calvin, *Institutes of the Christian Religion* (1960) 1.5.8.

[24] Calvin, *Sermons upon Ephesians,* fol. 87; Calvin, *Institutes* 1.14.20; 3.9.1; 3.9.2; see also *Institutes* 1.5.1, 5, 10; 1.6.2; 1.14.20; 2.6.1.

[25] Calvin, *Institutes* 1.5.1; 3.9.2.

[26] Gerald Strauss, "How to Read a *Volksbuch*" (1989). Harold Bloom, introduction to *Christopher Marlowe's* Doctor Faustus (1988), p. 8, writes that "it scarcely matters whether its [*Doctor Faustus*'s] overt theology is Catholic, Lutheran, or Calvinist, since the theology is there as a good, boisterous mythology that the hyperbolist Marlowe is happy to exploit." Leo Kirschbaum, "Religious Values in *Doctor Faustus*" (1969), p. 77, argues that Marlowe's

biographical question of Marlowe's alleged atheism. There is the romantic myth of the Renaissance Faustus, creative genius, prodigious
intellect, rebellious individual, a myth that celebrates a man capable of
freeing himself from the restraints of all religion. There is the vexed
problem of variant texts, the B version perhaps reflecting different doctrinal positions than the A version. And within the play itself, there is
the puzzling and seemingly inconsistent identification of Faustus with
Roman Catholicism, with Protestantism, and with atheism.

If Faustus doubts that there is a God and scoffs at the idea of damnation, he addresses the question of atheism as one trained in divinity
at a Protestant university: Wittenberg, a place associated, indeed, with
another rebel, Luther, and the very beginning of the Reformation. If
he sells his soul to the devil in exchange for certain temporal powers,
he uses his power—paradoxically, it would seem—to gaze upon and
take delight in the "sumptuous" images, relics, buildings, and monuments of the Roman Church. If his own magic is associated with the
ceremonies, rituals, and "magic" of the Roman Church, he delights in
using it to play the Protestant hero, exposing the pope and his religion
as superstitious, idolatrous, and impotent in scenes clearly calculated
to arouse the English audience's strongest antipapal sentiments.

Furthermore, the historical Reformation appears in Marlowe's play
in a series of topical allusions that conflate time periods and merge
fact, fiction, and myth. Faustus tricks Pope Adrian (who served as pope
from 1522 to 1523, making him the contemporary of the historical
Faustus). The pope bewails the presence of Lollards (usually fifteenth-
century followers of Wycliff) and cites the Council of Trent (1545–
1563). He condemns Bruno, a fictional character who becomes in the
play a rival pope, but whose name surely brings to mind the Italian
philosopher and magician Giordano Bruno (1548?–1600). The historical Bruno visited England in 1583 where his hermetical writing on
magic and the phantasmic elicited hostile Protestant attacks.[27]

---

play "is wholly conventional in its Christian values and is in no sense iconoclastic," and
he goes on to claim that Aquinas, Hooker, Luther, Calvin, and Knox would all agree with
its theological assumptions. See also Jonathan Dollimore, "*Doctor Faustus* (ca. 1589–1592):
Subversion through Transgression" (1988); L. C. Knights, *Further Explorations* (1965);
Arieh Sachs, "The Religious Despair of Doctor Faustus" (1964); Wilbur Sanders, "Doctor
Faustus' Sin" (1988); Edward A. Snow, "Marlowe's *Doctor Faustus* and the Ends of Desire"
(1988).

[27] Frances A. Yates, *Giordano Bruno and the Hermetic Tradition* (1964), pp. 275–90; see
also Hilary Gatti, *The Renaissance Drama of Knowledge* (1989).

We cannot even be certain what Faustus's ties to the University of Wittenberg might mean to Marlowe or an Elizabethan audience, for, in addition to its associations with Luther, Wittenberg was in the 1580s "a hot-bed of heterodoxy" and the center of a controversial late-Reformation movement of "crypto-Calvinists" whose beliefs, particularly about the nature of the sacrament of communion, were vehemently opposed and suppressed by orthodox Lutherans.[28] If, as the Reformation historian Gerald Strauss suggests, the Lutheran *Faustbuch* affiliates Faustus with Wittenberg rather than Württemburg, the university of the historical Faustus, to heighten his disgrace by associating him with the Wittenberg Calvinists, how might this association be understood by a London audience? Their queen was rebuffed by the Lutherans when she attempted to negotiate "a universal Protestant alliance" that would have prevented the persecution of these very Calvinists.[29] Their English Church was influenced far more by Calvin than Luther.

And what should we make of Giordano Bruno's appearance in Wittenberg shortly after his departure from England? In that city, as in England, Bruno becomes embroiled in controversy by participating in highly contested debates about the nature and function of images, debates that reiterate and reformulate the original iconoclastic controversies between the traditionalists and reformers in the early sixteenth century. According to the historian Hajo Holborn, the "bitter and divisive feuds between the Lutherans and the Calvinists" in Wittenberg during the 1580s center on "the doctrine of sacraments," the Lutherans objecting to the "symbolic and mystical interpretation" of the visible bread and wine that the Calvinists advanced.[30] So acrimonious are these feuds that Bruno abruptly leaves Wittenberg after "a Calvinist party gained the upper hand over" the Lutherans who had embraced him.[31]

While in England, Bruno also opposes Calvinism, advancing instead a "magical religion." He offers "the magic of the *Asclepius*" with its

[28] Strauss, "How to Read a *Volksbuch*," p. 34.

[29] Hajo Holborn, *A History of Modern Germany* (1959), p. 262.

[30] Ibid., p. 256. In his fascinating investigation of Marlowe's death, Charles Nicholl also speculates about the connections between Bruno and Marlowe (*The Reckoning* [1992], pp. 206–15). Nicholl's book persuasively connects Marlowe to anti-Catholic espionage and also serves as a reminder of how fluid and unfixed religious allegiances could be in Elizabethan England.

[31] Yates, *Bruno*, p. 307.

"talismanic images"[32] in place of the doctrine of justification by faith alone, a doctrine he ardently rejects. Bruno believes "in the primacy of the imagination as the instrument for reaching truth," advocates "the conditioning of the imagination or the memory to receive demonic influences through images or other magical signs," and seeks to discover the magical power of images, signs, seals, characters, emblems, hieroglyphs, and diagrams.[33] Although the Oxford doctors who debate him conclude he is mad, and the Calvinist writers who attack him accuse him of papistry, Frances Yates speculates that Bruno's "magical Hermeticism offered to sub-Catholics, discontented intelligentsia, and other secretly dissatisfied elements in Elizabethan society a new outlet . . . for their secret yearnings."[34]

Although we do not know Marlowe's response to Bruno's visit, it is surely in the religious controversies of the 1580s that we should locate *Doctor Faustus*. Like the historical Bruno, who embraces "Magus man" and celebrates "the miraculous and godlike power of man to know the world,"[35] Faustus is a "speculator," who, according to Marlowe's source (an English adaptation of the *Faustbuch*), "would throw the Scriptures from him" when he "fell into . . . fantasies and deepe cogitations."[36] Unable to resist its seductive appeal, Faustus commits himself to mastering the phantasmic world. In opposition to Faustus, the Good Angel and the Old Man—like the historical Calvinists—denounce magic and advocate faith in unseen things, urging Faustus to renounce the spectacles that delight him and the speculations that absorb him. Marlowe explores his culture's deeply conflicted attitudes toward the imagination, creating a protagonist whose imaginative powers are simultaneously marvelous and dangerous, godlike and presumptuous, immortal and deadly.

If, in his play, magic is the devil's domain, it is also the dramatist's. Through magic Faustus attains, among other things, the status of a court entertainer who delights the Emperor and his courtiers with enchanting shows. Marlowe associates the magical arts with the dramatic arts, the man who speculates in images with the playwright, magical

[32] Ibid., pp. 234, 326.
[33] Ibid., pp. 335, 266, 270–83, 308–34.
[34] Ibid., pp. 233–34.
[35] Ibid., p. 246.
[36] P. F., *The Historie of the damnable life, and deserved death of Doctor John Faustus* (1592), p. 136.

and demonic spectacle with theatrical spectacle. His theater interrogates its own theatricality, creating spectacles that dazzle and seduce his audiences while dramatizing the fall of a protagonist who is bedazzled by demonic shows and seduced by his own power to manipulate images. He thus dramatizes the dangers and limitations of spectacle, even as he induces, or even seduces, his spectators to look. Watching characters watch the magician's and the devil's theatrical shows, Marlowe's spectators cannot help but become self-conscious about their own relation to the theater.

This is especially true in the B version of the play, which calls attention to the different ways on-stage spectators respond to magical spectacles.[37] Leah Marcus believes that "the different versions of the play carry different ideological freight—the A text could be described as more nationalist and more Calvinist, Puritan, or ultra-Protestant, the B text as more internationalist, imperial, and Anglican, or Anglo-Catholic."[38] The clear-cut distinction Marcus draws between Calvinists and Anglicans, however, is a misleading one. She fails to acknowledge the pervasive influence of Calvin on the English Church in the late sixteenth and early seventeenth century, ignores the international dimension of Calvinism, makes inaccurate assumptions about the role of spectacle in the English Church of the time, and, most curiously, given the intense anti-Catholic sentiments among English Protestants in the Tudor and Stuart period, aligns Anglicanism with Anglo-Catholicism. In addition, Marcus does not adequately attend to the way the B version "anatomizes" or interrogates spectacle.

Many of the additional scenes in the B text reflexively examine ways of seeing and interpreting theatrical spectacle, juxtaposing the awed and dazzled spectator and the skeptic. When, for example, Benvolio is

[37] All citations are to the B text of 1616 in Christopher Marlowe, *Doctor Faustus*, ed. David Bevington and Eric Rasmussen (1993). Although the A text includes a knight who doubts Faustus, it does not elaborate on Benvolio's skepticism, nor does it include Faustus's warning to the Emperor.

[38] Leah Marcus, "Textual Indeterminacy and Ideological Difference" (1989), p. 5. Although her thesis that the variant texts may represent two fundamentally different but equally coherent doctrinal positions is compelling, I disagree with the way Marcus interprets the play's spectacle. The fact that the B text includes more spectacle does not, in and of itself, mean that it is more traditional. In addition, my research suggests that Wittenberg in the 1580s, far from being the conservative and Lutheran center that Marcus describes, was in fact a site of theological controversy aroused by the strong presence of a group of Calvinists.

aroused from sleep and encouraged to look out his window so that he can "see" Faustus—"Wonder of men, renowned magician" (4.1.48)—create a magical spectacle for the Emperor "As never yet was seen in Germany" (4.1.33), he doubts the power of the conjurer, saying "I do not greatly believe him." While the Emperor Charles celebrates Faustus' art and eagerly anticipates the moment when he can "behold" Alexander the Great and his paramour "in their true shapes and state majestical, / That we may wonder at their excellence" (4.1.77–78), Benvolio complains bitterly, "zounds, I could eat myself for anger, to think I have been such an ass all this while to stand gaping after the devil's governor, and can see nothing" (4.1.87–89). Faustus punishes Benvolio for his skepticism, turning him into a "wondrous sight," a "strange beast" that the other courtiers (and presumably the audience) are exhorted to "see, see." But he also chides the Emperor, whose "thoughts are so ravished / With sight of this renowned Emperor" (4.1.105–6) that he is deluded into believing he can embrace the great Alexander himself: "My gracious lord," warns Faustus, "you do forget yourself, / These are but shadows, not substantial" (4.1.103–4). Faustus calls attention to the Emperor's misjudgment, a kind of mis-seeing. He identifies as erroneous the assumption that a visible sign is identical to the substantial thing itself, which is the fundamental error that the Protestants ascribe to the Roman Church.

While Benvolio is ridiculed because, in his disbelief, he "can see nothing," and the Emperor Charles is chided because, in his looking, he confuses the sign or shadow of the thing with the thing itself, Faustus is depicted in this play as a man who at crucial moments chooses images, shows, pageants, and spectacles, all explicitly the craft of the devil, over a God he cannot see. Whenever Faustus thinks about God, mentions heaven, or despairs about the fate of his soul, Mephistopheles offers him something visible or created "to delight his mind." Faustus is so enamored of the phantasmic, the artificial, the theatrical, and the beautiful that he ultimately cannot sustain his faith in a God whose invisibility he interprets as absence.

He relinquishes the deed to his soul only after Mephistopheles creates a "show" in which devils present him with "crowns and rich apparel" and "dance" (2.1). He recants his renunciation of the devil when he remembers the "sweet pleasure" of Homer and the "ravishing sound of his melodious harp" (2.3.27). He turns away from the Good Angel and resists the urge to repent when Lucifer offers him a pageant of the seven deadly sins as a "pastime," telling him to forget his thoughts of paradise and instead "mark the show," a "sight" that Faustus proclaims "doth delight my soul!" (2.3). And he stifles a final impulse to repent by asking for, and receiving, Helen of Troy—or rather a vision of her—the most beautiful woman in the world (5.1). Although the chorus, the Old Man, and the Good Angel pronounce his choices sinful and damnable, the pleasure Faustus takes in all this theatricality is intense—and intensely shared by Marlowe's audiences.

Marlowe exploits the power of the stage to enchant, paradoxically, in order to disenchant. Faustus rhapsodizes about the beauty of "that heavenly Helen" in poetry so lyrical that the audience is necessarily caught up in his passion; but at the very moment that he asks, "Was this the face that launched a thousand ships, / And burnt the topless towers of Ilium?" (5.1.94–95), he admits that "her lips suck forth my soul." The ravishing Helen is both dazzling and demonic, the bewitching vision both irresistible and illusory. This climactic scene simultaneously displays and contains the magical potential of theater, arousing erotic fantasy only to disturb and destabilize it, stimulating the imagination only to curb and discredit it.

A similar pattern of enchantment and disenchantment operates throughout *Doctor Faustus*. Rather than identifying it as a thematic pattern, I wish here to consider its ritual function. Many of the play's comic scenes parody Faustus's magic, and in doing so they demystify it. They resemble certain acts of "ritual desacralization" performed by Protestant crowds in Germany during the turbulent years of the Reformation and may well fulfill the identical ritual task of transforming sacred images invested with magical properties into "profane objects, mere matter."[39] The action in the scenes in the pope's chambers and the tavern, in particular, closely parallel ritual acts of desecration documented by R. W. Scribner. He describes how people removed "crucifixes, the images of Christ and the host" from churches and holy shrines, brought them into the secular world of the streets and taverns, and tested their efficacy by interrogating and ridiculing them in carnivalesque rites of "inverted transubstantiation."[40]

In the scenes in the pope's chambers (3.1, 2), Marlowe similarly

---

[39] R. W. Scribner, *Popular Culture and Popular Movements in Reformation Germany* (1987), p. 114.

[40] Ibid., pp. 71–122; for the quotation see p. 114.

displays the theatrical grandeur of Roman Catholicism only to mock and, I suggest, ritually desacralize it, thereby altering his spectators' relation to it. Desiring "to see the monuments / And situation of bright splendent Rome," and promised "what Rome contains for to delight thine eyes," Faustus observes "the Cardinals and Bishops, some bearing crosiers, some the pillars, Monks and Friars singing their procession. Then the Pope . . ." (3.1.49–50, 31, s.d.). All the splendid ecclesiastical images of power and mystery that the spectators are invited to gaze upon, however, are rendered impotent by Faustus, who irreverently interrupts the pope's banquet and effortlessly and gleefully steals the pope's wine. The sacramental dimension of the banquet and wine are underscored, not only by the cardinal's sense that a sacrilege is being committed but also by the pope's defensive question, "What Lollards do attend our Holiness?" (3.2.69), and Faustus's impatient question, "Must every bit be spiced with a cross?" (3.2.86).

Although the friar attempts to reassert the power of the Roman Catholic rituals by bringing in bell, book, and candle to excommunicate the offender and reciting a "holy dirge," Faustus ridicules his holy gestures, physically beating the friars and setting off firecrackers in a carnivalesque disregard for the sacred rituals of the Roman Church. In the comic tavern scene that immediately follows, the eucharistic wine becomes fully desacralized. In a demystifying parody of Faustus's own magical power, the silly clowns steal a cup of literal wine from the vintner in a meaningless act of petty thievery. Marlowe has, in effect, fixed on the eucharistic wine of the Roman Catholic Mass—what the Calvinists declared the chief idol of papistry—removed it from the church, displayed it on the secular stage in a literal banquet surrounded by the external trappings of Roman Catholicism, transferred it from the hands of the pope to the hands of the magician whose power derives from the devil, and, finally, turned it into a mundane thing entirely devoid of mystery, sanctity, or power. The eucharistic wine is in this manner tested and examined, its mystery exhausted as it passes from pope to magician to clown. Displayed in the secular space of the common stage, the sacred eucharistic symbol, the very sight of which many lay Catholics believed to be salvific, is trivialized and domesticated.[41]

Critics deprive Marlowe's play of its motivating conflict and flatten

[41] Horton Davies, *Worship and Theology in England* (1970), 1:139–40.

out its disturbing ambivalences when they ignore the religious controversies that raged in England in the late sixteenth century or gloss over
the crucial distinctions that Elizabethans made among Roman Catholicism, Lutheranism, Calvinism, and other reformed theologies. Marlowe's *Doctor Faustus* is very much the product of Reformation England,
conflicted about its own artifice and disruptive to the spectators who
watch it, whether they are, like the Emperor Charles, enchanted by its
dazzling spectacle or, like Benvolio, skeptical and critical. It is disruptive
because it exploits the theater's potential to enthrall its spectators, even
as it demystifies and disenchants its own lavish and pleasing spectacles.
It is conflicted because it celebrates the human imagination and yet
forces a recognition of the insubstantiality, impotence, and silliness of
all imagined things—including, even, itself.

I do not wish to imply that Marlowe's play is either doctrine or doc-
trinaire. Perhaps it is a howl of protest against a God who endows humans with imagination but forbids them to create; perhaps it is an
impassioned plea for empathy toward the intellectual man driven to
know more than his God allows; perhaps it is a raw and powerful expression of the artist's intolerable position in an iconoclastic culture.
But I do want to argue that this play was shaped by (and, given its
popularity, surely helped to shape) an early Protestant English culture
disrupted by iconoclastic acts and antitheatrical polemics. *Doctor Faustus*
does not—indeed it cannot—escape the Calvinist paradigms that dom-
inate so much of Elizabethan thinking.

Hamlet, Interior Drama, and the Self-Censoring Spectator

In the intensely self-reflexive play *Hamlet*, the arrival of a troupe
of players raises for Shakespeare's spectators fundamental questions
both about the theater they watch and about their own watching. Why
does a malcontented and brooding Hamlet respond to the newly ar-
rived actors with "a kind of joy" immediately after he declares himself
unable to take delight in the visible world, a world he likens to a beautiful theater?[42] Why does an isolated and alienated Hamlet identify the
tragedians of the city as "old" and "good" friends" shortly after he

[42] All citations are to *Hamlet*, in Shakespeare, *The Complete Works*, ed. Alfred Harbage
(1969).

rejects the overtures of his schoolboy friends whom he accuses of hypocritical role-playing? And why does a doubting and skeptical Hamlet turn to imaginative fiction, granting a play the power to "catch the conscience of the king" even though he mistrusts and condemns the theatrical posturing of monarch and court?

Hamlet's interest in theater is rarely examined in the context of Protestant antitheatricality, despite the fact that many scholars have commented on how his Wittenberg education directly links Hamlet with Protestantism.[43] And yet, just as Hamlet's Wittenberg education is clearly pertinent to Shakespeare's exploration of such issues as authority and patriarchy, faith and knowledge, judgment and retribution, it is also relevant to Hamlet's distrust of theatrical posturing and interest in the dramatic arts. Hamlet returns to Denmark from the cradle of the Protestant Reformation alienated from its monarch, critical of its customs and ceremonies, and exhibiting many of the traits associated with the new religion: interiority, skepticism, guilt, and a philosophical melancholy believed in the sixteenth century to have afflicted St. Paul and Luther as well. He also returns with a keen interest in drama. Instead of addressing the play's thematic exploration of theological doctrine, constructing a "Lutheran Hamlet" or "allegorizing the play as a code for the Reformation itself," I want to show how Hamlet's dramatic theory is an expression of an emerging Protestant aesthetics that responds to a heightened distrust of images and the imaginary in both London and Wittenberg at the end of the sixteenth century.[44]

Through the character of Hamlet, Shakespeare self-consciously addresses the central concerns of the reformers when they critique plays, players, playwrights, and playgoers. Hamlet is obsessed with the empty theatricality of the court and the Machiavellian role-playing of the courtiers. Nevertheless, he embraces the actors and devises his own drama, one he hopes will have the power to stir the conscience and move the soul. Suspicious of cunning, he praises plays that mirror nature, actors who refrain from exploiting their creative powers, and audiences who distance themselves from spectacle and focus on the

---

[43] See, for examples, Walter Cohen, "The Reformation and Elizabethan Drama" (1984); Roland Mushat Frye, *The Renaissance Hamlet* (1984), p. 160; David Kaula, "Hamlet and the Image of Both Churches" (1984); Kenneth S. Rothwell, "Hamlet's 'Glass of Fashion'" (1988); and Raymond B. Waddington, "Lutheran Hamlet" (1989).

[44] Waddington, "Lutheran Hamlet"; Rothwell, "Hamlet's 'Glass of Fashion,'" p. 81.

meaning of the play. Hamlet, I am suggesting, articulates the qualities of an ideal *Protestant* theater.

Like sixteenth-century English apologists for poetry and stage, including the Protestant Sir Philip Sidney, Hamlet distinguishes good from bad art by applying the precise criteria used by the English reformers to distinguish between "unabused" (acceptable) and "abused" (idolatrous) images. The reformers denounce art that seduces or dazzles but permit images that "are signs and tokens," which put the people "in remembrance of the godly and virtuous lives of them that they do represent."[45] Sidney disapproves of paintings and poems that "please an ill-pleased eye with wanton shows" but defends the "figuring forth [of] good things" in art.[46] In Hamlet's advice to the players, Shakespeare critiques a superficial kind of theatricality, but he advocates a theater that mirrors nature in order "to show virtue her own feature, scorn her own image, and the very age and body of the time his form and pressure" (3.2.21–23). Rejecting art that is, in Sidney's words, *phantastike*, Shakespeare, Sidney, and the reformers all sanction art that is *eikastike*, or imitative.[47] In place of "wanton shows," "inexplicable dumb shows," and "phantastike" art forms, Sidney and Shakespeare advocate art that represents the natural world and figures virtue and vice—precisely the qualities of art endorsed by English reformers.

Although some of the more radical Protestants may wish to impose a total censorship of the imaginary, as Couliano argues, it is therefore inaccurate to assume that Renaissance English playwrights and poets write in opposition to an emerging Protestant ideology that is essentially hostile to art. Sidney, for example, is both a committed Protestant whose religious beliefs link him to an incipient puritanism and a celebrated poet and writer intent on rescuing literature from the accusations that it "abuseth men's wit, training it to wanton sinfulness."[48] Sidney's question, "But what, will the abuse of a thing make the right use odious?" reiterates a question that runs throughout Protestant dis-

---

[45] Edward H. Cardwell, *Documentary Annals of the Reformed Church of England* (1844), 1: 29, 27.

[46] Sir Philip Sidney, *An Apology for Poetry* (1970), pp. 59–60.

[47] Ibid., p. 59. For a summary of Renaissance English dramatic theory, see Virgil K. Whitaker, *The Mirror Up to Nature* (1965), pp. 56–93.

[48] Andrew D. Weiner, *Sir Philip Sidney and the Poetics of Protestantism* (1978); Sidney, *Apology*, p. 58.

course on images and appears as well in the arguments playwrights make in defense of playing. "Playes are good or bad, as they are us'd," explains a prefatory poem in Thomas Heywood's *An Apology for Actors*, "and best inventions often are abused."[49]

In his discussions of art, Calvin explores an identical question. Rather than forbid art, he focuses on its proper and improper uses. "And yet I am not gripped by the superstition of thinking absolutely no images permissible," he writes. "But because sculpture and painting are gifts of God, I see a pure and legitimate use of each, lest those things which the Lord has conferred upon us for his glory and our good be not only polluted by perverse misuse but also turned to our destruction."[50] When he condemns certain kinds of art but approves others, Calvin not only arouses anxiety about the legitimacy of art, he also creates a self-consciousness about the aesthetic experience. If "a false imitation is a corruption" capable of polluting and even destroying the soul, what is a true imitation? If artists foolishly "bragge and boast themselves to have wrought wonders . . . [and] will allege their own abilities," how can they put art to "a pure and legitimate use"? If people are exhorted to "shake off all vayne imaginations that may come in [their] heads," how can they use the divine gift of imagination for "God's glory" and their "good"?[51]

Although he condemns images that purport to have magical power, art that calls attention to its creator's skill, and artists who attempt to rival God's creativity, Calvin explicitly approves of art that represents things "which the eyes are capable of seeing" and art that depicts "histories and events."[52] In this he agrees with Luther, who allows "pictures in which one sees merely past events and things, as in a glass," and most other sixteenth-century reformers.[53] Even the radical Zwingli permits images that are "the likeness of anything that is visible" and "representations of historic events . . . so long as they do not give rise to reverence."[54] All these early Protestant reformers carefully distinguish

[49] Sidney, *Apology*, p. 60; Heywood, *Apology*, sig. A4[r].

[50] Calvin, *Institutes* 1.11.12

[51] Ibid. 4.18.8; Calvin, *Sermons of M. John Calvin upon the Epistle of Saincte Paule to the Galathians*, (1574), fol. 120; Calvin, *Institutes* 1.11.12; Calvin *Sermons upon Ephesians*, fol. 76[v].

[52] Calvin, *Institutes* 1.11.12.

[53] Qtd. in Carl C. Christensen, *Art and the Reformation in Germany* (1979), p. 53; see also Martin Bucer, *A treatise* (1535?), sig. E8[r]; Perkins, *Warning*, sig. D5[r-v].

[54] Qtd. in Charles Garside, *Zwingli and the Arts* (1966), pp. 172, 149–50.

between art that glorifies the fancy or artifice of its creator and art that mirrors nature or represents the past. Condemning the former as "man-made" and therefore subject to the errors of the human imagination, they nonetheless advocate the latter, arguing that it shows forth the glory and heavenly design of the divine Creator.

In *Hamlet* Shakespeare articulates an aesthetics of the stage that I believe takes account of these very distinctions. In his advice to the players, Hamlet carefully distinguishes bad theater from good according to whether it mirrors nature (God's creation) or calls attention to human invention. Criticizing "affectation," de-emphasizing "cunning," Hamlet calls for "an honest method, as wholesome as sweet, and by very much more handsome than fine" (2.2.432–34). His aesthetics, based on "the modesty of nature" rather than elegance, ornamentation, or embellishment, explicitly privileges what God has made over what man is capable of making. Anticipating seventeenth-century theories of art that develop in the wake of the Reformation and endorse the "plaine and honest worke agreeing with Nature" while condemning "phantastically capricious devices" and cautioning against "fancying things abhorring from Nature," Hamlet's dramatic theory reveals how fully Shakespeare has reconciled his dramatic art to the Protestant's deep distrust of the imagined and man-made.[55]

When he calls for the players to "reform" their acting "altogether," Hamlet identifies as his own early Protestant concerns about the imagination, its excesses and dangers. Contemptuous of the "barren spectators" for their love of "inexplicable dumb shows and noise" (3.2.11–12), he reiterates Calvin's scorn for "the untutored crowd [which] . . . is marvelously captivated by ceremonial pomp" and those "hypocrites and lightheaded women [who] think that nothing [can be] more beautiful" than theatrical "trifles."[56] Hamlet distrusts the very kind of theatricality that seduces Faustus. Disgusted by players who overact, thereby calling attention to their own artifice, he accuses them of violating nature: "O, there be players that I have seen play . . . that neither having th'accent of Christians, nor the gait of Christian, pagan, nor man, have so strutted and bellowed that I have thought some of Nature's journeymen had made men, and not made them well, they imitated humanity so abominably" (3.2.27–33). For Hamlet, actors who

---

[55] François Du Jon, the Younger, *The painting of the ancients* (1638), p. 43.
[56] Calvin, *Institutes* 4.17.41.

exploit their own creative talents, foregrounding their craft and skill, fail to represent human beings, and instead appear as perverted, unnatural, artificial copies of human beings, not made by God but by "Nature's journeymen." Bad art, for Hamlet as well as the Calvinists, foolishly rivals, rather than accurately represents, divine creation, for it, in the words of a Protestant preacher, "dothe onely commende and sette forth the vayne and unprofitable science and cunnyng of the workeman."[57]

Like Protestant artists in seventeenth-century Holland, Shakespeare self-consciously eschews artifice and artfulness and claims instead to mirror, or "describe," the visible and historical world, developing in his audiences a sense that the play they watch reflects and refracts the world they inhabit.[58] Rather than exhibit the spectacular or glorify the artificial, he proposes a drama whose purpose is "to hold, as 'twere, the mirror up to nature" (3.2.20–21). For him, theatrical images are reflections (shadows, figures) of a world beyond the stage, and viewing a play is not an idolatrous but an ethical act that drives the spectator inward.

If theater is understood to mirror a natural world that is itself a divinely created theater the faithful are exhorted to gaze upon, the playwright is no presumptuous rival of God but someone who simply records what God causes to be done in the world. And if theater focuses its spectators' gaze on the acts of men and women in history, the playwright is no cunning artificer but someone who directs attention to "God's workmanship." By embracing the notion, cherished by Calvinists, that the visible world is itself a "magnificent" theater created by the great "Artificer," Shakespeare deflects his own capacity to inspire wonder onto a deity Calvin calls the "wonder-worker."[59] Shakespeare's

---

[57] John Veron, *A stronge battery against the idolatrous invocation of the dead Saints* (1562), fol. 103ʳ–103ᵛ.

[58] Svetlana Alpers, *The Art of Describing* (1983); I disagree with Annabel Patterson, who argues in *Shakespeare and the Popular Voice* (1989), pp. 11–31, that Hamlet's scorn for the groundlings' love of dumb shows and his praise of the "judicious few" manifests elitist assumptions that would not be shared by his author. Hamlet delivers here a harsh critique of playgoers and their attachment to spectacle, but his desire to reform the theater suggests a firm belief in the public's capacity to change, a belief ardently shared by the reformers who, although they ridicule popular piety, are also committed to reaching, educating, and thereby "saving" the masses. Shakespeare's own position should be inferred not from the popularity but from the aesthetics of his plays, which do not rely primarily on spectacle but rather on the power of their verbal texts.

[59] Calvin, *Sermons upon Ephesians*, fol. 77ʳ; Calvin, *Institutes* 2.6.1; 1.14.21; 1.5.2; Calvin

remarkable achievement redeems art, rescuing theater (at least temporarily) from antitheatrical threats by transforming (before our very eyes in *The Winter's Tale*) the bewitching image—painted and stony, dead and man-made—into a living person, wrinkled by time.

Because the reformers believe that nature and history manifest God, it is not only legitimate to represent them but also essential that people learn to discover the divine through them. Calvin repeatedly urges the faithful to discover signs of God in the visible world, a world he likens to a "most beautiful theater," "a spectacle of God's glory," and a "Glasse, wherein we maie beholde" God. For him, human beings are themselves representations, *images* that God made " 'according to his likeness' as if he were saying that he was going to make man, in whome he would represent himself as in an image, by means of engraved marks of likeness." Calvin urges people to "enter intoo" and contemplate themselves in order to know God: "If a man looke but uppon one of his fingers," Calvin asserts, "what workmanship and what goodnesse of God is there."[60]

Sight therefore has a significant spiritual dimension for Calvin. Turning one's eyes from the man-made images of the Roman Catholic Church to nature is not, for him and other early Protestants, a movement from the sacred to the secular, as most literary historians assume, but the reverse. In fact, Protestant divines who literally competed with Shakespeare on Sunday afternoons exhort the faithful to engage in "the earnest beholding of the majesty of god, shining most brightly in his living creatures, which are always, and everywhere sene with the eye."[61] They appeal to their listeners to redirect their vision away from the "dead" images of the Roman Catholic Church to those "true," "living," and "lively" images of God: to "Jesus Christ who is the expressed image of God"; to the "true reliks [the saints] which are, the exaumple of theyr steadfast fayth and beliefe, their godlye lyfe and

---

writes that "This magnificent theater of heaven and earth, crammed with innumerable miracles, Paul calls the 'wisdom of God.' Contemplating it, we ought in wisdom to have known God" (*Institutes* 2.6.1). For discussions of the *theatrum mundi* trope and the drama, see Frances Yates, *The Theatre of the World* (1969); Charles Cannon, " 'As in a Theater': *Hamlet* in the Light of Calvin's Doctrine of Predestination" (1971). Frye reviews critical discussions of Hamlet's dramatic theory in *Renaissance Hamlet*, pp. 281–92.

[60] Calvin, *Institutes* 1.14.20; 1.5.5; Calvin, *The Catechisme* (1582), sig. A4ᵛ; *Institutes* 1.15.3; Calvin, *Sermons upon Ephesians*, fol. 87ʳ.

[61] Veron, *A stronge battery*, fol. 103ʳ.

conversation"; and to their fellow human beings who are the "living image of God, and made by the very hand of God."[62]

The religious practices of Elizabethan England may well have predisposed Shakespeare's audiences to interpret the characters portrayed on stage as lively images of virtue and vice, their stories as manifestations of divine will. And Shakespeare's representational theater may well have thrived in an early Protestant culture that was hostile to other forms of human artifice because it directed its spectators' attention to human characters played by human actors—the living images of God—rather than to the imaginary and erroneous, ornamental and lifeless images made by the hands of men. In contrast to painted images of Christ, humans are "flesh of his [Christ's] flesh, and bone of his bone; and in them is a lively resemblance of him, and they have a bodie and a reasonable soule, as hee hath, and the graces of his spirit in them."[63]

Even though Hamlet teaches his viewers to distrust certain kinds of theater, he imagines a profitable way of seeing, commending the "judicious" few who are not blinded by the spectacular or deluded by the mystified and can therefore attend to what is significant. Like the few whom Calvin singles out for praise because they "more deeply investigate" the matter, Hamlet's ideal playgoers concentrate on interpreting the meaning of what they see, considering "some necessary question of the play" rather than taking pleasure in the superficial, the spectacular, or the trivial.[64] Ideally, for Hamlet and presumably Shakespeare, watching a stage play is therefore an experience that develops moral awareness, deepens self-knowledge, and elicits ethical choices.

Although he frets about the tendency of spectators to overvalue spectacle, Hamlet does not reject the theater because so many abuse it, but rather chooses it as his instrument. Interested in the capacity of drama to stir its spectators, he believes, in fact, that plays can elicit self-recognition, confession, even repentance:

> I have heard that guilty creatures sitting at a play
> Have by the very cunning of the scene

---

[62] Calvin, *Sermons upon Ephesians*, fol. 40^v; Veron, *A stronge battery*, fol. 37^r; Perkins, *Warning*, p. 45.

[63] John Dod and Richard Cleaver, *A Plaine and Familiar Exposition of the Ten Commandments* (1606), sig. G5^r.

[64] Calvin, *Institutes* 4.10.12.

Been struck so to the soul that presently
They have proclaimed their malefactions.

(2.2.575–78)

Hamlet expresses here a belief that watching a play can strike the soul and provoke self-examination. Theater is for him an agent of reform.

Apologists for the stage make similar claims when they insist that what a play's spectators see when they look upon the stage is their own moral condition. "A Play's a true transparant Christall mirror, / To shew good minds their mirth, the bad their terror," asserts a prefatory poem to Heywood's *Apology for Actors*, echoing Hamlet. In it the play-goer can "see his vertue or his crime / Layd open."[65] The assertion that seeing one's "crime / Layd open" can be beneficial—can, in fact, "new mold the harts of the spectators"—is shared by the reformers who stress the value of viewing sin.[66] According to Calvin, the faithful can confront their own unworthiness, a necessary initial phase of re-pentance, only if they are able to acknowledge how they have "de-faced," "mutilated," and "almost blotted out" the divine image. The fallen condition, for Calvin, is therefore a persuasive picture, a "sorry spectacle" that, when contemplated in the context of the *Imago Dei*, is so horrifying that "thence is kindled a new zeal to seek God."[67]

The English Calvinists consequently approve of art that reminds peo-ple of their sins, disrupting moral complacency and stimulating self-examination. In addition to images that "be representers of virtue and good example," they allow images that "by occasion, may be stirrers of men's minds, and make them to remember themselves, and to la-ment their sins." And they explicitly approve of art that "provoke[s]" us, as spectators, to "consider ourselves . . . and to condemn and abhor our sin."[68]

Certainly Hamlet's own play, "The Murder of Gonzago," affects Claudius in this way, reminding him of his cruel deed, arousing guilt, and fostering an intense self-scrutiny.[69] When he views the dramatic

[65] John Taylor, qtd. in Heywood, *Apology*, sig. A3ᵛ.

[66] Heywood, *Apology*, sig. B4ʳ.

[67] Calvin, *Sermons upon Galathians*, fol. 193ʳ–194ᵛ; Calvin, *Institutes* 1.15.4; 2.1.1.

[68] "The Contents of a Book of Articles devised by the King," qtd. in Foxe, *A&M* 5: 163; qtd. in Phillips, *Reformation of Images*, p. 57.

[69] Arthur McGee, *The Elizabethan Hamlet* (1987), pp.110–22, argues that Hamlet is a Roman Catholic; he believes that the players disobey Hamlet, change the prepared text,

reenactment of the murder he has committed, sees his act mirrored in the play action, Claudius abruptly flees the performance and, in the following scene, attempts to pray. Hamlet's play thus arouses Claudius from his moral stupor, overwhelming him with guilt and sending him to his knees in prayer. Although he struggles mightily against the potential of this scene to remold his heart (like Calvin's hardened sinners who "furiously repel all remembrance" and therefore "in seeing see they not"), his intense response to watching his crime reenacted and his subsequent attempt to pray exemplify the extraordinary power Shakespeare attributes to theatrical representation.[70] Clearly Shakespeare imagines here a theater that is fundamentally different from Mephistopheles' seductive theatricality, one that, far from pleasing a wanton eye, disrupts and disturbs the sinful spectator. An occasion for self-examination, a goad to the guilty, a mirror for the soul, Hamlet's theater does not dazzle its spectators with external spectacles, but rather drives them inward.

The play-within-a-play creates a sustained experience of self-reflexivity for Shakespeare's audiences. They watch actors play players cast in dramatic roles, observe Hamlet observing his uncle observing a dramatic reenactment of his secret crime, see a playlet that mirrors the ghost's narrative in a play that is said to mirror nature. Shakespeare fosters in his spectators the very self-scrutiny that sets Hamlet apart from his world. Forced to share Hamlet's heightened self-consciousness, Shakespeare's spectators turn their gaze upon themselves, see themselves seeing and being seen. As a consequence, they identify with both the observing subject and the observed object of the gaze. By replicating in its spectators Hamlet's divided self, Shakespeare's theater distances itself from the theatricality that Calvin and the English Calvinists condemn, a theatricality characterized, in contrast, by visual splendor and inauthenticity.

Hamlet's tortured and unrelenting analysis of his own motives and actions manifests a distinctly Protestant habit of mind, one that the play of *Hamlet* induces in its spectators as well. Calvin advocates just such an

---

and "frustrate Hamlet's design." James R. Siemon, *Shakespearean Iconoclasm* (1985), p. 236, holds that the playlet is a failure and argues that the "representation turns out to be idolatrous self-deception." For discussions of Shakespeare's metadrama, see James L. Calderwood, *To Be or Not to Be* (1983); Maurice Charney, *Style in* Hamlet (1969); and Robert Egan, *Drama Within Drama* (1975).

[70] Calvin, *Institutes* 1.4.2.

open-ended, self-scrutinizing, reflective interiority as the antidote to the theatricality he abhors. He urges the faithful to "diligently inquire into all the winding recesses with which human minds are filled and perplexed," and "to compose and examine themselves deeply and seriously and to converse freely with themselves."[71] In championing an ongoing, interior self-examination that exhibits the self to itself, Calvin imagines the judging spectator and performing player as dialectical voices within the individual. William Bouwsma argues that by so splitting the self into the "observer and observed, audience and actor," Calvin "was driven back to theatricality even by his effort to escape it."[72] The interior drama Calvin advocates, however, surely does not replicate the inauthentic masks, flamboyant role-playing, or dazzling spectacle that the reformers seek to abolish. Rather, by making the individual highly self-conscious of his own propensity to posture and deceive while confronting him with his own susceptibility to seduction and bedazzlement, it undermines and controls his idolatrous impulses.

It is, I suggest, just this self-conscious and alienating sense of a split self that Shakespeare nurtures in his spectators. Conceived in opposition to the kind of artifice that postures, deceives, and seduces, his play serves as a defense against the duplicity of a deeply ingrained theatricality. He creates a drama that contains its own power to dazzle and seduce by requiring his spectators to internalize the dialectic of the stage, thereby denying them any direct or unmediated access to the magical, the erotic, or the imaginary. Shakespeare's reflexive attention in *Hamlet* to the gaze of both his characters and his spectators draws on early Protestant notions of the conscience, a topic I explore in Chapter 7. In privileging interiority and self-reflexivity over the theatrics of the court and the spectacle of earlier modes of drama, Shakespeare explores the potential of the stage to reform his spectators, disrupting their trust in externals and nurturing an awareness of themselves as both actors and spectators in the great theater of the world.

Although the antitheatricalists ultimately succeeded in closing the London theaters, their hostility toward the stage, based on their mistrust of all that is imaginary and man-made, thus paradoxically helps to shape the drama of Elizabethan and Jacobean England. That drama, which began to flourish soon after the popular religious drama of the

[71] Qtd. in Bouwsma, *John Calvin*, p. 179.
[72] Ibid., p. 180.

late Middle Ages was suppressed, not only addresses but, I believe, also attempts to redress the objections of the reformers who would also abolish it.

Products of a culture traumatized and energized by iconoclastic attacks on the magical, artificial, and phantasmic, the plays of Shakespeare, Marlowe, and their contemporaries display dazzling spectacle, but they also destabilize their spectators' relation to it. In *Doctor Faustus* Marlowe explores the seductive power of his own theater, captivating his audiences with stunning spectacles even as he mocks their propensity to believe what they see. Though he features wondrous magic, he also insists on its illusory nature and demonic origins. Dramatizing the compulsive attempts of an imaginative man like Faustus to rival God's creative power, Marlowe interrogates the magician's and the playwright's art even as he celebrates it.

Shakespeare critiques the prodigious displays of cunning that characterize Faustus's magical entertainments. In place of the histrionic and phantasmic, he develops a drama that represents the natural world. If he strives to mirror nature in a playhouse called the Globe, he imagines the world itself as a stage, thereby fostering a dual awareness in his playgoers of themselves as both actors and spectators. Although he recognizes that theater, like the great theater of the world itself, may dazzle and deceive, Shakespeare insists on its potential to manifest truths. In opposition to the seductive theatricality that thrills and enthralls Faustus, causing his ruin, he imagines a drama so powerful and persuasive that it can elicit a profound emotional and ethical response in its spectators, initiating an inward process of self-examination, and perhaps even moral reformation.

In its rehearsal of the kind of spectacles and theatricality that the reformers condemn, *Doctor Faustus* illustrates one of the strategies frequently used by Renaissance playwrights to explore the idolatrous potential of the stage. In my next chapter I show how Thomas Kyd and Thomas Middleton also stage dangerous forms of theater, displaying and demystifying elaborate spectacles that bear a striking resemblance to the Roman Mass as the reformers understand it. *Hamlet*, in contrast, provides an alternate model of the theater. Affirming the power of representational drama, it articulates a Protestant aesthetics that, I argue in Chapter 4, is deeply informed by a Protestant sacramental theology. Despite their differences, both plays reflexively address the antitheatrical biases of the English reformers, and both respond to early

Protestant culture's growing distrust of the imaginary. However disruptive and destabilizing, that distrust proves to be a stimulus rather than an obstacle to dramatic production, so much so that the drama of the English Renaissance can also be understood as the drama of the English Reformation.

CHAPTER FOUR

Rehearsing the Eucharistic Controversies: The Revenge Tragedies

Whereas it was forbidden, in the old law, that any man should eat or drink blood, the apostles, notwithstanding, took the cup at Christ's hands and drank of it; and never staggered, or shrank at the matter: whereby it may be gathered, that they took it for a mystery, for a token and a remembrance, far otherwise than it hath of late been taken. Again, when the sacrament was dealt, none of them all crouched down, and took it for his God forgetting him that sat there present before their eyes, but took it, and ate it, knowing that it was a sacrament and remembrance of Christ's body.

—John Foxe, *Actes and Monuments*

Observing The Lord's Supper and the Lord Chamberlain's Men

In a provocative essay, "The Purpose of Playing: Reflections on a Shakespearean Anthropology," Louis Adrian Montrose explores the relation between the London commercial stage and the suppression of late medieval religious rituals during the Reformation. Noting how easily the distinction between drama and ritual can become blurred in performance, he argues that the drama appropriates and transforms the forbidden Roman Catholic rituals, rituals he associates with "the material efficacy of magic."[1] He thus sees the theater of Elizabethan England as an institution that preserved and perpetuated the magic of the traditional Church. Emphasizing the antitheatrical biases and iconoclastic impulses of early English Protestantism, Montrose constructs the reformed religion as essentially hostile to the stage. The drama that emerged soon after Elizabeth reestabli-

[1] Louis Adrian Montrose, "The Purpose of Playing" (1980), p. 62.

shed Protestantism, he suggests, may provide "another form of compensation" for the suppressed images, rituals, and ceremonies of the medieval Church, offering an eager populace what the new religion deprived them of: mystery, magic, spectacle, theatricality.[2]

Although Montrose explores the relation between religious rituals and secular plays from the perspective of cultural anthropology, he denies the *reformed* sacraments the power anthropologists attribute to religious rituals to shape the way their participants experience and interpret their world. With many other literary scholars, he assumes that the newly instituted reformed rituals were empty, evacuated of meaning, and thus profoundly unsatisfying. If, however, the regular observance of a religious ritual has, as Clifford Geertz argues, the capacity to "induc[e] in the worshipper a certain distinctive set of dispositions (tendencies, capacities, propensities, skills, habits, liabilities, pronenesses) which lend a chronic character to the flow of his activity and the quality of his experience," then the central ritual of the English Church, the Protestant Lord's Supper, surely exerts a powerful, shaping force in the lives of Elizabethan and Jacobean Londoners.[3] Montrose ignores the new Protestant rituals in favor of the older Roman Catholic ones because he assumes that the Reformation was primarily experienced as loss. Interested in how the suppression of the Roman Mass might have contributed to the emergence of the commercial stage, he fails to ask how the institution of the Protestant Lord's Supper might have shaped—in a constructive way—the new drama and its audiences.

Nevertheless, his thesis that Elizabethan drama replaces the lost medieval religious rituals presumably because the reformed religion fails to create viable ritual forms in place of the ones it destroys has gained wide acceptance.[4] Martha Tuck Rozett, in her book on the relation

---

[2] Ibid., p. 60.

[3] Clifford Geertz, *The Interpretation of Cultures* (1973), p. 95.

[4] Dissenting from Montrose are Robert Knapp, *Shakespeare—The Theater and the Book* (1989), and C. L. Barber, *Creating Elizabethan Tragedy* (1988). Knapp writes, "Surely there is truth to the hunch that a philosophical doctrine of exemplarism and a theological doctrine of real presence sort better with metaphors of readability [and the Corpus Christi plays], while notions of God's unsearchable grandeur, the spiritually defective reason of human beings, and the superiority of historical types to other kinds of allegory better suit the image of the Globe, that *theatrum mundi* in which divine intentions are not so visible as divine magnificence and vengeance" (p. 20). Barber speculates that there is a relation between the experience of communion in the Elizabethan Church and of play going in the Elizabethan theater (p. 46), but he does not fully develop this insight, turning instead to psychoanalytical analyses of plays by Marlowe and Kyd. See also An-

between the doctrine of election and the emergence of Elizabethan tragedy, comments that "ironically, the reformers drove their audiences to seek in the theatre what the Church no longer provided."[5] Michael O'Connell goes even farther, arguing in his essay "The Idolatrous Eye: Iconoclasm, Anti-Theatricalism, and the Image of the Elizabethan Theater" that Elizabethan drama emerges in opposition to the reformed religion, appropriating and reinvigorating the forbidden rituals, spectacles, and theatricality of the traditional Church. He therefore suggests that the drama "could be viewed as a competing—idolatrous—religious structure."[6] All three critics imagine the Protestant religion of early modern England as essentially devoid of meaningful rituals, ceremonies, images, and communal experiences. And they imply that sixteenth-century Londoners, or at least the ten thousand or so who flock weekly to the theaters, are hostile to, and deeply dissatisfied by, the official Protestant religion they are required by law to worship.

Certainly, many experience the suppression of the Roman Mass as a profound loss. Many others, however, are as profoundly affected by the power of the revised Protestant sacrament. That power is too often unacknowledged by literary critics who view the Reformation from the perspective of four centuries of continued demystification of the sacred, four hundred years of greater and greater rationalization of religion. The beginning of that process is all too often confused with the end, a modern age that declares God absent, rituals empty, signs meaningless, community dead. But if the reformers, in their denunciation of the Roman Mass, anticipate, and set in motion, the anxieties of modernism, they do not empty the Protestant sacrament of the Lord's Supper of its meaning or deprive it of its ritual status.

In fact, many people in sixteenth-century England experience the Lord's Supper as meaningful, mysterious, and deeply satisfying. The

---

thony B. Dawson's speculations on the relation between the body of the actor and "the debate surrounding the question of the 'real presence of Christ in the sacrament'" ("Performance and Participation" [1996], pp. 37–39).

[5] Martha Tuck Rozett, *The Doctrine of Election and the Emergence of Elizabethan Tragedy* (1984), pp. 21–22.

[6] Michael O'Connell, "The Idolatrous Eye" (1985), p. 307; see also Clifford Davidson, "The Anti-Visual Prejudice" (1988), pp. 33–46, and Steven Mullaney, *The Place of the Stage* (1988), pp. 92–93, who finds a "grudging and politic admiration" in Protestant England for the efficacy of the suppressed rituals, and then notes "what a given culture excludes as alien can . . . come back to haunt it."

degree of resistance to Mary's attempt to reinstate the Mass suggest
how passionately some Englishmen and women embraced the new religion, how fully they have—by the mid-1500s—internalized the teachings of the reformers. This is *particularly* true in London and its
surrounding parishes, where the influence of the Continental Reformation is felt most strongly and the conditions of urban life predispose
citizens to accept the new reformed ideology. Recent historical studies
reveal that the citizens of London accepted the reformed religion earlier and with far less resistance than people in rural and northern parts
of England. "Nowhere in the kingdom," Gina Alexander writes, "had
there been a greater circulation of Protestant ideas of many varieties,
nowhere had Protestant modes of worship taken firmer root than in
the [London] diocese to which Bonner was restored in September
1553."[7]

If we grant that the reformed Lord's Supper is a viable and widely
practiced religious ritual in late sixteenth-century London, one that
shares with other such sacred rituals the capacity to "alter, often radically, the whole landscape presented to common sense," how might its
regular observance affect the way its worshipers see, interpret, and in-
teract with the visible world?[8] More specifically, how might the practice
of the Protestant ritual of the Lord's Supper shape the way London
playwrights imagine and London playgoers experience the spectacle
and theatrics of Elizabethan and Jacobean drama?

Although the sacred space of the English Protestant church may
seem very far removed from the secular space of the London theater
in Shakespeare's time, both the religious ritual and the popular play
function as "cultural performances," those powerful cultural forms
that symbolic anthropologists believe have the capacity to shape human
consciousness. Both are public and performative genres. Both occupy
a communal space specifically designed for them, one that is marked
off and set apart from the everyday world. Both are "central and re-
current" events in the lives of the citizens of London. Both are "or-
chestrations of media"—images, words, music—"not expressions in a
single medium." And both are reflexive forms that create what Victor

---

[7] Gina Alexander, "Bonner and the Marian Persecutions" (1987), p. 166. See also
Horton Davies, *Worship and Theology in England* (1970), 1:62, who confirms that Londoners
embraced Protestantism earlier and with less resistance than people living in northern
and rural regions of England.

[8] Geertz, *Interpretation*, p. 122.

Turner has described as a " 'discontinuum' of action" during which
their spectators "become conscious, through witnessing and often participating in such performances, of the nature, texture, style, and given
meanings of their own lives as members of a sociocultural community."[9] Observing (celebrating) the Lord's Supper in the Elizabethan
Church and observing (watching) the Lord Chamberlain's Men in the
Elizabethan theater are, from an anthropological perspective, related
cultural activities that structure the way Londoners in the early modern
period know and understand their world.

Rather than honor the distinctions between sacred and secular—
distinctions that are themselves early Protestant constructions—I
therefore propose to treat both ritual and play as reflexive cultural
forms that have the capacity not only to mirror but also to shape the
lived experience of their participants. In observing the reformed Lord's
Supper in the late sixteenth-century English Church, worshipers must
acknowledge that the sacramental bread and wine are signs, and not
the transubstantiated body and blood of Christ. They must consciously
repudiate the old religion's belief that *viewing* the Host is salvific. In
the absence of any such miraculous spectacle, they must attend to the
figurative power of the communal bread and wine. And, they must
cultivate a receptivity to the spoken word rather than worship the image. In observing a theatrical performance by an acting company such
as the Lord Chamberlain's Men, the spectators must recognize (as the
Mechanicals in *A Midsummer Night's Dream* are so anxious to demonstrate) that what they see is a representation, and not the literal presence of what is represented. They must consciously accept the illusory
nature of theatrical images and yet believe in the figurative truth of
those very images. And they must attend closely to the oral recitation
of poetic verse while being careful not to overvalue spectacle.

In this chapter I explore the relation between these two experiences,
one religious and one aesthetic, focusing on the function of visible
signs in both. Both the Protestant ritual and the Renaissance play, I
argue, destabilize their spectators, denying them any unmediated experience of visible things and fostering a distrust of externals. Nevertheless, both also insist on the figurative power of the visible sign,
inculcating a new mode of seeing that, while it requires people to be

---

[9] For a detailed discussion of the anthropological term *cultural performance*, see Victor
Turner, *The Anthropology of Performance* (1987), pp. 23–27, 81–82.

skeptical about what they see and self-reflexive about their own looking, also encourages them to be receptive to the capacity of signs, in conjunction with spoken words, to move, persuade, and transform. I focus on the genre of revenge tragedy, for in its intense focus on representation and remembrance, it explores key terms in the debate over the meaning of the sacrament of communion.

The Rhetoric of the Roman Mass and the Reformed Lord's Supper

If the iconoclastic impulses of the early Protestant reformers are in part a response to the iconophilia that pervades late medieval popular culture, nowhere is this dialectic more fully articulated than in the eucharistic controversy of the sixteenth century. Because the early Protestants believe that the most heinous and blasphemous idol of the Roman Catholic church is the Mass itself, a ritual that many Catholics had come to view as a "mysterious spectacle," the Reformation debate over images necessarily addresses that central sacrament in both faiths, what the Catholics call the Mass and the reformed Protestants the Lord's Supper.[10] Rejecting the sacrament of the altar as "an abominable idol" and a "foul idol," English reformers condemn the emphasis in popular devotion on *viewing* the sacred Host, an experience that for many had become "the principal, if not the exclusive, concern of worshippers," so much so that "people frequently left the church after the eleva-

---

[10] Davies, *Worship and Theology*, 1:139; for a comprehensive analysis of the various Protestant eucharistic theories, and their relative importance in English theology, see Davies, 1:76–123. Davies describes the three main theories developed as alternatives to transubstantiation—consubstantiation or the real presence, virtualism, and memorialism—and he shows how the major English reformers adopted, interpreted, combined, and subtly altered all three of these theories. My discussion here is necessarily more general than Davies's and therefore cannot attend to all the distinctions among the various theologians and sects. I concentrate on what I believe are the dominant features of the reformed Lord's Supper as understood by most early English Protestants, and I emphasize the central issues that separated Roman Catholics from almost all early English Protestants. In relying closely on Calvin and citing extensively from Foxe, I accept the arguments of recent historians that early English Protestantism was most strongly influenced by Calvin and therefore that English theories of the Eucharist tended toward virtualism. See Davies, *Worship and Theology*, 1:111–20; Patrick Collinson, *Godly People* (1983), pp. 213–44; A. G. Dickens, *The English Reformation* (1964), pp. 197–201.

tion."[11] The Roman Mass deeply offends the reformers because the priest, in elevating the Host, presumes to offer a salvific vision of God, a God the reformers insist is invisible. How to see, what it is possible to see, and the power of what one sees are thus central issues in any interpretation of the eucharistic sacrament.

In their condemnation of the Roman Catholic Mass, the English reformers explicitly repudiate the devotional gaze. Dismissing the adoration of the elevated host as mere gaping, John Foxe, for example, ridicules "our mass-men" for "gazing, peeping, pixing, boxing, carrying, re-carrying, worshipping, stooping, kneeling, knocking, with 'stoop down before,' 'hold up higher,' 'I thank God I see my Maker to-day.'"[12] Protestants object to the Mass because it deflects the worshiper's attention away from an invisible God, focusing instead on material objects and "man-made" images. In an effort to break the habit of "seeing and adoring the body in the form of bread," John Foxe ridicules worshipers who "imagine a body were they see no body" and condemns the Mass as "altogether corporeal and extern" because it encourages "the outward seeing and touching of him, of itself, without faith."[13] The Protestant martyrs he portrays defiantly resist pressure from the Roman clergy to see Christ "flesh, blood, and bone" when the pyx is displayed, claiming instead to see "nothing but a few clouts hanging together on a heap" and challenging their inquisitors with the question, "whom seest thou yonder?"[14]

Through such anecdotes, the English reformers nurture in their readers a reflexive attention to sight, often depicting the clash of different modes of seeing and analyzing what they believe to be the errors and inadequacies of traditional—bodily—seeing. Foxe, for instance, relates a conversation between two friends, a man named William Rivelay, who believes he has "seen his Lord God in form of bread and wine over the priest's head," and a man named John Southwick, who impatiently corrects him, exclaiming, "Nay, William! thou saw'st not the Lord God, thou sawest bread, wine, and the chalice." When Rivelay persists in his belief that he sees God, stubbornly asserting that "I trust verily that I saw my Lord God in form of bread and wine, and this I

---

[11] Foxe, *A&M*, 8:464, 492; Davies, *Worship and Theology*, 1:140; Margaret R. Miles, *Image as Insight* (1985), p. 97.

[12] Foxe, *A&M*, 6:361; see also 7:198.

[13] Ibid., 1:528.

[14] Ibid., 8:242, 158.

doubt not," Southwick attempts to teach his friend to see in a more analytical, self-conscious, and mediated way: "Nay, I tell thee thou sawest but only a figure or sacrament of him, which is in substance bread and wine."[15] In Foxe's polemical work, William Rivelay's way of seeing—one informed by what Gail Gibson describes as a late medieval belief in "the sanctifying presence of God's image in the *world*"—is challenged and ridiculed by his friend Southwick, who carefully distinguishes between the visible sign and the invisible God it signifies.[16] Foxe champions Southwick's interpreting strategies, depicting them as enlightened and even heroic.

The reformers warn that the Roman religion draws its worshipers away from spiritual considerations and focuses them instead on the material and corporeal. In a typical anecdote in a Protestant sermon, a Catholic priest offers a dying goldsmith "a cross of fine silver being double gilted" and tells him it is "your maker, your saviour, and redeemer, look upon hym." The goldsmith gazes silently at the cross before replying, unmoved and unrepentant, "What is the price of an ounce?" In an attempt to demystify such images, the preacher asks sarcastically, "Was not thys manne well edified by the syght of this goodly crosse?"[17] Such narratives are clearly intended to disrupt the devotional gaze.

However contemptuous of the devotional gaze, Calvin and the English reformers he influences do *not* eliminate the visible from the Lord's Supper. Rather, they identify the visible images of bread and wine as divine signs and repeatedly call attention to their power. Insisting that the Lord's Supper is a promise and a memorial, not a sacrifice or a miracle, they grant images an important, indeed essential, mnemonic function. Because they believe that Christ's words, "Do this in the remembrance of me" (Luke 22:19), are the "key" to the sacrament that "opened and revealed" its meaning, they view the sacramental bread and wine as powerful reminders of Christ's sacrifice.[18] By calling to mind the Last Supper, the bread and wine renew and reinforce an

---

[15] Ibid., 4:206–07.

[16] Gail Gibson, *The Theater of Devotion* (1989), p. 14; see also Carolyn Walker Bynum, "The Body of Christ in the Later Middle Ages" (1986), pp. 407–23, who demonstrates how in late medieval spirituality the physical was often inseparable from the spiritual.

[17] John Veron, *A stronge battery against the idolatrous invocation of the dead Saintes* (1562), fol. 102ᵛ.

[18] Nicholas Ridley, "A Brief Declaration of the Lord's Supper" (1843), 39:22.

understanding of the original event. Their display at the celebration of the Lord's Supper helps Protestant worshipers recall not only Christ's sacrifice but also their own unworthiness. Arguing that the sacramental signs "are the true pictures that we ought to have," Calvin explains that looking on them helps people remember their sinful state: "Like as when we see the water of baptism it is a picture which sheweth us that we be full of filth and uncleannesse."[19] Only by remembering their own sins can they fully grasp the meaning of the sacrament as a "perpetual memorie" and experience it as a promise of the redemption of sins.[20]

Far from forbidding images, the early Protestants thus teach worshipers to see the visible elements of the sacraments as divine signs that can lead them to an invisible God. Even though they condemn as idolatrous any human attempt to render God visible, they teach that God chooses to represent himself in images, so that he "may after a sorte be sene and felte of us" and the faithful may "behold and se[e] him" in the sacraments "as it were in the face."[21] The sacraments for Calvin are "the true pictures" and "the good images that God hath set afore us," and reformed Christians are encouraged to discover God in "such tokens and sygnes" and to "turne our eyes to that countenance . . . that we should behold it with great heade, care and diligence."[22]

In fact, Calvin emphasizes that God communicates with human beings through images, using "earthly and visible signs" because he deems them "fitteth for us" as "souls engrafted in bodies." Accommodating "our feeble capacity," he "condescends to lead us to himself even by these earthly elements, and to set before us in the flesh a

---

[19] Calvin, *Sermons of M. John Calvin upon the Epistle of Saincte Paule to the Galathians* (1574), fol. 114ᵛ.

[20] Martin Bucer, *A treatise declaryng and shewing dyvers causes that pyctures and other ymages ar in no wise to be sufferd in churches* [1535?], sig. Dviiiᵛ; see also Calvin, *Institutes of the Christian Religion* (1960) 4.17.40; Calvin, *The sermons of M. John Calvin upon S. Paule too the Ephesians* (1574), fol. 76ᵛ-77ʳ; William Perkins, *A Warning against the idolatrie of the last times* (1601), p. 126; Abraham Scultetus, *A Short Information, but agreeable unto Scripture, of Idol-Images* (1620), sig. C3ʳ; Ridley, "Lord's Supper," 39:15; Foxe, *A&M*, 5:163, 7:654.

[21] John Calvin, *Four godlye sermons agaynst the pollution of idolatries* (1561), sigs. Kiiiʳ, Kiiiᵛ.

[22] Calvin, *Sermons upon Galathians*, fol. 114ᵛ; Calvin, *Four sermons*, fol. Kiiʳ. In his recent biography of the French reformer, William Bouwsma notes how Calvin "often seemed much impressed by the special value of sight" (*John Calvin* [1988], p. 72). Calvin relies heavily on the visual mode of perception, favors metaphors of sight, and even likens the word of God to a corrective lens, a pair of spectacles for "bleary-eyed men and those with weak vision" (*Institutes* 1.6.1).

mirror of spiritual blessings"; he thus "imparts spiritual things under visible ones." The sacraments—those "physical signs . . . thrust before our eyes"—thus represent "God's promises as painted in a picture," which God "sets . . . before our sight, portrayed graphically and in the manner of images."[23] Although they must not be confused with the things they signify, the sacramental images are thus vehicles that are essential to faith, God-given tokens and signs the believer is encouraged to contemplate, interpret, and, above all, experience.

Calvin thus conceives of the visible element as a necessary rhetorical tool by which God "exhorteth us to come unto him," making "him selfe lowe, too the ende wee shoulde not have any excuse, to say wee were not able to mount up to suche a heighth."[24] Images like the bread and wine of the Lord's Supper or the water of baptism are the "ladders and stayres" by which humans, creatures of the flesh, may climb to God.[25] Worshipers are admonished not to "pluck down Christ from heaven, and put him in your faith, as in a visible place," but instead to "rise and spring up to him" by means of images.[26] In opposition to the Mass, which the reformers believe encourages its worshipers to see, ingest, and adore an incarnate God, the sight of whom is salvific, the Protestant Lord's Supper therefore invites its worshipers to remember, receive, and rise up to a transcendent God who cannot be seen, eaten, or touched. But if God is invisible, the Protestant devout are "lifted up to heaven with our eyes and minds" by means of visible signs.[27]

That transcendent moment when "the divine essence infuseth itself unspeakably into the faithful receiver of the sacrament" cannot be achieved by means of the visible image alone.[28] Calvin accuses the Catholics of emptying the sacramental signs of meaning by divorcing them from words, thereby mystifying them. He is especially contemptuous of the use of Latin in the Roman Catholic Mass, so that words are "whis-

[23] Calvin, *Sermons upon Galathians*, fol. 118; Calvin, *Institutes* 4.14.3; 4.17.11; 4.14.3; 4.17.11; 4.14.6.

[24] Calvin, *Sermons upon Galathians*, fol. 118ʳ.

[25] Calvin, *Four sermons*, sig. Kiiᵛ.

[26] Foxe, *A&M*, 6:339.

[27] Calvin, *Institutes* 4.17.18; Calvin thus notes that "the apostle condemns as blind and accursed those who, content with present shadows, did not stretch their minds to Christ" (*Institutes* 2.11.10); and Bucer asks rhetorically if Roman Catholic worshippers "do beleve that god and the sayntes are in heven, why do they not rather lyft up their eyes to that place than to the deed ymages?" (*Treatise*, sig. E.iiʳ).

[28] Foxe, *A&M*, 6:312.

pered without meaning," and he ridicules the Mass for its primary emphasis on spectacle devoid of any explanatory words: "Nothing more preposterous could happen in the Supper than for it to be turned into a silent action, as has happened under the pope's tyranny. . . . Here we should not imagine some magic incantation, supposing it enough to have mumbled the words, as if they were to be heard by the elements; but let us understand that these words are living preaching which edifies its hearers, penetrates into their very minds, impresses itself upon their hearts and settles there, and reveals its effectiveness in the fulfillment of what it promises."[29] For Calvin and the English Calvinists, then, the Mass is an abuse of God's sacrament not because it is dramatic or visual (in fact, in important ways the Lord's Supper is both) but because it is performed in "silence" or with "a mere noise." They complain that "the priests do so champ [the words] and chaw them, and post so fast, that neither they understand what they say nor they that hear them." And they insist that without words that "make us understand what the visible sign means," the eucharistic bread and wine are "utterly meaningless signs."[30]

Literary scholars often assume that when Protestants condemn the theatricality and spectacle of the Mass, they condemn theater and image per se. Stephen Greenblatt, for example, asserts in his essay on *King Lear* and religious exorcism that for early Protestants "the difference between true and false religion is the presence of theater."[31] The reformers, however, use the language of the theater pejoratively almost exclusively to refer to the silent actions, gestures, and visual displays of the Mass, that is, to images and ceremonies that are *divorced from words.*

The poetic drama of the English Renaissance stage, with its rich and powerful verbal and vernacular texts, is hardly what Calvin has (or could have) in mind when he ridicules Catholic sacraments and ceremonies as "lifeless and theatrical trifles" that "draw the eyes of the common people to wonderment by a new spectacle," "theatrical props . . . where nothing appears but the mask of useless elegance and fruitless extravagance." For Calvin, the Roman sacraments are lifeless, useless, and fruitless because "there is no woorde that sanctifyeth them."

---

[29] Calvin, *Institutes* 4.14.4; 4.17.39.
[30] Calvin, *Institutes* 4.17.39; 4.14.4; Foxe, *A&M* 8:476; Calvin, *Institutes* 4.14.4; 4.10.15.
[31] Stephen Greenblatt, *Shakespearean Negotiations* (1988), p. 126.

They are nothing more than "bare signs" because "the sacrament requires preaching to beget faith."[32]

For reformers like Calvin, the Roman Mass is deeply flawed not because it is theatrical but because it features a particular kind of theatricality—one that privileges spectacle unaccompanied by the interpreting word, traffics in stage illusions, and uses artifice to beguile the eyes of its worshipers. They accuse priests of perverting the sacramental bread and wine by turning them into theatrical properties. The elements of the Mass, they insist, are merely "puppets, maumats [idols], and elfes," and the host is nothing more than a "patched monster, and a disguised puppet." And they construct Roman Catholic priests as cunning performers—"false theves and Juglers"—who "hath bewitched the mindes of the simple people" with "tricks" and "delude[d] the eyes of the spectators with empty pomp."[33] By means of such theatricality, the priests, they argue, deceive a credulous people, intentionally manipulating sacred images, as a popular song of the era laments, to fool the eyes of the devout:

> Thus were we poore soules
> Begyled with idolles,
> With fayned myracles and lyes,
> By the devyel and his docters,
> The pope and his procters;
> That, with such, have blerid our eyes.[34]

Although Calvin creates distrust for theatrical actions and spectacular images unaccompanied by explanatory words, mystified by unintelligible incantations, or divorced from the divine Word, he imagines the Lord's Supper as a dramatic representation in which the spoken word has the capacity to render fully what the visible signs symbolize, thereby creating the felt experience of the original event and communicating its meaning. The sacrament of the Lord's Supper, he writes, "does not feed our eyes with a mere appearance only, but leads us to the present

---

[32] Calvin, *Institutes* 4.17.43; 4.10.29; Calvin, *Sermons upon Ephesians*, fol. 85ʳ; Calvin, *Institutes* 4.14.4.

[33] Foxe, *A&M*, 5:409, 8:464; Nicholas Ridley, *A friendly farewell* (1559), sigs. Biiʳ; Calvin, *Institutes* 4.10.12.

[34] Qtd. in Foxe, *A&M*, 5:409.

reality and effectively performs what it symbolizes."[35] God's use of visible signs to represent himself endows that representation with mystery, those signs with the power to effect an inner, spiritual transformation. When reformed theologians insist that the sacramental bread is a figure—"one thing spoken, and another meant"—they therefore also assert the potency of that figure.[36]

In their sustained critiques of the Roman Mass, the reformers thus describe and evaluate competing theories of representation. They condemn the doctrine of transubstantiation because they believe it confuses the visible sign (the bread) for the thing it is meant to signify (Christ's body), deluding worshipers into "imagin[ing] a body where they see no body" and causing them to focus on "corporeal and extern matters." Arguing instead that the sacramental bread is a "sign," a "figure," a "token," a "seal," a "trope," and a "symbol," they vehemently deny that it is the very body of Christ. It "feedeth, it tasteth like bread, it looketh like bread, the little silly mouse taketh it for bread, and, to be short, it hath all the properties and tokens of bread: ergo," writes one reformer, "it is bread."[37] Another, quoting Augustine, concludes, "As to follow the letter and receive the signs for the things themselves are marks of servile weakness, so unprofitably to interpret the signs is a mark of badly straying error."[38]

Analogy is therefore crucial to the Calvinist reinterpretation of the Lord's Supper. Because the sacrament depends on the correspondence between earthly bread and Christ's body, between physical eating and spiritual nourishment, Calvin declares it meaningless *unless* the bread is literal bread, a sign of something it is not:

> The nature of the Sacrament is therefore canceled, unless, in the mode of signifying, the earthly sign corresponds to the heavenly thing. And the truth of this mystery accordingly perishes for us unless true bread represents the true body of Christ. Again I repeat: since the Supper is nothing but a visible witnessing of that promise contained in the sixth chapter of John, namely, that Christ is the bread of life come down from heaven [John 6:51], visible bread must serve as an intermediary to represent that

---

[35] Calvin, *Institutes* 4.15.14.
[36] Foxe, *A&M*, 8:244.
[37] Ibid., 1:528; 6: 344.
[38] Calvin, *Institutes* 4.14.16.

spiritual bread—unless we are willing to lose all the benefit which God, to sustain our weakness, confers upon us.[39]

Insisting that "The analogy and resemblance between the sacrament, and the thing signified, must ever be kept in all sacraments," the reformers argue that if the visible sign is mistaken for the thing it signifies, the sacrament loses its efficacy and its observation becomes an idolatrous "adoration" instead of a divinely sanctioned "commemoration."[40]

To realize the commemorative power of the sacrament, the English reformers therefore advocate the use of a simple table like the one that might have been used at the original supper, and a whole loaf of bread, like the one Christ might have broken. In place of the ornate altars of the Roman Church, which were shrouded in mystery, they thus propose substituting "an honest table, decently covered." Although Roman Catholic believers found the Protestant communion tables to be so thoroughly demystified and plain they ridiculed them as "oyster boards," the reformers insist on the appropriateness of an ordinary table because it calls to mind the historical Last Supper. They use visible objects like the table and bread to create a representational scene, much as stage properties do on the bare Elizabethan stage, and they firmly believe that the simple, visible signs they display have the capacity to stir the memory of the participants. They also seek to redesign the sacred space of the church, placing the minister in the midst of his congregation where he can be easily seen and heard, very much like actors on the thrust stage of the Elizabethan theaters, rather than separating him from the lay worshipers as in the Roman Church.[41]

Early Protestants believe the reformed ritual—simple, unadorned, figurative, and accessible—communicates the true mystery of the sacrament of the Lord's Supper, whereas the Roman Mass is a perversion of the sacrament, featuring nothing but empty spectacle and useless

[39] Ibid. 4.17.14.

[40] Peter Martyr, qtd. in Foxe, *A&M*, 6:300; John Philpot accuses the Roman Catholics of taking "away the substantial parts of the sacrament, as, 'Take ye, eate ye, Drink ye all of this; Do ye this in remembrance of me' [and replacing them with] 'hear ye, gaze ye, knock ye, worship ye, offer ye, sacrifice ye for the quick and the dead' " (qtd. in Foxe, *A&M*, 7:654).

[41] For a discussion of the communion tables in English Protestant Churches, see Davies, *Worship and Theology*, 1:204, 355, 363–65; quotations are from 1:364, 238.

mystifications. For them, the figurative interpretation of the sacrament thus does not deprive the Lord's Supper of either its drama or its mystery but instead restores both its dramatic and spiritual power. Literary scholars, however, tend to deny or minimize the sacred power most reformers attributed to signs—to representations. Stephen Greenblatt, for instance, argues that, in reinterpreting the ritual of the Lord's Supper as metaphor, the early Protestants transform the sacred into the literary and the aesthetic, thereby evacuating the ritual of its meaning.[42] But for sixteenth-century English Calvinists, the reinterpretation of the sacramental bread and wine as signs emphatically did not empty the Lord's Supper of its meaning or turn the sacred into the aesthetic. To the contrary, it reclaimed an original ("true") meaning and heightened the divine mystery of the sacrament.

Calvin directly answers the accusations of his "adversaries" who "heap unsavory witticisms" upon him and his fellow reformers by calling them "tropists" and claiming they rob the sacrament of its mystery:

> There is no reason for anyone to object that this is a figurative expression by which the name of the thing signified is given to the sign. I indeed admit that the breaking of bread is a symbol; it is not the thing itself. But having admitted this, we shall nevertheless duly infer that by the showing of the symbol the thing itself is also shown . . . if the Lord truly represents the participation in his body through the breaking of bread, there ought not to be the least doubt that he truly presents and shows his body. And the godly ought by all means to keep this rule: whenever they see symbols appointed by the Lord, to think and be persuaded that the truth of the thing signified is surely present there. For why should the Lord put in your hand the symbol of his body, except to assure you of a true participation in it? But if it is true that a visible sign is given us to seal the gift of a thing invisible, when we have received the symbol of the body, let us no less surely trust that the body itself is also given to us.[43]

Calvin insists on the power of the figure to call forth what it represents. For him the sacramental bread is not a mere sign but a divinely given symbol, an assurance of the truth of the representation and of the worshiper's participation in the sacred mystery.

---

[42] Greenblatt, *Shakespearean Negotiations*, pp. 121–28.
[43] Calvin, *Institutes*, 4.17.21; 4.17.10.

Greenblatt senses a "felt difference between Shakespeare's art and the [Protestant] religious ideology to which it gives voice," but I am not persuaded by his argument. When he describes Shakespeare's theater as "an institution that calls forth what is not, that signifies absence, that transforms the literal into the metaphorical," he identifies precisely the ways in which Shakespearean theater most closely resembles the sacred rituals of the sixteenth-century English Church and most markedly adheres to Calvinist doctrine. If, as he contends, Shakespearean theater "makes for itself the hollow round space within which it survives," he does not fully acknowledge the ways this hollow theatrical space resembles the hallowed sacred space of the early Protestant Church.[44] In fact, when the reformers repudiate the theatricality of the Roman Mass and reinterpret the sacrament of the Lord's Supper, they create the conditions for another kind of theater, one that is logocentric, representational, and powerful enough to awaken memory, trouble the conscience, and perhaps even reform the soul.

Metadramatic Spectacles of Bodies and Blood

The tragedies of the early modern English stage reflexively explore the nature of their own representations. Through metadramatic devices like the play-within-a-play, they raise questions about the reliability, efficacy, and status of visible signs. In their frequent representations of playgoers, many of whom fundamentally misinterpret what they see performed before their very eyes, they also scrutinize different modes of seeing, making their own spectators highly self-conscious about their own looking. They thus engage many of the key issues in the theological debates about the sacraments, and may even be understood to participate in those debates. Elizabethan and Jacobean revenge tragedies, especially, seem intent on rehearsing the eucharistic controversies that rage outside the walls of the theaters, using the secular stage to work through the deeply divisive conflicts concerning their culture's most meaningful religious ritual. Far from being compensatory or providing their audiences with secular versions of the forbidden images and rituals of the traditional church, they serve as "active agencies of change," holding older forms up for scrutiny while rethinking the re-

[44] Greenblatt, *Shakespearean Negotiations*, pp. 126–28.

lation between letter and figure, image and word, action and representation.[45]

In Chapter 3 I show how *Hamlet* articulates an emerging Protestant aesthetics of the stage. I would like to return for a moment to Shakespeare's revenge tragedy, because I think Shakespeare explores in *Hamlet* the possibility that a language-centered, representational drama can aspire to achieve, in a secular, aesthetic space, the same kind of effect that the reformers attribute to The Lord's Supper: edifying its audiences, penetrating their minds, impressing upon their hearts, and settling there.[46] Shakespeare uses "The Murder of Gonzago" to interrogate the nature and power of his own representations, representations that he seems to deliberately align with reformed rituals. By reflexively attending to the way the play-within-a-play represents an action, works by analogy, uses images and words, and arouses the memory, he addresses the reformers' radical reinterpretation of the sacraments and its implications for the secular stage.

"The Murder of Gonzago" represents a past action: the killing of Hamlet's father as reported by the ghost. In his additions to the original script, Hamlet is remarkably careful to preserve the distinction between the dramatic narrative and the "real" events it mirrors: the setting is Vienna, not Denmark; the murderer is a nephew, not a brother of the king (creating, of course, another powerful analogy); and Hamlet describes the play's action as being "something like the murder of my father" and a story that "comes near the circumstances" of that murder.[47] By insisting that the play-within-the-play works by means of analogy, Shakespeare fosters an awareness of the gap between the figurative and literal: the king who has murdered his brother and now watches the play is not the king who is shown murdering his uncle (and, of course, both the king in the audience and the king on the stage are fictions, played by actors before another audience). Nevertheless, the recognition of this gap does not diminish the power of the play; in fact, it may enhance it. Indeed the play of *Hamlet* repeatedly calls attention to its own representations, and yet it achieves an extraordinary power over its audiences. Why?

[45] Turner, *Anthropology of Performance*, p. 24.
[46] I am paraphrasing Calvin, *Institutes* 4.17.39.
[47] *Hamlet*, in Shakespeare, *The Complete Works*, ed. Alfred Harbage (1969), 5.2.581; 3.2.73; all further citations are to this text.

Like the reformed sacrament of the Lord's Supper, Hamlet's play (and, by inference, Shakespeare's) uses representation to awaken memory. When Claudius watches a fictional scene that resembles (but is not identical to) his own secret treachery, he is forced to confront his own sinfulness. The staged reenactment awakens his conscience and arouses guilt. Shakespeare thus claims for his representative theater an aesthetic power that corresponds to the power Calvin claims for the sacraments. Asserting no magical or supernatural powers and making no effort to deny or disguise its figurative nature, the play-within-the-play nevertheless has the capacity to awaken memory, arouse guilt, elicit self-reflection, precisely the powers that the reformers attribute to the sacrament—the representative drama—of the Lord's Supper.

That power, Shakespeare makes clear, does not reside primarily in the visual images of the theater, but rather in the words that interpret and enliven them. Hamlet's play thus conforms to the reformed sacrament in another, crucial way, its emphasis on the role language plays in representation. In his advice to the players to "suit the action to the word, the word to the action" (3.2.17–18), Hamlet imagines a theater in which word and image reinforce each another. Throughout the performance of the playlet, Shakespeare explores the relationship between the visual and verbal elements of the drama, testing, it would seem, the separate and combined powers of image and word. First, the Prologue delivers a brief speech unaccompanied by theatrical images. Then, the Players present a dumb show that depicts their play's entire story in mime without any explanatory words. Neither *hearing* a retelling of the story nor *viewing* a reenactment of his crime and his courtship, however, unsettles or moves Claudius. Nor does the continuous verbal commentary of Hamlet, who, Ophelia observes, is "as good as a chorus," alone have the power to stir Claudius. Yet, as soon as the character of Lucianus enters the garden prepared to kill the king and begins to speak, Claudius bolts from his chair, "struck so to the soul" by this combination of dramatic image, poetic text, and choral commentary, that he can no longer repress or conceal his guilt. Rather than privileging spectacle, Hamlet's play emphasizes the capacity of language to realize, or bring into being, what the images signify. It uses images "for memorie and representation," purposes approved even by Protestant reformers who advocate iconoclasm.[48] Shakespeare's protagonist thus

[48] Perkins, *Warning*, sig. C8ᵛ.

uses drama as a powerful tool in his quest for the truth, a means of exposing the hypocrisy and fraudulent theatricality of the king. His play is attentive to the relation between words and images, the function of absences and gaps, and the capacity of representation to awaken memory. It suggests that by the beginning of the seventeenth century, English dramatists have internalized sacramental theories of the Protestant reformers and have begun to examine their relevance to dramatic theory.

In fact, many revenge tragedians exhibit a remarkable familiarity with the eucharistic controversy in their plays, often employing metadramatic devices to rehearse the difference between literal action and figurative representation. In contrast to the play-within-a-play in *Hamlet*, however, they often feature dramas that mystify and deceive. In *The Spanish Tragedy*, a play that precedes and influences *Hamlet*, Thomas Kyd, for instance, stages a play-within-a-play that incorporates many of the elements of the Roman Mass as constructed by its Protestant detractors. His protagonist exploits the theater for his own dark purposes, using it to kill when it purports to represent killing, then displaying the bodies of the dead as the stuff of theater. Through his perverted drama Kyd expresses in a startling and unsettling way a profound anxiety about the very theatricality that *The Spanish Tragedy* everywhere displays.

It is surely significant that Kyd sets his play in Roman Catholic Spain, a country that in the 1580s not only attempted to invade England but sought as well to return it to the Roman Church. In marked contrast to Shakespeare, who identifies his protagonist with the university from which he has been summoned—Wittenberg, the original site of the Reformation—Kyd thus identifies Hieronimo's theatricality with the Roman religion.[49] Whereas Shakespeare's play appropriates the conventions of the reformed rituals and articulates Protestant theories of representation, Kyd's features the excesses of Roman rituals (as English Protestants in the late 1580s understood them) in an effort to critique and contain them.

---

[49] "In the 1580's," Ronald Broude writes, "England was facing a religious and political crisis of the utmost gravity: 'The Enterprise,' the grandiose Catholic scheme of the invasion of England and the extirpation of English Protestantism, was being implemented by Spain, encouraged by Rome and France, while England was responding with a wave of nationalism and prayer" ("Time, Truth, and Right in *The Spanish Tragedy*" [1971] p. 130). See also Frank Ardolino, "'In Paris? Mass, and Well Remembered!'" (1990); Steven Justice, "Spain, Tragedy, and *The Spanish Tragedy*" (1985).

The Spanish Tragedy concludes with a spectacular performance of "Soliman and Perseda," a play-within-a-play that Hieronimo uses as a cunning vehicle to kill the men who murdered his son while their fathers watch, unaware that the fictional story is being literally enacted in their presence. In striking contrast to Hamlet's play, Hieronimo's emphasizes the spectacular and visual dimension of drama at the expense of the verbal. As both the playwright bent on revenge and the actor cast in the role of murderer, Hieronimo cunningly fools the eyes of his spectators who assume they are watching their sons "fabulously counterfeit" death when, in fact, they are witnessing them die. He mystifies his spectacle of blood by having his actors perform their parts in various "unknown languages"—Greek, Latin, Italian, and French—despite their objections that "this will be a mere confusion, / And hardly shall we all be understood."[50] Although he promises to interpret the play at its conclusion, his final oration relies heavily on visual images, becoming the occasion for the theatrical display of the body of Horatio, that "strange and wondrous show" to which Hieronimo directs his audience's attention: "See here my show, look on this spectacle" (4.4.89).[51]

He also displays a handkerchief "dyed" in "the dearest blood" of his son. Calling it a "propitious" object that he has faithfully preserved, like a holy relic, near his "bloody heart," he commands his stage audience to "behold" it as well. For Hieronimo, the *sight* of the handkerchief has explanatory power, and the visual display of his son's body and blood renders his violent act (and his play) both understandable and justifiable. Preparing to "end my play" with his own suicide while asserting that he has "no more to say," he attempts to display himself,

[50] Kyd, *The Spanish Tragedy*, in *Drama of the English Renaissance*, ed. Russell A. Fraser and Norman Rabkin (1976), 4.1.179–180; all further citations of Kyd's play are to this text.

[51] Surprisingly, many critical discussions of Hieronimo's play praise its spectacle. Michael Hattaway, *Elizabethan Popular Theater* (1982), p. 111, asserts that "only recently . . . have dramatic critics been able to react without condescension or embarrassment to the basic satisfaction this kind of popular show can provide." Defending Hieronimo's use of sundry languages as the playwright's means of communicating with the illiterate, he speculates that "it is possible that he [Kyd] was trying to see whether he could employ a theatre language that would, to the unlettered at least, communicate by its mere sound" (p. 110). Of Hieronimo's show, Carol McGinnis Kay, "Deception through Words" (1977), p. 137, asserts that "it is clear that this is not spectacle for spectacle's sake alone." Donna B. Hamilton, "*The Spanish Tragedy*: A Speaking Picture" (1974), p. 215, goes so far as to suggest the bloody spectacle approaches the Renaissance ideal of a speaking picture: "Hieronimo's playlet goes beyond his other attempts by being truly a speaking picture."

hanging by his own rope, as a culminating spectacle: "Behold Hieron-imo, / Author and actor in this tragedy" (4.4.146–47). Initially pre-vented from killing himself, he vows to remain silent and, to make good on that vow, bites out his tongue, creating by his willful and ultimate rejection of language another corporeal image. Pressured further to "reveal" the mystery of his drama, to explain himself in language ("Yet can he write"), he gestures for a knife to sharpen his pen and uses it instead to kill the Duke of Castile and himself, again substituting dead bodies for explanatory words. Although students of Kyd's play often puzzle over what it is, exactly, that Hieronimo thinks he is refusing to reveal, since he explains his motives before he bites out his tongue, I suggest that his stubborn insistence on silence, like his polyglot play, assures that the spectacle of bodies and blood he has so elaborately staged will retain its primacy over the interpreting word.

In that spectacle Hieronimo substitutes actual killing for the reen-actment of a killing and literalizes, in a grotesque manner, the action he purports to represent. His play blatantly violates the distinction be-tween visible sign and the thing it signifies, turning the analogous into the identical, the symbolic into the literal, the represented into the real. Kyd thus uses the play-within-a-play to explore the relation between letter and figure. He stages the horror that ensues when a represen-tation of an action is quite literally realized.

Kyd adopts here a favorite rhetorical strategy of the reformers who seek to disrupt the devotional gaze by exploring, in startling and often shocking detail, a literalist understanding of the host. Convinced that the doctrine of transubstantiation is a ridiculous literalization of a trope, they, in effect, out-literalize the literalists in order to demonstrate what they see as the error in the papists' carnal understanding of the eucharist. By confronting their readers with the violent, grotesque, and absurd implications of transubstantiation, they aggressively seek to de-naturalize Roman Catholic beliefs in the nature and efficacy of the Mass.

Throughout *Actes and Monuments*, for example, Foxe accuses Roman Catholics of killing and eating God. He mocks them for worshiping a "bready God" who is "grated with the tooth," "conveyed into the belly," even vomited overboard by seasick sailors. He ridicules them for shutting God up in a box where the eucharistic wafer "breed[s] worms" and becomes "mouldy and overgrown with vermin." His mar-tyrs repeatedly use such strategies in their adamant denials that the

body of Christ is literally in the sacramental bread. "How is that possible," demands one martyr when she is interrogated by the Catholic
authorities, "to be the body of Christ, to whom all power is given, and
which is exalted above all heavens, when we see the mice and rats, apes
and monkeys, play with it, and tear it in pieces?"[52] Foxe's own literalizations—exaggerated, ridiculous, outrageous—attempt to undermine
belief in the Mass by rendering its mystery irrational and untenable. By
imagining, in grotesque detail, a literal enactment of the sacrament of
communion—including the killing, chewing, swallowing, and digesting
of God's body—he coerces his readers into accepting a figurative understanding of Christ's words, "This is my body." Through such stra-
tegic literalizations of figures and tropes, the reformers not only
"prove" the "error" of transubstantiation, they also rehearse competing—Roman Catholic and Protestant—theories of representation, dis-
crediting traditional modes of interpretation and inculcating reformed
ones.

In an emblem book that draws its images from Protestant sermons,
Thomas Jenner adopts such a strategy in order to render the devotional
gaze of Roman Catholic worshipers ridiculous. Under the title "The
foolishnes of Transubstantiation," he presents a picture of a tavern with
a sign on which a cluster of grapes is painted (Figure 10). Against the
outside wall of the tavern, a man has placed a ladder and climbed up
to the commercial sign where he foolishly attempts to drink the image
of the grapes. In an extended poem, Jenner likens the man who mis-
takes the tavern sign for the spirits sold within to Roman Catholics.
Both, he argues, fundamentally misunderstand the nature of signs:

> Suche mad men *Papists* are, which verefie
> That in a *little Wafer (hid)* doth lye
> *Christs very flesh*; While th'*elements* (there) be
> Hung out to Commers in, that they might see,
> In *Christ* alone stands that *spirituall food*;
> Which must not of these *signes* be understood.[53]

He mocks transubstantiation as an absurd literalization of a trope that
fosters a carnal understanding of the Eucharist, and he seeks to disrupt

[52] Foxe, *A&M*, 8:498, 6:341, 5:511, 5:546, 6:341, 4:432.
[53] Thomas Jenner, *The Soules Solace* (1631), sig. F7ᵛ.

FIGURE 10. "The foolishnes of Transubstantiation." Thomas Jenner, *The Soules Solace* (London, 1626), emblem #28. By permission of the Huntington Library, San Marino, California.

traditional ways of seeing. In doing so, he forces his readers to become self-conscious about how they interpret signs and how they experience representations, including, I suggest, dramatic representations.

Kyd's playlet seems to function in much the same way, interrogating the difference between sign and thing signified, representation and literal act. Instead of representing the history of Soliman and Perseda and staging a reenactment of their deaths, it collapses the distinctions between letter and figure, character and actor, and stages "real" deaths. Although its on-stage audience members initially assume they are watching a representation of murder and admire the skill of the actors (who include their own children), the audience in the theater understands that the actors are "really" killing and being killed. When the on-stage spectators realize that the spectacle of bodies and blood they have witnessed is, in fact, not a theatrical representation at all but the very slaughter of their loved ones, they are forced to confront the "truth" of the reformers' repeated assertions that "a letter (meaning a literal sense) . . . killeth."[54]

[54] Ridley, "Lord's Supper," 39:31–32.

The play's rehearsal of the issues surrounding the doctrine of transubstantiation—that is, whether the Eucharist is an actual sacrifice or a remembrance of a past killing, and whether the communicants see the body of Christ or only a figure of that body—should not be obscured by its secular content. By mystifying and privileging spectacle, literalizing mimetic action, and displaying "real" bodies and blood, Kyd's playlet "Soliman and Perseda" manifests the very qualities of the Roman Mass that the Calvinist reformers condemn when they complain that "of the sacrament [the papists] make an idol; of commemoration make adoration; instead of receiving, make a deceiving; in place of showing forth Christ's death, make new oblations of his death."[55] It thus uses the popular stage to address one of the most disruptive theological controversies of its age.

Though Hieronimo celebrates his sacrificial theater, reveling in the way his drama has produced "real" bodies and blood, Kyd positions his own audiences at one remove from this carnal spectacle and asks them to judge it. His play-within-a-play thus functions reflexively. It can, I think, be understood to be a cultural performance, one of those "magical mirrors of social reality" that according to Victor Turner "exaggerate, invert, re-form, magnify, minimize, dis-color, re-color, even deliberately falsify" the central conflicts of its culture in order to reflect upon them.[56]

Dramatists after Kyd continue to stage plays-within-plays that feature mystifying spectacles and collapse the distinction between letter and figure, like Kyd using the theater to rehearse the terms of the Reformation debate on the sacraments. The deadly masque in Middleton's *Women Beware Women* is perhaps the most fully realized example.[57] Cast as mythological and allegorical figures in the masque, central characters in the main play carry out multiple acts of revenge against one another while confused audience members, including the Duke of Florence, his new bride, and his brother the Cardinal, watch without understanding that the masques's stage properties are being used as literal weapons of revenge. Middleton uses irony to complicate his metadrama. In contrast to Hieronimo's play, where the characters carry out the plot in a straightforward manner, his masque characters pretend to bestow symbolic gifts—a cup of nectar, a burning treasure, Cupid's

[55] Foxe, *A&M*, 5:303.
[56] Turner, *Anthropology of Performance*, p. 42.
[57] Middleton, *Women Beware Women*, ed. Charles Barber (1969), act 5.

darts, incense burned on Juno's altar—all of which literally kill their recipients. The irony contributes to the play's exploration of a dangerous kind of theater, and Middleton uses it to develop connections between that theater and an idolatrous Roman Church. Drawing on antitheatrical tracts condemning the representation of pagan gods on the English stage as idolatrous and on iconoclastic tracts denouncing Roman Catholic saints as pagan gods, Middleton stages a spectacular masque that exposes pagan gods, their worshipers (played by Italian— Roman Catholic—characters), and the theater itself as fraudulent and dangerous. In it the deities are murderous, their followers are cunning and cruel, and both the gifts of the gods and the sacred offerings of men and women are lethal. Middleton uses the stage to critique abuses of it, and he codes those abuses as Roman Catholic.

Like *Women Beware Women* and many other plays that employ metadramatic devices to critique fraudulent theatricality, Kyd's play fosters in its spectators a reflexive awareness of their own seeing. As audience members, they find themselves uncomfortably aligned with a series of on-stage audiences. They watch the King of Spain and Viceroy of Portugal naively watch Hieronimo's play without understanding that their sons are being killed before their very eyes. They watch the King and Ambassador of Portugal watch a masque that according to the King "contents mine eye, / Although I sound not well the mystery" (1.4.138–39). That masque portrays three separate conquests of Portugal or Spain by Englishman, but the Spanish king inexplicably (and surely, to an English audience, foolishly) finds the spectacles comforting rather than disturbing. And they watch the ghost of Andrea watch the action of the larger play, as well as the playlets, while imposing narrow, naive, and perverse interpretations onto what he sees. Kyd's play thus encourages its spectators to evaluate the flawed and unselfconscious looking of on-stage audiences even as it invites them to "sit . . . down to see the mystery" (1.1.90). Again, Kyd explores a central concern of the reformers, appropriating a rhetorical strategy from Protestant discourse to disrupt older modes of seeing and foster new ones.

Even minor characters in *The Spanish Tragedy* focus the audience's attention on acts of seeing. Arrested for murder, Pedringano, for example, gazes upon an empty box, so confident it contains his pardon that he "flout[s] the gallows, scorn[s] the audience, and descant[s] on the hangman, and all presuming of his pardon from hence" (3.5.12– 14). Critical efforts to identify sources for Pedringano's box in classical myths about Pandora's or Silenus's box ignore contemporary Protestant polemics ridiculing priests who claim to carry God in a box or pyx and mocking the Mass as a "Jacke of the boxe."[58] Pedringano's presumption that the physical presence of the box guarantees his pardon even though he is guilty and flagrantly disregards the law reiterates precisely the error Protestants believe Roman Catholics make when they trust in externals, believing the sight of the host will save them, regardless of their behavior. Kyd juxtaposes Pedringano's execution with the last-minute reprieve of Alexandro. In striking contrast to Pedringano, who trusts in externals while refusing to repent, the wronged Alexandro renounces all earthly things, puts his faith in "heaven," and prepares to die. Whereas Pedringano is executed, still believing that "in that box is balm for both" his body and soul (3.6.81), Alexandro is miraculously saved from death and acquitted.

At the end of the play, the ghost of Andrea announces that "these were spectacles to please my soul" (4.5.12), but Kyd's audiences have learned to distrust spectacles of blood, strange shows in sundry languages, dramatic displays of boxed pardons, and silent mysteries. Hieronimo effectively turns its uncritical delight in spectacle and theatrics back against the Spanish court, exposing its violence and corruption by displaying them on the stage. Although he is disaffected from the Spanish court, Hieronimo is, as Knight Marshal, closely identified with its legal practices and aesthetic forms, and Kyd portrays him as an abuser of images as well. Although his play demonstrates—in a grotesque, graphic, and outrageously literal way—how the letter kills, it does so by exhibiting the very qualities of the Mass that so offend the Protestant reformers. Hieronimo's show baffles, confuses, and ultimately ruins all who behold it. By foregrounding the very issues that lie at the heart of the eucharistic controversy, *The Spanish Tragedy* calls attention to a dangerous and fraudulent kind of theatricality—a "Catholic" theatricality—in order to demystify and discredit it. Its repeated performance on the London stages surely must have contributed to the demystification of the Roman Mass in Elizabethan England.

Although the playlets in *The Spanish Tragedy* and *Hamlet* both investigate the nature of representation, they present examples of strikingly

---

[58] See, for instance, Frank Ardolino, "The Hangman's Noose and the Empty Box" (1977); Barbara J. Baines, "Kyd's Silenus Box and the Limits of Perception" (1980); Davies, *Worship and Theology*, 1:238.

different kinds of theater. "Soliman and Perseda" features a carnal spectacle of literal deaths, mystified by strange languages and silence. Kyd creates and sustains an ironic distance between his spectators— English playgoers in the public theater—and on-stage spectators— Spanish and Portuguese courtiers who are credulous and confused— and he dramatizes the abuse of theater even as he invents a drama that scrupulously avoids replicating that abuse. "The Murder of Gonzago," in contrast, represents a past murder that, through a union of theatrical signs and spoken words, has the capacity to reveal truths, profoundly affecting its spectators and eliciting painful self-examination. Shakespeare's own spectators watch as Hamlet and Horatio "observe"—indeed, "rivet" their eyes on—Claudius, who in turn watches first a dumb show and then a fully realized dramatic scene that reenacts a ghost's tale of murder and represents a killing he himself has committed. How the spectators see all this watching and mirroring, especially in the context of the troubling vision of the ghost, the orchestrated spectacle of the monarchy, and the duplicitous role-playing of the courtiers, is integrally related to the way the reformed religion structures the experience of the Lord's Supper. Shakespeare fosters a mode of sight that is skeptical, mediated, self-reflexive, analogical, and, I submit, distinctly Protestant.

Remembrance and Revenge

I have shown how Kyd, Shakespeare, and Middleton all use plays-within-plays to investigate the relation between the representation of a killing and literal killing. Their intense interest in representation is matched by an equally intense interest in memory, another key term in the reformed sacrament of the Lord's Supper and, I suggest, in the reformation of early modern English culture. The revenge tragedies explore the power that the dead exert over the living. Revengers meditate on skulls, bones, and corpses; they cling to bloody tokens of the dead; they see ghosts. What might be the relation between this obsessive attention to the dead, with its focus on the decaying skulls and blood-soaked mementos of fathers, sons, and mistresses, and the revenge tragedies' reflexive attention to its own representations, its own theatrical displays of bodies and blood?

The revenge tragedies, I suggest, rehearse a divisive and deeply disturbing struggle occurring in reform culture between a traditional mode of commemorating the dead that emphasizes presence and a reformed mode that emphasizes absence. This struggle is grounded in the controversy over the interpretation of the sacrament of communion and whether the bread and wine are the transubstantiated body and blood of Christ or figures—remembrances—of that body. It is fueled by the reformers' tirades against idolatry, especially their distinctions between a "carnal" or "corporeal" devotion to the body and a ritual remembrance of it. And it addresses the central challenge of the reformed religion: how to relinquish the (idolatrous) body and sustain faith in an invisible God. Protestant inquiries into the nature and function of memory are thus integrally related to Protestant theories of representation. Both concern the use and abuse of images, the function of signs, and the tension between body and spirit—compelling concerns in Elizabethan and Jacobean revenge tragedies.

Hieronimo preserves the corpse of his son and keeps the blood-drenched handkerchief close to his heart. Vindice in Middleton's *The Revenger's Tragedy* carries with him the skull of his mistress, killed nine years earlier.[59] They are two examples of the way protagonists in revenge tragedies fetishize the dead. From the perspective of reform theology, their attachment to the bodies and relics of their dead loved ones would not only be a perverse form of love but also an idolatrous one, focusing as it does on external and corporeal things and substituting the adoration of a physical body for faith in an invisible God. According to Martin Bucer, images "do rather plucke away the memorie and mynde of man from god and do turne the eyes of the minde backwardes to behold and considre erthly thinges."[60] Hieronimo and Vindice, I suggest, are depicted as men whose eyes are turned backward, fixed on earthly things.

In depicting Hieronimo as a man who is tragically unable to relinquish the body of a beloved son, Kyd may even have in mind the grieving father in the *Book of Wisdom*—a favorite text of the iconoclasts who repeatedly identify the father who loved his son too intensely as the original idolater. Unable to console himself when his son died, that man—the archetypal father—kept an image of his dead son upon

---

[59] Thomas Middleton, *The Revenger's Tragedy*, in *Drama of the English Renaissance*, ed. Russell A. Fraser and Norman Rabkin (1976), act 1.

[60] Bucer, *Treatise*, sig. Eii[r].

which he "conferred . . . honor on the dead, and thus superstitiously worshiped [his son's] memory."[61] Commenting on this anecdote, John Foxe warns his readers about the dangers of excessive grief, cautioning them not to let "the remembrance of your children keep you from God."[62] Like the grieving father in the *Book of Wisdom*, Hieronimo seeks to remember his dead son through images, carrying the bloody hand-kerchief close to his heart and gazing on it whenever he is overcome by his loss. His desperate attempt to hold on to the physical remains of his murdered son and to find solace in Horatio's handkerchief is, from an early Protestant point of view, a form of idolatry, for Hieron-imo privileges the body over the spirit, trusts only in what is present, and exhibits excessive love for another mortal.

But why locate the impulse to avenge the death of a loved one in the human propensity to idolatry? Although both Hieronimo and Vind-ice elicit deep sympathy from the viewer, their devotion to the relics of their dead loved ones is depicted as a kind of madness, one that drives them to violence—and to the further abuse of images. Hieronimo "re-members" his son by killing more sons in a play that violates the dis-tinction between body and sign. Vindice "remembers" his mistress by disguising her skull so that it appears to be the head of a beautiful woman, then tricking the Duke into kissing its poisoned lips. By linking the idolatrous desire to hold onto the body with vengeance and mur-der, these revenge tragedies raise provocative questions about how the living should remember the dead, questions that lie at the heart of the reformation of religion.

In his study of the Reformation of the English Church, Eamon Duffy points out that traditional funeral rituals were the most "recalcitrant" of the older religious practices, persisting long after they had been officially banned. He speculates that the deep resistances to the changes in funeral practices instituted by the reformers indicate the degree to which the Protestant reforms disrupted the collective mem-ory, cutting the living off from the dead. In the traditional Church, he explains "the dead could still be spoken to directly . . . because in some sense they still belonged within the human community," their presence sustained by prayers and Masses to the dead, their names "recited week

---

[61] Calvin, *Institutes* 1.11.8; Nicholas Ridley, "A Treatise . . . Concerning Images" (1843), 39:85; Foxe, *A&M*, 8:702.
[62] Foxe, *A&M*, 8:174.

by week in the bede-roll at the parish Mass," and their memories preserved by "the objects they had left for use in the worship of that
community." In abolishing all those ritual practices, banishing the objects that the dead had bequeathed to the living, and "ripping out . . .
the memorials of the dead," the reformers, Duffy argues, deliberately
silenced the dead and distanced them from the living. The dead, he
writes, "could neither be spoken to nor even about, in any way that
affected their well-being. The dead had gone beyond the reach of human contact, even human prayer . . . [and] the [funeral] service was no
longer a rite of intercession on behalf of the dead, but an exhortation
to faith on the part of the living. Indeed, it is not too much to say that
the oddest feature of the 1552 burial rite is the disappearance of the
corpse from it."[63]

Duffy's observations provide a fascinating insight into the culture that
produced Elizabethan and Jacobean revenge tragedy. At a time when
radical reforms in the ritual commemoration of the dead are being
imposed on the English people and "the boundaries of the human
community have been redrawn," when "the dead became as shadowy
as the blanks in the stripped matrices of their gravestones," and when
"the dead person is spoken not to, but about, as one no longer here,
but precisely as departed," a popular new form of drama emerges.[64] It
interrogates a world inhabited by shadowy ghosts, probes the need to
honor the bodies of the dead, and questions the human capacity to
remember what is absent, thereby exploring and perhaps reestablishing
the boundaries between the living and the dead.

Kyd and Middleton examine older forms of cultural remembrance.
Their protagonists desperately try to hold on to the bodies of their dead
loved ones—hoping to keep them present in their lives—and as a consequence perversely kill in the name of love. Their single-minded devotion to the relics of the dead, their inability to relinquish the body,
and their inconsolable grief may well speak to Elizabethan audiences
about their own anxieties and their own losses in the wake of reform.
But *The Spanish Tragedy* and *The Revenger's Tragedy* also participate in the
reformation of memory by dramatizing the dangers inherent in "carnal" devotion, the fatal error of trusting the image. In his revenge
tragedy Shakespeare seems to deliberately shift the focus, inverting

---

[63] Eamon Duffy, *The Stripping of the Altars* (1992), pp. 577, 475, 495, 475.
[64] Ibid., pp. 475, 495, 475.

Kyd's emphasis on spectacle and body (as he also turns the grieving father into the absent one, the dead son into the living, grieving one) and attending instead to signs, representations, absences. In the eery appearances of the ghostly figure of Hamlet's father, in the careful preservation of the distinction between letter and figure in Hamlet's play, in the way Hamlet uses the skull of Yorick to meditate on death, and in the crucial moment when Hamlet, delivering his provocative "death of a sparrow" speech, asserts his faith in an unseen God, Shakespeare depicts the challenge of a radically different—a reformed—way of remembering the dead.

All three plays, however, are doing important cultural work. They challenge the intensely felt desire of traditionalists to experience the spiritual in the material world. They question the human capacity to sustain faith in what is absent. And they reflect upon a deep sense of cultural loss—a silencing of the dead, a disruption of the collective memory—caused by the iconoclastic reforms of the church. All three also participate in reform culture's inquiry into the status of signs, the subject of my next chapter.

CHAPTER FIVE

Ocular Proof in the Age of Reform: *Othello*

Be sure of it; give me the ocular proof.

— Othello

"So Remote a Trifle"

When Thomas Rymer examines the merits of Shakespeare's *Othello* (1603) in his *Short View of Tragedy* (1693), he finds a seriously flawed play with a narrative so improbable that it can only work "to delude our senses, disorder our thoughts, addle our brain, pervert our affections, hair our imaginations, corrupt our appetite, and fill our head with vanity, confusion, *Tintamarre*, and Jingle-jangle." Chief among its improbabilities, according to Rymer, is the handkerchief that Othello accepts as the "ocular proof" of Desdemona's infidelity. "So much ado, so much stress, so much passion and repetition about an Handkerchief!" he laments, adding pointedly, "Had it been *Desdemona's* Garter, the Sagacious Moor might have smelt a Rat; but the Handkerchief is so remote a trifle, no Booby, on this side *Mauritania*, cou'd make any consequence from it."[1]

In mocking *Othello* as "the Tragedy of the Handkerchief," Rymer assumes that Desdemona's napkin is a "trifle" so insignificant that its use as evidence to prove adultery defies logic and strains credulity. He does not point out that Shakespeare's villain Iago also insists that the handkerchief is a trifle, nor does he analyze Iago's conviction that "trifles light as air / Are to the jealous confirmations strong / As proofs of holy writ."[2] Rymer ignores altogether Othello's story that a "sibyl" sewed the napkin "in a prophetic fury" and an Egyptian "charmer"

---

[1] Thomas Rymer, "A Short View of English Tragedy" (1957), 2:254–55, 251.

[2] *Othello*, in Shakespeare, *The Complete Works*, ed. Alfred Harbage (1969), 3.3.319–24; all further references are to this text.

gave it to his mother, and he gives no credence to the charmer's warning, as recounted by Othello, that the handkerchief had the magical
power to:

> subdue my father
> Entirely to her love; but if she lost it
> Or made a gift of it, my father's eye
> Should hold her loathed, and his spirits should hunt
> After new fancies.

(3.4.53–57)

Certain that the handkerchief is merely a piece of linen, a material
object so inconsequential that Cassio's possession of it proves nothing,
Rymer refuses even to entertain the possibility of Othello's claim that
"there's magic in the web of it" (3.4.69).

Writing at the beginning of the Enlightenment, Rymer articulates an
empirical view of magic that, until recently, has dominated critical interpretations of *Othello*.[3] Even critics who defend Shakespeare's use of
the handkerchief against Rymer's objections usually do so by insisting
that the napkin "must be read in terms of symbolic logic" and thus
view it primarily as a literary symbol, not a magical object.[4] Most scholars implicitly share Rymer's view that Othello's belief in the magical
properties of the handkerchief is preposterous. They thus do not take
seriously Othello's claim that "to lose't or give't away were such per-
dition / As nothing else could match" (3.4.67–68). One concludes that
the Moor suffers "symptoms of delusion," another that he is
"grip[ped]" by an "exotic and barbarous female superstition." Determined to rescue Othello from any taint of magical thinking, some even
argue that he concocts the narrative about the Egyptian charmer to

---

[3] Two books published in 1994 take seriously the magic of Othello's handkerchief and
are indicative of the way scholars today have begun to critique the assumptions of modernist critics; see John Gillies, *Shakespeare and the Geography of Difference* (1994), pp. 25–34,
and Linda Woodbridge, *The Scythe of Saturn* (1994), pp. 65–67. Other recent works that
address the role of magic in Renaissance drama include: Anthony Harris, *Night's Black
Agents* (1980); John Mebane, *Renaissance Magic and the Return of the Golden Age* (1989);
Barbara Traister, *Heavenly Necromancers* (1984); David Woodman, *White Magic and English
Renaissance Drama* (1973).

[4] Lynda B. Boose, "Othello's Handkerchief" (1975), p. 367.

terrify Desdemona, apparently finding deception and cruelty more fitting attributes of a hero than magical beliefs.[5]

I will return to the interesting way the magical, the feminine, and the strange are linked not only in modern commentary but also in *Othello* and in early Protestant culture, but here I simply want to point out how, beginning as early as Rymer, critics appropriate the language of Iago—his talk of trifles, his identification of the magical with the erroneous, his racist and misogynous sentiments—in order to rationalize and estrange the magical elements of the play. But if Iago's dismissive attitude toward magic is shared by nearly all post-Enlightenment readers of the play, it is not shared by many of the other characters in the play world of Venice. Brabantio believes Othello has used "charms," "spells," "medicines," and "witchcraft" on his daughter, in effect, binding her to him with "chains of magic." And Desdemona treats the napkin as if it were a magical talisman or a sacred relic, kissing and talking to it. According to Emilia, the Moor's wife:

> so loves the token
> (For he conjured her she should ever keep it)
> That she reserves it evermore about her
> To kiss and talk to.
>
> (3.3.293–96)

After she misplaces it, she concludes that "sure, there's some wonder in this handkerchief" (3.4.101). Like Othello, she asserts her belief in the magical efficacy of the napkin.

In this chapter I use Othello's handkerchief to illustrate how Renaissance English tragedies enact, as well as thematize, a problematic of sight characteristic of early Protestant English culture. Shakespeare entertains the possibility that the napkin is a mere trifle, but he also entertains the possibility that it is a magical thing of "wonder" capable of enthralling and ensnaring the lovers and a sign or "remembrance"

---

[5] David Kaula, "Othello Possessed" (1966), p. 127. Kaula believes that Othello is ultimately purged of his belief in the magical power of the handkerchief, and he argues that Shakespeare's play "implies that the belief in witchcraft is a delusion" (p. 113). For a review of critical literature on the magic of the handkerchief, see Michael C. Andrews, "Honest Othello" (1973); Karen Newman, *Fashioning Femininity and English Renaissance Drama* (1991), pp. 90–92. For a example of the way critics rationalize the magic of the handkerchief, see Eldred Jones, *Othello's Countrymen* (1965), p. 102.

that has the power to sustain love. Though he employs a chilling dramatic irony to reveal how Iago manipulates the napkin to deceive Othello, tricking him into accepting it as empirical evidence of Desdemona's infidelity, he also encourages his audiences to interpret it symbolically. Whether Desdemona's napkin is a magical totem or a meaningful image or a trivial thing, whether it is a superstitious idol or a sacramental sign or a handcrafted object, whether it has the power to enthrall or the capacity to call to remembrance or the propensity to delude are vital issues in 1603 that have been fully resolved by 1693. Might the theater of early modern England participate in the process of resolving such issues by investigating the validity of magical objects, visible signs, and empirical proof?

Veronica's Napkin and Paul's Handkerchiefs: "Trifles Light as Air" / "Proofs of Holy Writ"

Although Rymer's world, like our own, has been thoroughly rationalized, Shakespeare writes at a time when the reformers' iconoclastic assaults on magic and the imagination have not yet completely suppressed premodern beliefs in an enchanted world, "saturated with sacramental possibility and meaning."[6] In his book, *Religion and the Decline of Magic*, Keith Thomas demonstrates that magical beliefs were both widespread and passionately contested in early modern England. He documents how many people in sixteenth- and seventeenth-century England, including the educated and elite, engaged in a range of magical practices: the interpretation of dreams, visions, portents, prophecies, and astrological charts; the manipulation of amulets, talismans, wax effigies, aphrodisiacs, and love charms; and the consultation of cunning men and women as a means of seeking protection from witchcraft and the devil. Thomas shows how magical practices continued, and even flourished, during the years following the Reformation when Protestant reformers were mounting aggressive attacks on the "magic" of the Roman Church and on popular magic. He argues that by eliminating the intermediaries of the Roman Church, early Protestantism may well have intensified the people's need for cunning men and women. Thus, even though the reformers eventually succeeded in

---

[6] Gail McMurray Gibson, *The Theater of Devotion* (1989), p. 6.

eliminating many of the magical practices, the new religion coexisted with the old magic throughout the sixteenth and much of the seventeenth centuries.[7]

Attentive to the transitional nature of early modern thought, Debora Shuger finds just such a coexistence of modern and medieval ideas in late Renaissance English culture, a culture she describes as manifesting "both a troubled modernity and a drastic archaism." She identifies "a central tension in Renaissance habits of thought" between a premodern consciousness she calls "participatory" and a modern consciousness she calls "rational." Shuger finds this tension operating "as much within individuals as between sects or parties," and she concludes that "in some respects, the dominant culture was more radical, probing, and self-critical than has often been assumed, in others it seems more primitive, more alien from our own habits of thought, closer perhaps to those of traditional societies."[8]

Shuger demonstrates how the people of early modern England do not completely or unproblematically embrace the empirical, rational, and scientific or fully sever their ties with the magical and mysterious when they convert to Protestantism. Their world—Shakespeare's world—is one in which the conflicting truth claims of empiricism and magic often coexist and appeals to skepticism compete with appeals to mystery. Because it is so much easier for post-Enlightenment readers to recognize what is familiar than what is alien, however, many scholars, Shuger argues, tend to focus only on the modern dimension of Renaissance texts and thus fail to discern "the simultaneous existence of both" modern and premodern habits of thought.[9]

In the critical literature of *Othello*, that tendency appears as early as Rymer. Although he writes just a century after Shakespeare, Rymer clearly cannot fathom the Renaissance fascination with the magical and phantasmic. His failure to imagine the preceding era's beliefs in the magical efficacy of images and objects is, in part, a testimony to the ultimate success of the Reformation. For it is in the discourse of the reformers that images and relics commonly believed to have magical powers are denounced as "trifles" that "delude the eyes of the spec-

---

[7] Keith Thomas, *Religion and the Decline of Magic* (1971), pp. 232–33, 278, 265.

[8] Debora Shuger, *Habits of Thought in the English Renaissance* (1990), pp. 13, 44–45, 14–15.

[9] Shuger makes this point about modern readings of Hooker in *Habits of Thought*, p. 44.

tators," "lifeless and theatrical trifles, which serve no other purpose than to deceive the senses of a people stupefied ... dulled and befooled with superstition." It is in the discourse of the reformers that the magical becomes inextricably linked to the strange and the feminine, identified with error and superstition, and repudiated as witchcraft. And it is in the discourse of the reformers that holy images and sacred relics beloved and worshiped by the populace, including numerous well-known handkerchiefs, are systematically and relentlessly demystified.[10] Rymer implicitly acknowledges that he is a product of the Reformation when he distances himself from Shakespeare's play about a magical handkerchief and asks disdainfully whether *Othello* might not affect its audiences "beyond what all the Parish Clarks of *London* with their old Testament farces and interludes, in *Richard* the seconds time, cou'd ever pretend to?"[11]

Shakespeare's contemporary audiences would surely be familiar with Protestant attempts to discredit the "magic" of the Roman religion and would be sensitive to the religious implications of any claim that a visible object like a handkerchief has magical properties. Calvin's lament that "the worlde hath gone a maddyng after reliques" that "hath had [the] power to blind the whole earth" is echoed throughout the sixteenth century by English reformers who document and catalogue thousands of images worshiped for their miraculous, efficacious, or magical properties.[12] Among those images are relics like Veronica's napkin, Abagarus's cloth, and many lesser known handkerchiefs, all believed to be miraculously imprinted with the image of Jesus Christ, and pieces of cloth believed to be fragments of the veil, or "kerchief," that the Virgin Mary supposedly used to swaddle the Christ child and subsequently as a shroud to cover Christ's body. Popular devotion to such cloths was based on the belief that they had the power to protect, heal, or save. In the late Middle Ages, holy relics like these kerchiefs were frequently used as magical talismans in domestic life, to enhance fertility, for example, or aid in childbirth.[13]

---

[10] Calvin, *Institutes of the Christian Religion* 4.10.12, 4.17.43; see also, Calvin, *A very profitable treatise* (1561); Philip Melancthon, *A newe work concerning both partes of the sacrament* (1543).

[11] Rymer, "Short View of Tragedy," p. 255.

[12] Calvin, *A very profitable treatise*, sigs. A6ʳ, A8ʳ.

[13] See, for example, John Veron, *A stronge battery against the idolatrous invocation of the*

The fury with which various reformers denounce and seek to destroy such relics suggests something of the intensity with which the populace worships, honors, and trusts in them. When, for instance, Nicholas Ridley praises a man who, upon seeing such a cloth hanging at the door of the church, "did not only remove it, but with a vehemency of zeal cut it in pieces," his iconoclastic sentiments are grounded in his awareness that such relics continue to elicit awe and reverence among many laypeople who fervently believe them to be magical.[14] Such anecdotes indicate how pervasive popular beliefs in the magical properties of handkerchiefs and other objects are in the sixteenth century, and they suggest how upsetting, even threatening, the persistence of magical beliefs is to reform-minded theologians. The theologians declare religious relics to be "lying signs," the fraudulent creations of Roman priests, who, they complain, intentionally "blear the people's eyes, making them believe they see that they see not, and not to see that which they see."[15] So successful are the English reformers in equating Catholic priests with trickery and church spectacle with magic that according to Thomas, "the term 'conjurer' c[o]me[s] to be a synonym for recusant priest" and even some of the Elizabethan clergy are mocked as "Egyptian enchanters" by more reform-minded radicals.[16] Magic thus becomes inseparably linked to Roman Catholicism in Protestant discourse and associated with fraud, illusion, superstition, and error.

Calvin suggests that people who believe in the magical efficacy of relics and images are blinded by their own a priori assumptions so that "many beholdying a relique shut their eyes through superstition to the ende, that they se[e]ing shoulde see nothyng at all: that is to say that they dare not looke in good earnest to consider what the thing is."[17] He asserts that a false belief in the magical efficacy of images impedes visual perception, preventing people from performing any kind of em-

---

dead Saintes (1562), fols. 82ᵛ, 91ᵛ; Nicholas Ridley, "A Treatise . . . Concerning Images" (1843), 39:91; Gibson, pp. 51–65.

[14] Ridley, "Treatise Concerning Images," 39:92; Veron recounts a similar story about encountering a "vaile died or painted, and having the ymage as it were of Christ, or of som saint," which "when I dyd see that the image of man, did hange in the churche contrary to scriptures, I rente it" (*A stronge battery*, fol. 91ʳ–92ᵛ; see also fol. 78ᵛ).

[15] John Foxe, *A&M*, 5:589; 1:83.

[16] Thomas, *Religion and the Decline of Magic* (1971), pp. 68–69.

[17] Calvin, *A very profitable treatise*, sig. B1ʳ.

pirical examination of a relic. Calvin is particularly concerned that magical thinking causes people to trust in "the appearance of a physical thing rather than in God himself."[18] Whether a hoax perpetrated by the Roman Church or a superstition imposed by the misguided worshiper, the widespread belief that objects like Veronica's handkerchief provided the ocular proof of God's power is declared to be a dangerous illusion, one that seduces and ensnares unsuspecting souls.

Protestant fears of superstition extend even to the interpretation of images recorded in the Bible. They are particularly acute when the reformers consider the Biblical narrative about the miraculous handkerchiefs that Paul uses to cure the sick. According to the book of Acts, "God wrought no smale miracles by the hands of Paul. So that from his bodie were brought unto the sicke, kerchefs or handkerchiefs, and the diseases departed from them, and the evil spirits went out of them" (19.11–12). Paul's napkins receive a great deal of nervous attention from the reformers who are clearly disconcerted by what seems to be a scriptural confirmation of magic practiced by a mere man. Even though Protestants believed that miracles had occurred in Biblical times, and only afterwards had ceased to be, Protestant commentators strenuously deny that Paul's handkerchiefs were the source of miraculous cures. Their anxious interpretations of the episode reported in Acts tend to be defensive, revealing how much they have at stake in the image controversies.

In their gloss on Acts 19, the translators of the *Geneva Bible* make a point of asserting that Paul's handkerchiefs are neither magical nor idolatrous. Instead of interpreting them as powerful in themselves, the commentators insist on their status as divine signs. Paul's handkerchiefs, they explain, were sent "to autorize the Gospel, and to confirme Pauls ministerie, not to cause men to worship him or his napkins." They insist that the physical objects are not curative agents but rather visible signs—"proofs of holy writ," to borrow a phrase from Shakespeare—that authorize and confirm God's word. In his *Commentary on Acts*, Calvin, too, distinguishes between a magical and a symbolic interpretation of Paul's handkerchiefs. He explicitly warns against idolatry, arguing that the handkerchiefs should be understood as divine signs and not revered as magical totems: "For which cause the Papists are more absurd, who wrest this place unto their relics; as if Paul sent his

---

[18] Calvin, *Institutes* 4.14.14.

handkerchiefs that men might worship and kiss them in their honor; as in Papistry they worship Francis' shoes and mantle, Rose's girdle, St. Margaret's comb and such like trifles.'' William Tyndale likewise draws a sharp distinction between Paul's handkerchiefs, which he interprets as divine signs meant to affirm belief in God's word, and magical or efficacious objects that are worshiped for themselves and are therefore idolatrous. "Paul," he notes, "sent his napkin to heal the sick, not that men should trust in his napkin, but believe in his preaching.''[19] For Tyndale, Calvin, and the translators of *The Geneva Bible*, Paul's handkerchiefs raise the specter of idolatry, and they strive mightily to disassociate the physical objects from any hint of the magical or miraculous, lest people put their faith in a visible thing. And yet, even as they seek to divorce Paul's napkins from any taint of magic, they insist on their potency as signs that help sustain faith in an unseen God.

The handkerchief is thus a contested site in Reformation disputes about the nature, power, and validity of ocular proof. What is centrally at issue in the commentaries on Paul's handkerchiefs, as well as in popular devotion to relics like Veronica's and Abagarus's napkins, is the role of sight in the practice of faith. In refuting popular beliefs in the magical napkins of Veronica and Abagarus, John Veron cites the Biblical image of the brass serpent. Although it had originally served an appropriate function as "a memorial or remembrance," it had to be destroyed when the Israelites superstitiously began to worship it.[20] According to reformers like Veron, some images are frauds and others are meaningful signs; some images trick people into believing lies, others draw people to God; and some images, like Paul's handkerchiefs and the brass serpent, may be abused by the superstitious while used properly by the godly.

In placing "so much stress" on a handkerchief, Shakespeare thus features an object that is repeatedly used in the theological discourse of his day to explore many of the same troubling epistemological questions raised in *Othello*. Although he locates such questions in the domestic world of marriage and in the secular realm of the theater, his

---

[19] Marginal commentary on Acts 19:11–12 in *The Geneva Bible* (1560); John Calvin, *Commentary on Acts*, qtd. in Carlos M. N. Eire, *War against the Idols* (1986), p. 223; William Tyndale, *An Answer to Sir Thomas More's Dialogue* (1850), pp. 74–76, 83.

[20] Veron, *A stronge battery*, fol. 81ʳ.

play, like the theological writings of the reformers, examines the truth claims of magic and empiricism, the limits of visual evidence, the basis of faith, and the function of memory and imagination in acts of knowing. Read in the context of the religious controversies of the Reformation, and in particular the radical reinterpretations of the validity of ocular proof in acts of faith, *Othello* may be said to rehearse the epistemological crisis created by the reformers when they deny the magical efficacy of images and relics and yet assert the power of visible signs. Othello's trust in a visible object he believes is magical proves fatal; equally dangerous, I suggest, is the Moor's failure to remember what the handkerchief originally signified to him.

Described as Desdemona's "first remembrance of the Moor," the handkerchief may be understood to be neither trivial nor magical but rather memorial, a potent sign of love capable of renewing, rather than disrupting, faith. The use of the word *remembrance* to describe the handkerchief resonates with the play's language of trifles and magic. As I show in my discussion of the reformed sacraments in Chapter 4, Protestant theologians insist on the value of images when they are used as vehicles of memory. Contemptuous of idols—those "triflying unprofitable helpes which ar rather hindereres of true fayth"—they nevertheless approve of images that function as "tokens to put us in remembrance of godly thinges."[21] And they carefully distinguish between abused images—that is, images that tempt people to worship them as idols—and unabused images, or "remembrances"—that is, images that function as signs, calling to mind what is invisible. Calling the memory "the Gallery of the soul, hang'd with so many, and so lively pictures of the goodness and mercies of thy God to thee, as that every one of them shall be a catechism to thee," Donne, for example, emphasizes the role of memory images in acts of faith, even asserting that "the art of salvation is but the art of memory."[22] Properly used as aids to memory, certain images were believed to have the capacity to remind the individual of God's grace and to help him or her to sustain faith in an invisible deity.

---

[21] John Phillips, *The Reformation of Images* (1973), pp. 57–77, 88–91, 147–50; Martin Bucer, *A treatise declaryng and shewing dyvers causes that pyctures and other ymages ar in no wise to be suffred in churches* [1535?], sigs. B7^r–B7^v.

[22] John Donne, *The Sermons* (1953–1962), 2.11.237. For a discussion of Luther's defense of memory images, see Carl C. Christensen, *Art and the Reformation in Germany* (1979).

Although Shakespeare applies the notion of a remembrance to a love token, not a sacred image, he clearly entertains the possibility that Desdemona's handkerchief could function as a memory image, renewing and strengthening the love between Othello and his wife. Calling the handkerchief "a recognizance and pledge of love"—that is, an emblem or visual sign of the bond between the lovers—he uses it to explore the nature of visible signs, opening up the possibility that a sign—a remembrance—might have the power to strengthen and sustain faith in the absence of any external proofs. If the "antique token" is understood to be a meaningful sign, Othello's obsession with the literal object is deeply ironic, a flagrant abuse of an image that might have functioned, like Paul's handkerchiefs, as a sign or "memorial" that affirms and strengthens faith.

Shakespeare sustains just such an ironic reading by staging the scene when Desdemona loses the handkerchief, for she neither gives it away to a rival lover nor drops it carelessly, but rather offers it to Othello in an attempt to soothe his aching head. Racked by doubt, overcome with jealousy, Othello rejects her loving and caring gesture with the dismissive words, "Your napkin is too little / Let it alone" (3.3.286–87). He thus refuses to accept—literally or figuratively—the gift of the handkerchief. As a medicinal aid for the body, it is entirely inadequate to cure his psychic pain; as a sign of his wife's love, it falls unappreciated and unacknowledged. The handkerchief is lost in the middle of a scene that begins with Othello insisting that "I'll see before I doubt; when I doubt, prove" (3.3.190) and ends with him demanding of Iago, "Villain, be sure thou prove my love a whore! / Be sure of it; give me the ocular proof" (3.3.359–60). One of the greatest ironies of this profoundly ironic play is surely that in his quest for certainty Othello rejects as "too little" an object that is a visible sign of Desdemona's love for him and his for her, and then construes it as the literal proof of her infidelity. In dramatizing the story of a man who stakes his "life upon [his wife's] faith" only to trust a handkerchief as "the ocular proof" of her infidelity, Shakespeare explores the problem of sustaining faith in "an essence that's not seen."

That problem preoccupies people in the wake of the Reformation. In their efforts to discredit the images and relics of the Roman Church, the reformers repeatedly cite scriptural passages that problematize not only ocular proofs of God but also the role of sight in all acts of faith. In his commentary on Hebrews 11:1, Calvin, for example, dwells on the paradoxical nature of this important text, showing how Paul uses metaphors of sight to define faith as belief in the invisible. "Paul," he writes, "speaks as if to say that faith is an evidence of things not appearing, a seeing of things not seen, a clearness of things obscure, a presence of things absent, a showing forth of things hidden." Although the word *evidence* "commonly refers only to what is subject to our senses," he continues, Paul uses it to refer to "hidden things, the knowledge of which cannot reach our senses." Calling attention to the relation of faith to knowledge, Calvin thus examines the challenge of knowing what is hidden, absent, obscure, and invisible.[23] That challenge, Katherine Eisaman Maus argues in *Inwardness and Theater in the English Renaissance*, arouses a distinctive set of "epistemological anxieties." According to Maus, "Renaissance religious culture . . . nurtures habits of mind that encourage conceiving of human inwardness . . . as at once privileged and elusive, an absent presence 'interpreted' to observers by ambiguous inklings and tokens. . . . Faith itself encourages a kind of mistrust: for what is most true about human beings in such a system is simultaneously least verifiable."[24]

Othello's initial faith in Desdemona—his confident declaration that she is chaste and true—may thus paradoxically arouse in him a desire to verify what he believes. The desire makes him vulnerable to Iago, who undermines the Moor's faith in his wife by engaging him in an intense observation of her behavior and encouraging him to interpret "ambiguous inklings"—small gestures, simple acts, casual conversations—as meaningful signs that reveal the innermost truth about her. Othello's faith in Desdemona cannot survive his compulsive need to verify her chastity. His insistent demand that Iago produce visible evidence of his wife's impurity and his acceptance of the handkerchief as the ocular proof he seeks expose the inadequacy of his own faith.

By demonstrating both the insufficiency of visible evidence and the difficulty of sustaining faith in what cannot be seen, Shakespeare's play thus addresses fundamental questions about seeing, knowing, and believing, questions that are at the heart of the sixteenth-century religious reforms. One striking example of the way these questions challenged

---

[23] Calvin, *Institutes* 3.2.41; John Calvin, "The Epistle of Paul the Apostle to the Hebrews" (1963), p. 157.

[24] Katherine Eisaman Maus, *Inwardness and Theater in the English Renaissance* (1995), pp. 2, 11–12.

and disrupted late medieval assumptions is the biblical story of Doubting Thomas, a story that underwent a radical reinterpretation during the Reformation. In the later Middle Ages Thomas was cited as a positive example; his need to see and touch the resurrected Christ before he could believe in the resurrection demonstrated how humans required some kind of ocular proof to bolster their faith in God. But the reformers saw Thomas's demand for visible evidence of the resurrection as a profound flaw. For them, Thomas's insistence on seeing before believing was a terrible failure of faith.[25]

Othello was written at a time when late medieval interpretations of Doubting Thomas were giving way to Reformation versions, and the English people, newly inspired by the writings of the apostle Paul, were themselves caught up in Thomas's struggle to sustain their faith in the absence of any visible proof. The play seems at once to embrace, question, and protest against the Pauline paradox that faith is based on "the evidence of things which are not sene." Rather than simply affirm Protestant teaching, it dramatizes a resistance to the notion that faith can be sustained in the absence of visible proof, for it constructs the doubting Othello as tragic in his misperceptions and all too human in his desire for certain knowledge. Othello's demand for ocular proof is, I suggest, a typical response to the renewed emphasis in reform culture on faith.

Lying Signs and True Spectators

The removal of external aids to faith had the paradoxical effect of heightening attention to images and intensifying people's need to make sense of the visible world. The reformers exhibit an obsessive concern with visible signs, and they invest an enormous amount of energy investigating their validity. They examine a bewildering array of images—sacramental signs, portents and prodigies, demonic illusions, man-made frauds, natural phenomena—and they focus on the contested status of images. Compelled by their own polemical arguments to confront the ways images have historically been misunderstood and abused, they urgently attempt to sort out the authentic from the false, the divine from the demonic.

[25] Gibson, *Theater of Devotion*, p. 16–17.

In an essay on the status of preternatural signs and miracles in early modern Europe, Lorraine Daston identifies the late Renaissance as a transitional period in which interest in portents and visible signs intensified as part of a process of reconceptualizing facts and evidence. Distinguishing sixteenth- and early seventeenth-century assumptions about prodigies from both medieval and modern assumptions, she finds a growing tendency among people in early modern Europe to associate the magical with the demonic and to fear "the religious peril of becoming a dupe to a counterfeit miracle, staged by the devil to trap the unwary." The association of visible signs with the devil is, she argues, an important phase in "the gradual naturalization of the preternatural in the early modern period," for it provoked "ever more concerted attempts to distinguish genuine (that is, divine) portents from demonic counterfeits and superstitious divination." Citing Protestant theologians who repeatedly address the problem of distinguishing true from false signs, she comments that "it is striking that those seventeenth-century writers most exercised by the topic of miracles [that is, Protestant reformers] were those who insisted that miracles had long ago ceased." In the transition from medieval beliefs about miracles to a modern scientific view of facts and evidence, there is, she concludes, a period during the sixteenth and early seventeenth centuries in which the preternatural grew "in extent and intellectual importance," occupying the attention of theologians, philosophers, and other thinkers who insistently seek to distinguish among the divine, the demonic, and the merely insignificant.[26]

Ocular proof of God is thus not eliminated, or even marginalized, in the years immediately following the Reformation; but it is destabilized, and the interpretation of images becomes a critical, if difficult and dangerous, act. In their attempts to distinguish between true and fraudulent signs, the reformers rely on a confusing and often contradictory mixture of what we would call primitive and modern assumptions, simultaneously declaring some signs divine or demonic while demystifying others. The belief that Satan uses images to enchant and ensnare the naive is pervasive. William Perkins, for example, constructs Satan as a magician who manifests himself "by workes of wonder . . . sometime by inchantment, sometime by rare sleights and delusions . . .

---

[26] Lorraine Daston, "Marvelous Facts and Miraculous Evidence in Early Modern Europe" (1991), pp. 106–107, 95, 101, 114, 99.

all to purchase unto himselfe admiration, feare, and faith, of the credulous world which is usually caried away, with affectation and applause
of signes and wonders." For Perkins, the ability to discern false signs
from true is not only crucial for salvation but also exceedingly difficult
because the devil's images are so appealing and humans so credulous.
He imagines a world filled with images that require interpretation and
complicate faith. "As God hath his word and Sacraments the seals of
his covenant unto beleevers," he writes, "lo, the devill hath his words
and certaine outward signes," signs he identifies as "charmes, figures,
characters, and other outward ceremonies" that entice and delude
credulous spectators. Protestant iconophobia thus often manifested itself as a magical belief that the devil "lurked and dwelled" in images.[27]

Early Protestants also ardently believed that God manifested himself
through signs. John Foxe, for example, meticulously records the "tokens," "portents," "signs," and "prints" that Protestant reformers believe reveal God's cosmic plan, and he uses eyewitness accounts to verify
the truth of their claims, noting of one supernatural sign, for instance,
that one Master Dean "did see it with his eyes."[28] He identifies scores
of portents that he claims provide ocular proof that God supports the
reform project. "A miraculous white cross" appears on the chest of a
martyr before his death; "divers prints and tokens of the nails, of the
sponge, of the spear, of the Lord's coat, and of bloody crosses" mys-
teriously appear on the clothing of men and women in Germany, "portents" that Foxe interprets as signifying the coming Reformation of the
Church; "a tempest of thunder and lightning in Rome, which so struck
the church where the cardinals were made, that it removed the little
child Jesus out of the lap of his mother, and the keys out of St. Peter's
hand," a sign, originally recorded by John Bale, that Foxe believes indicates the coming "subversion and alteration of the see of Rome"; a
"monstrous owl" that terrifies the Pope and his clergy which Foxe identifies as an "evile signe" and "an ill favored token." He even interprets
the sudden death of a "Popish Priest" as a sign of God's displeasure.[29]
John Veron goes even further, arguing that God sometimes creates false
signs to punish evil men, sending them "strong delusion, that they

[27] William Perkins, *A Discourse of the Damned Art of Witchcraft* (1608), pp. 22, 43, 46–47,
43; John Foxe, *A&M* (1570), p. 787.

[28] Foxe, *A&M*, 8:481–82.

[29] Ibid., 4: 482; 4:257–58; 4:257; Foxe, *A&M* (1570), pp. 706, 1731.

should beleve lyes, that all they might be damned, whiche beleved not the truth.''[30]

Although he wants to persuade his readers of the authenticity of particular images, Foxe fully understands how his own religion has challenged the authority of all ocular proof, making any interpretation based on visible evidence uncertain and open to question. When he records a series of Protestant dreams and visions he interprets as divine prophecies, he admits that not every dream is a prophecy, and he acknowledges that "the papists, in their books and legends of saints, have their prodigious visions and apparitions of angels, of our Lady, of Christ, and other saints"—visions he wishes to discount. "Why," he asks in a self-reflective moment, "should I then more require these [Protestant images] to be credited of them [the Catholics] than theirs of us."[31] He seems painfully aware of Roman Catholic complaints that "where every man will be master, there must needs be uncertainty. And one thing is marvellous that at the same time it is taught that all men be liars, at the selfsame time almost every man would be believed."[32] And he openly and self-consciously confronts the doubt and uncertainty Protestantism arouses.

Acknowledging the difficulty of distinguishing between the "fained lyes" and "craftie juglings of men," on the one hand, and divine signs, on the other, Foxe ponders whether he should even report Protestant accounts of visible signs believed to be divine.[33] Before describing the "godly" dreams of one Cutbert Symson, he confesses: "I stand in no little doubt whether to report abroad or not considering with myself the great diversity of men's judgments in the reading of histories, and variety of affections. Some I see will not believe it; some will deride the same; some also will be offended with setting forth things of that sort uncertain, esteeming all things to be uncertain and incredible, whatsoever is strange from the common order of nature; others will be perchance aggrieved, thinking with themselves, or else thus reasoning

---

[30] Citing scripture, Veron asks rhetorically, "Do we not learne by these words of the apostle, that in the later days there shall be wonders and signes in the kingdome of Antichriste? And doubtelesse, as they are by the righteous judgement of God, ordeined for to deceive them ... that the ungodly contemners of the truth may the more be blynded and confirmed in their error?" (Veron, *A stronge battery*, fol. 8ᵛ).

[31] Foxe, *A&M*, 8:456.

[32] Stephen Gardiner, qtd. in Foxe, *A&M*, 6:31.

[33] I quote from "An Homily Against perill of Idolatrie and superfluous decking of Churches in the time of Queen Elizabeth I" (1623), pp. 52–53.

with me, that although the matter were as is reported, yet forsomuch as the common error of believing rash miracles, fantasies, visions, dreams, and apparitions, thereby may be confirmed, more expedient it were the same to be unset forth." Rather than insist on his own, authoritative analysis of such images, Foxe calls attention to the problematic nature of visible proof, the uncertainty of human interpretation, and the multiplicity of individual perspectives. In conscious opposition to the papists, whom he accuses of "binding" men "precisely to believe" their particular interpretation, he explicitly leaves "the judgment" of the visions he reports "free unto the arbitrement of the reader."[34]

The certainty with which Thomas Rymer distinguishes superstition from truth in 1693 is thus vastly complicated a century earlier by the Calvinist conviction that God manifests himself to the faithful through signs and by the reformers' heightened sense that both men and the archenemy Satan, understood to be "a natural Magician," manipulate images, counterfeit false signs, and stage fraudulent miracles to trick the unwary.[35] If seeing, for early Protestants, no longer provides direct access to the divine, if the eyes are prone to error and superstition, if evil men deliberately set out to deceive others, and if the devil uses enticing images to ensnare unsuspecting souls, images may nevertheless also be divine signs of great significance.

Rather than impose a rigorous and consistent set of criteria for determining what constitutes ocular proof, Foxe invokes the inscrutability of God and insists on the inadequacy of human reason in the face of divine mystery. "And if any shall muse, or object again," Foxe writes, "why should such visions be given to him, or a few singular persons, more than to all the rest, ... I say, concerning the Lord's times and doings I have not to meddle nor make, who may work where and when it pleaseth him. . . . of the Lord's secret times I have not to reason."[36] He thus relies on faith to prove the divinity of Protestant visions and the error of Roman Catholic ones. Rejecting empiricism, he claims his interpretations are valid because they are inspired by God. Although Foxe's position seems hopelessly inconsistent and illogical to readers today, it is fairly typical of the way early Protestants explain the visible

---

[34] Foxe, *A&M*, 8:456.
[35] Thomas Browne, "Pseudodoxia Epidemica," 1:188.
[36] Foxe, *A&M*, 8:456–57.

world. Calvin, for instance, teaches that faith precedes physical seeing. Reason is therefore not the basis of a "correct" interpretation. Human beings, he insists, "have not the eyes to see unless they be illumined by the inner revelation of God through faith."[37]

Eyesight is for Calvin both a metaphor for an interior and spiritual kind of seeing—one of his favorite figures of speech—and a physical act utterly dependent on that inner, divinely given sight. He uses the kerchief as a metaphor for the essential blindness of every person who has not been illuminated by God. "Wee bee blynd," he writes in a sermon on the book of Ephesians, unless God "open our eyes, and take away the kercheefe or veyle that is before them, yea and give us a newe sight."[38] Calvin is essentially pessimistic about the human capacity to interpret. In what might be called the Protestant paradox of perception, God in his goodness creates visible signs to lead humans to him, but humans in their depravity are too blind to recognize them. The universe may be "a magnificent theater," but, Calvin laments, "scarcely one man in a hundred is a true spectator of it."[39] Emphasizing the enormous gap between the meaningful signs inscribed in the visible world and error-prone humans, Calvin casts humans as obtuse spectators, so blinded by "their fatal errors," so driven by their own narcissistic desires, so dazzled by the world and their own imaginings that they fail to understand the signs that God displays in the great theater of the world.[40] The challenge of distinguishing false images from true signs is both complicated by a Calvinist emphasis on original sin and made all the more urgent.

"Free Unto the Arbitrement of the Reader"

Our experience of early modern drama would, I think, be enriched if we recognized how vexed and unresolved the questions con-

---

[37] Calvin, *Institutes* 2.2.20; 1.5.14. "Even Moses," Calvin writes, "reproaching the people for their forgetfulness, nevertheless notes at the same time that one cannot become wise in God's mysteries except by his gift. He says: 'Your eyes saw those signs and great wonders; but the Lord has not given you a heart to understand, or ears to hear or eyes to see.' What more could he express if he called us 'blocks' in our contemplation of God's works?" (*Institutes* 2.2.20).

[38] John Calvin, *The sermons of M. John Calvin upon the Epistle of S. Paul too the Ephesians* (1577), fol. 43ᵛ.

[39] Calvin, *Institutes* 2.6.1; 1.5.8.

[40] Ibid. 1.5.14.

cerning the nature of images were in Shakespeare's day, how pressing the problem of distinguishing false sign from true. Exhibiting an anxious attention to images, Renaissance tragedies engage their audiences in an open-ended inquiry into the status of visible signs. They both replicate in the theater their culture's dialectic of belief and skepticism and contribute to the formation of Enlightenment assumptions about the visible world. Investigating a range of ambiguous images, they explore the problem of knowing in a world poised between the medieval and modern ages. The epistemological crisis they address is in large part a product of the Reformation and its adherents' articulation of a set of theological assumptions about the visible world, God's inscription in it, and the limitations of human sight. By depicting fictional worlds filled with natural, preternatural, and supernatural images, many of them ambiguous or confusing, they dramatize the difficulty of knowing in an age when the old symbolic system is breaking apart and a new one has not yet solidified.

The images they display—mysterious, magical, monstrous—confound the characters who behold them and challenge the spectators in the theater to make sense of them. Witches, ghosts, hallucinations, and dangerously misleading apparitions haunt Macbeth, who repeatedly overdetermines the meaning of what he sees. Ominous dreams, portents, prophecies, and prodigies trouble Julius Caesar, the title character of Shakespeare's tragedy, conveying a sense of the mysterious and apocalyptic that is heightened by the multiple and conflicting interpretations various characters give them.[41] Characters in *The Duchess of Malfi* compulsively "read" everything as a visible sign: a bloodshot eye, a nosebleed, a pregnant woman's physiological response to apricots, the astrological signs at a child's nativity, a "malevolent star," a fake pilgrimage, a dream, and a ghost. Webster's audiences, however, never know whether the stated interpretations are true or merely superstitious, and they are constantly confronted with the limitations of any knowledge based on sight. Even in a play like *The Changeling,* where a sustained dramatic irony exposes the interpretive errors of the characters, audiences are engaged in sorting out the false from the accurate interpretations of characters who repeatedly attempt to "read" inner qualities and feelings in an individual's face, gestures, behavior, and friends, who find omens in the visible world they inhabit, and who

---

[41] For an interesting discussion of images and prodigies in *Julius Caesar,* see Mark Rose, "Conjuring Caesar" (1992), pp. 256–69.

determine innocence and guilt by means of visual evidence. Misinterpretation in Middleton's play, as in so many other Renaissance tragedies, leads to ruin. Alsemero misreads Beatrice-Joanna's character in her beautiful face, wrongly concludes his wife is "chaste as the breath of heaven" when he sees her imitate the physical reactions of a virgin in response to the virginity test he administers, and fails to discern the substitution of another woman for his wife in his marriage bed.[42]

Although post-Enlightenment critics typically seek to explain the remarkable images displayed on the Renaissance English stage, declaring many to be superstitious and fixing the precise meaning of others, the plays themselves rarely achieve the closure provided by the critics. They do not so much teach their audiences how to interpret as arouse anxiety about any act of interpretation. Visible evidence in them is unreliable and easily manipulated by malicious men and cunning women. Spectacles are fraudulent and illusory and sometimes demonic, seducing and ensnaring viewers with dazzling but insubstantial images. And signs, though they are sometimes meaningful, are all too often dangerously indeterminate. The act of interpreting is both critical and potentially tragic, for any reliance on sight as a basis of knowledge results in uncertainty and, often, disastrous errors.

By featuring images that simultaneously promise and withhold meaning and portraying protagonists who tragically (and sometimes willfully) misinterpret them, the tragedies of Shakespeare and his contemporaries thus participate in an ongoing inquiry into the status of signs and actively contribute to the process of demystification that Daston describes. But if their exposés help to construct a modern understanding of facts and evidence, they do not fully embrace such an understanding, for they also feature mysterious and compelling images that are sometimes divine, sometimes demonic, and always potentially significant. The presence of such images complicates early modern notions of sight and works against the emerging rationalism.

Theatrical representations of ghosts, for example, rarely resolve the questions raised by the frightening appearance of spectral figures claiming to be spirits of the dead. Instead, a character's encounter with a ghost typically elicits an open-ended inquiry into the nature of the image. Is it a superstition, a hallucination, an illusion, or a supernatural vision? And how does a person know? In the course of Cyril Tourneur's

---

[42] John Webster, *The Duchess of Malfi*, ed. John Russell Brown (1964); Thomas Middleton and William Rowley, *The Changeling*, ed. George Walton Williams (1966).

The Atheist's Tragedy, a spectral figure is believed to be a supernatural being, the actual ghost of a murdered man; a character dressed in a sheet is mistakenly taken for a real ghost; a living person who had been presumed dead is thought to be his own ghost when he reappears; a cloud is interpreted as a haunting ghost by a guilty man; and the existence of all ghosts is categorically denied.[43] Such an extended exploration of the phenomenon of ghosts may seem silly or ludicrous to readers today who embrace scientific paradigms that close off the possibility that ghosts, demons, and prodigious signs exist. But as I have argued, early modern culture is a transitional one in which modern and premodern beliefs coexist. Even as D'Amville confidently articulates a modern, scientific understanding, insisting that ghosts are nothing more than "mere imaginary fables. There's no such thing in *rerum natura*," Charlement encounters an image of his father he fervently believes to be a ghost. And, although D'Amville takes what we today recognize as a modern or enlightened position, he is the villain of Tourneur's play, the atheist who realizes too late the error of his way of seeing.[44] *The Atheist's Tragedy* engages its audiences in the problem of distinguishing among false, superstitious, and true signs, but it does not resolve the problem according to Enlightenment thinking. Indeed, the confusion about how to interpret the various ghost-like figures in Tourneur's play works against the rationalist perspective of D'Amville, whose disbelief in the phenomenon of ghosts, like his atheism, is portrayed as foolish.

Because Tourneur's play is schematic, its didacticism explicit, it makes visible its own inquiry into the status of visible signs. Working with the genre of revenge tragedy, Tourneur is surely inspired by Shakespeare's *Hamlet*, where a similar inquiry is far more disturbing. Shakespeare displays and examines, but never fully explains, the ghost that appears to the young Hamlet. Its ambiguity drives his audiences into the mystery of the play. The "bodiless" ghost of Hamlet's father appears three times. It is variously described as a "figure," "a form," "a mote to trouble the mind's eye," an "illusion," "a king of shreds and patches," a "gracious figure," and "nothing at all."[45] The play explores the possibility that the spectral figure is a dead man's ghost who speaks

---

[43] For a discussion of visible signs in Tourneur's play, see my essay, " 'Reduce Thy Understanding to Thine Eye': Seeing and Interpreting in *The Atheist's Tragedy*" (1981).

[44] Cyril Tourneur, *The Atheist's Tragedy*, ed. Irving Ribner (1964), 4.3.275–76.

[45] *Hamlet*, in Shakespeare, *The Complete Works*, ed. Alfred Harbage (1969), 1.1; 3.4.

from the invisible world beyond, a dangerous demon intent on ensnaring Hamlet's soul, a psychic manifestation of loss and guilt, and a
metaphoric speck of dust that irritates and perhaps clouds inner sight.

When Hamlet sees the ghost of his father in his mother's chamber while Gertrude sees "nothing at all" yet insists "all that is I see"
(3.4.133), the play entertains two sharply conflicting ways of interpreting the ghost. Gertrude accuses her son of "bend[ing his] eye on va-
cancy"; he accuses her of having "eyes without feeling, feeling without
sight" (3.4.118, 79). She thinks he is mad, the ghost a hallucination.
He insists that what he looks upon has the power to make stones re-
sponsive. Unable to reconcile what they see, Hamlet demands of his
mother, "Have you eyes? . . . Have you eyes?" In a scene that directly
addresses issues of moral blindness, hallucinatory madness, self-
reflection, espionage, mistaken identity, and the reading of character
in physiognomy and portraiture, Shakespeare raises, but does not resolve, fundamental questions about the relation of sight and knowledge. Depending on how a director chooses to stage the ghost, the
play's spectators may themselves see or not see the ghost, but all that
they see on stage is, by definition, a theatrical illusion. And theater in
Hamlet is sometimes condemned as fraudulent artifice, sometimes celebrated as a true mirror of nature. The experience of the spectators is
thus unsettling, for the ghost confronts them with the limits and fallibility of their own seeing.

In dramatizing multiple and competing ways of seeing and knowing,
Shakespeare seems intent on opening up, rather than closing off, possible ways an image like the ghost in *Hamlet* or the handkerchief in
Othello might signify. In a manner far more reminiscent of John Foxe
than of Thomas Rymer, he interrogates its nature while leaving its interpretation "free unto the arbitrement of the reader" or audience
member, and he seems far more interested in exploring the process by
which an image is interpreted or misinterpreted than in fixing its exact
meaning. The attempt by Rymer and subsequent critics to declare Desdemona's handkerchief a trifle thus seems misguided, for it ignores the
very deliberate way Shakespeare uses the handkerchief to initiate an
open-ended investigation of visible signs.

The handkerchief passes from hand to hand, is subjected to various
and conflicting interpretations, is read and reread as a signifier, and
accrues significance until it becomes the crucial factor determining
whether Othello believes or doubts his wife, and thus whether he cher-

ishes or kills her. Rather than provide a single set of criteria for understanding the handkerchief, Shakespeare complicates his audiences' own seeing by entertaining different ways it might signify or falsely signify or fail to signify. In addition to thematizing the problem of sustaining faith in the invisible, *Othello* thus reproduces in the theater reform culture's epistemological anxiety about the nature and validity of images.

Othello and Desdemona believe the handkerchief has the magical power both to enthrall the lover and to release him from the enchanted web of eros. If they are right, the handkerchief is mysterious, wonderful, and exceedingly dangerous, and Desdemona may well be, as her father fears, under the magical spell of an exotic stranger. If the handkerchief is indeed powerful enough to determine Othello's feelings toward his wife, the Moor himself is under its spell, and their love cannot survive its loss. Iago, however, believes the handkerchief is a trifle that can nevertheless be used to trick the man who trusts in it. Contemptuous of both magic and eros, he cynically pretends the object is empirical evidence of adultery, thereby manipulating Othello into believing what is patently false: Desdemona is unfaithful. Iago succeeds in part because he maliciously stages a fraudulent narrative in order to trick Othello into trusting what he sees rather than exercising his faith in Desdemona. As I have shown, the handkerchief is also constructed as a token or remembrance of the love between Othello and Desdemona, and as such it serves to remind Shakespeare's audiences of what Othello forgets, Desdemona's love for him. By entertaining multiple ways Desdemona's handkerchief might function within the world of the play—as a magical totem, a potent sign, and an insignificant trifle—Shakespeare engages his spectators in its vexed interpretation.

Displayed on the stage, the handkerchief embroidered with strawberries also functions as a richly suggestive theatrical sign that insists on being "read," yet has no stable or fixed meaning. During the critical scene in which it is lost, Desdemona gives the handkerchief to Othello to relieve his headache. If she binds it around her husband's head, he would temporarily appear to the audience like the erring and fallen characters in late Tudor morality plays who wear handkerchiefs tied around their heads as iconographic signs of their moral or spiritual disease. It would thus signal that his pain is psychological or spiritual, not physiological, and Desdemona's curative "too little" because it administers only to the body. If the napkin temporarily covers his eyes, it might also function as a traditional icon of moral or spiritual blindness. Perhaps it would remind Shakespeare's audiences of the Pauline metaphor of the "kercheefe or veyle" that hinders human sight. Or perhaps it would call attention to the inadequacy of the ocular proof that Othello begins to demand in this scene.[46]

In addition, the white handkerchief is embroidered with red strawberries, a fruit rich in symbolic associations. If the image operates as a conventional Renaissance icon of deceit—the fruit attracts the eye while the leaves conceal a dangerous serpent—its use as ornamentation on the napkin would be ironic, a reminder that the handkerchief is untrustworthy, a tool of the serpent Iago, a sign that Othello fails to read. If instead the strawberry evokes associations with the fertile female body (nipples, lips, clitoris, menstrual blood), its appearance on the handkerchief might reinforce the connection between the napkin and its magical origins with the Egyptian charmer and Othello's mother. It might also serve to locate Othello's distrust of Desdemona in a fear of women and female sexuality, and thus heighten the audience's sense of the dangerous and magical power of eros. But the image of the strawberry is also a conventional attribute of both the Virgin Mary and the fallen Eve, and it is also sometimes used as an attribute of the falsely accused Susanna. In its association with such divergent archetypes as Mary and Eve, the strawberry might simultaneously suggest both female chastity and sexual betrayal and thus call attention to Othello's confusion of the two, his inability to distinguish between virgin and whore. In alluding to the story of Susanna, it might also underscore the vulnerability of innocent women to slander and misrepresentation.[47] As Linda Boose has argued, the white cloth "spotted" with red strawberries may also call to mind the bloodied wedding sheets that were traditionally displayed as a visible proof of the newly married woman's virginity. If so, its link in the play to the wedding sheets Desdemona asks Emilia to lay on what becomes her deathbed would be powerfully suggestive. As a substitute for the wedding sheets that signal both vir-

---

[46] For discussions of the handkerchief in this scene, see my essay, "Irony, Parody, and Inversion" (1982); Steven Baker, "Sight and a Sight in *Othello*" (1987).

[47] For discussions of the iconography of strawberries, see: Boose, "Othello's Handkerchief"; Karen Newman, *Fashioning Femininity* (1991), pp. 90–92; Michael Neill, "Unproper Beds" (1989); Lawrence J. Ross, "The Meaning of Strawberries in Shakespeare" (1960); Peter L. Rudnytsky, "The Purloined Hankerchief in *Othello*" (1985); Edward A. Snow, "Sexual Anxiety and the Male Order of Things in *Othello*" (1980).

ginity and sexual consummation, the handkerchief might be understood to underscore the complex relation between ocular proof and an unseen essence.[48]

To read the handkerchief as an iconographic sign, spectators in the theater must try to make sense of a range of competing and sometimes contradictory meanings, in effect, participating in the problem of knowing by means of visible signs. Desdemona's napkin simultaneously invites and thwarts interpretation, and it thus engages its spectators in questions about what they see and how they know. Made keenly aware of the way Iago manipulates Othello's sight by displaying the handkerchief as a lying sign, they nevertheless cannot escape their own reliance on visible signs. They are, after all, watching a play, observing a man tragically misinterpret what he sees. Because all that they see is a representation, Othello's repeated errors—substituting the sight of the handkerchief in Cassio's hands for the sight of Desdemona in Cassio's bed, collapsing the sign and the thing signified, misreading the signs— may serve to remind them of the gap between the representation and the real. The handkerchief, variously read as a magical talisman, a remembrance, a trifle, and a damning piece of empirical evidence, and displayed on stage as an iconographic sign, forces them to confront the uncertainty of human knowledge and the fallibility of their own interpretive acts.

Instead of nurturing a mode of seeing that we would identify as modern—unified, focused, privileged—early modern tragedy elicits multiple and often incompatible ways of seeing, fracturing vision and decentering the spectator. Although plays like *Hamlet* and *Othello* arouse an intense desire for clarification, explanation, and illumination, they do not provide the paradigms by which these acts can be accomplished. Instead, they create for their spectators the troubled, confused, and sometimes exhilarating experience of *not* knowing. The aesthetic experience of Renaissance tragedy thus replicates the lived experience of people in early modern England, as described by Datson, Thomas, and others. It is a destabilizing and even transformative experience, forcing audiences to question received ideas, evaluate opposing ways of seeing, and test their own epistemological assumptions. Out of such experiences, Enlightenment notions of facts and evidence eventually emerge. But the immediate effect is not one of enlightenment. Spectators in

[48] Boose, "Othello's Handkerchief," 360–74.

the theaters of early modern London repeatedly find themselves identified with characters like Othello and Hamlet, Bosola and Macbeth,
characters who come to the realization that they operate in "a general
mist of error," never knowing anything for certain. Like these tragic
protagonists, they are forced to question not only whether they have
read the signs correctly but also whether the signs are meaningful at
all.

"What Mighty Magic"

Renaissance tragedy's inquiry into the status of signs extends to
the medium of the theater itself, linked in premodern thought to
magic. It thus destabilizes audiences' relation to the very stage they
watch. In *Othello* Shakespeare explores an assumed bond between magic
and theater. By investing Othello with the poet's power to move and
enchant while identifying him with the mysterious and magical, he
raises disturbing questions about his own art. When Brabantio charges
that Othello has enchanted Desdemona, imprisoning her against her
will in "chains of magic," Othello does not altogether deny the charge.
Instead, he promises to explain exactly "what drugs, what charms, /
What conjuration, and what mighty magic" he used in his courtship
(1.3.91–92). He then tells how he wooed Desdemona by recounting
the stirring narratives of his adventurous past. His stories, he explains,
so excited and moved Desdemona, who "swore, i' faith, 'twas strange,
'twas passing strange; / 'Twas pitiful, 'twas wondrous pitiful" (1.3.160–
61), she fell in love with him. Although Othello disingenuously denies
his power to bewitch by pleading, "This only is the witchcraft I have
used" (1.3.169), his retelling is seductive and compelling, a theatrical
performance that captivates both the on-stage listeners and the theater
audiences. "I think this tale would win my daughter too," the Duke
responds, siding with the Moor and surely articulating the feelings of
the audience. Shakespeare does not completely close off the possibility
that Othello—that "extravagant and wheeling stranger / Of here and
everywhere" (1.1.135–36)—is indeed a practitioner of the magical arts,
capable of enthralling not only his beloved and the Venetian aristocracy, but also the theater audience, and he vividly demonstrates the
seductive power of the player and dramatist.

Why does Shakespeare identify the Moor and his strange and wondrous tales with the theatrical arts? Does he himself claim the power

of the magician or does he renounce it? How are his audiences to understand the appeal of Othello's mighty magic? *Othello* is, I think, deeply conflicted in its attitudes toward the theater. Like *Doctor Faustus*, it invokes, but also exhausts and contains, the seductive power of the stage, demonstrating the magical allure of the theatrical even as it unleashes the demystifying power of reason, skepticism, and doubt. It arouses and mocks the imagination, it compels and ridicules magical belief, and it displays and domesticates the strange.

Rymer, it is true, seems impervious to the magic of Shakespeare's play, but in resisting its allure, he is deaf to the powerful language of romance that dominates the early scenes of this play. Shakespeare uses the conventions of romance to create an imaginative world in which the most beautiful woman of a highly civilized society falls in love with a great warrior, a noble and exotic stranger. The lovers defy the possessive father, transcend the petty prejudices of the woman's insulated world, and assert their love in the face of envy, suspicion, disbelief, in the shadow of an impending war, and in the darkness of the night. Shakespeare plays the magician with this romance narrative, eliciting in his audiences a sense of wonder and excitement, arousing desire, and captivating the imagination. But he also plays the iconoclast, deploying Iago to destroy the very fantasy he has conjured. *Othello* is almost unbearably painful to its audiences because it enacts what it represents, seducing its audiences with erotic images while exposing them as dangerous and illusory.

Read in the context of Protestant polemics against images and plays, Shakespeare's play can be understood to address a constellation of issues—about magic, erotic desire, ocular proof, and human perception—pertinent to early modern anxieties about the stage. The charge that the theater is a form of magic implicates the audience members themselves in magical practices. The horror Shakespeare's play arouses in its audiences surely derives in part from the way it requires them to entertain the possibility not only that the handkerchief is a silly and trivial thing, and Othello's trust in it a fatal error, but also that all products of the imagination—erotic passion, romantic narratives, internal images, indeed the very theater they watch—are, as the reformers preach, "lifeless and theatrical trifles," "utterly meaningless signs," "a sea of lies," "the worke of errours," "thynges of nought."[49]

---

[49] Calvin, *Institutes* 4.17.43, 4.10.15; Foxe, *A&M*, 5:588; Veron, *A stronge battery*, fols. 76^r, 98^r.

Not the least of the imaginative products Shakespeare examines is his own creation of the romantic Moor. At the beginning of the play Othello manifests the traits of a great hero, a skilled military officer, and a consummate actor. His presence commands respect; his dignity dwarfs the men who revile him; his eloquence moves all who hear him; his compelling narrative persuades even those predisposed to distrust him. But, having captivated his audiences with an idealized image of Othello, Shakespeare begins to disrupt their relation to it. Othello becomes rattled and suspicious, then insanely jealous and uncontrollably passionate, and finally murderously violent. In response to Iago's evil machinations, he thus comes to resemble the savage "other" the Venetians have all along feared. Before he dies, Othello identifies with "a malignant and turbaned Turk" he once killed, stabbing himself as he once stabbed "the circumcised dog" (5.2.353–56).

How are we to understand the mixture of admiration and fear, wonder and horror that Othello arouses? Recent studies of *Othello* have focused critical attention on issues of race and gender, using anthropological theories of the "other" to illuminate Shakespeare's constructions of the Moor in interesting and valuable ways.[50] I wish to call attention to a dimension of early modern culture these studies neglect—the "othering" of the imagination in the theological discourse of the reformers—and I shall suggest that Iago's ugly racist slurs and Brabantio's racist horror of miscegenation are related to Protestant tirades against images, plays, and magic in early modern England.

Drawing on biblical injunctions against idolatry, the Protestant reformers name idols "strange gods" because they displace God in the hearts of idolaters. They use the metaphor of the stranger to warn against the strong allure of anything—images, plays, fantasies, even loved ones—that alienates a person from God, and they caution against the human propensity to substitute the strange gods of their imaginations.[51] The biblical passages they cite often warn against marriage to

---

[50] See, for example, Frances E. Dolan, *Dangerous Familiars* (1994), pp. 109–19; Gillies, *Shakespeare and the Geography of Difference*, chapter 1; Ania Loomba, *Gender, Race, Renaissance Drama* (1989), chapter 2; Timothy Murray, "*Othello*'s Foul Generic Thoughts and Methods" (1985); Neill, "Unproper Beds"; Newman, *Fashioning Femininity*; Martin Orkin, "Othello and the 'plain face' of Racism" (1987).

[51] Ridley, "Treatise Concerning Images," 39:84; Henry Ainsworth, *An Arrow Against Idolatrie* (1624), p. 46; Calvin, *Four godlye sermons agaynst the pollution of idolatries* (1561), sig. A5ᵛ; Bucer, *Treatise*, sigs. A5ʳ, A6ʳ; William Perkins, *A Warning against the idolatrie of the last times* (1601), sigs. A2ᵛ, B4ʳ; Richard Porder, *A sermon of Gods fearefull threatnings . . .* ,

strangers, thus implicating the person who marries outside the tribe/ nation/faith in idolatry and impurity. The strange and the stranger, the magical and the magician, are understood to be dangerously seductive fantasies, and people are believed to be naturally prone to place their trust in them. Sixteenth-century English reformers draw on these biblical metaphors. By associating the Roman Church with the strange and the other—with that which is not English—they drive a wedge between it and the English people, arousing xenophobia and fears of pollution to convert them to the new faith.[52]

Without denying the importance of race in *Othello*, I suggest that sixteenth-century Protestant polemics—relying on early modern fears of the racial other, broadly defined—arouse a troubling suspicion of all forms of the imaginative, including erotic love, magic, and the theater, all central concerns in *Othello*. In his critique of the handkerchief, Rymer appropriates this strategy, scoffing at magical beliefs by associating them with ignorant Africans, when he asserts that "no Booby, on this side Mauritania," would place any trust in a magical handkerchief. In my next chapter I show how the reformers also construct the imagination and its products as feminine; they thus arouse misogyny as well as racial prejudice to counter the appeal of the imaginative and magical. The reformers' strategy of estranging magic by appealing to racist and misogynist sentiments is still operating in the critical literature on *Othello*, as the recent comment that Othello's belief in the magic of the handkerchief is an "exotic and barbarous female superstition" illustrates.[53]

In creating a protagonist who is a Moor and a stranger in the city he inhabits, who captures the heart of a Venetian lady with spellbinding stories of his exotic past, who invokes the magical powers of a love token made by an Egyptian charmer, and who is passionate and susceptible to insinuations that he is effeminate, Shakespeare seems to deliberately align Othello with the theater as it is increasingly being constructed by the antitheatricalists in early modern London. He is, I think, deeply ambivalent about the extraordinary appeal of his noble

---

fol. 38[r]. For scriptural references to strange gods, see Deuteronomy 7, Exodus 20, 1 Samuel 7: 3, Hosea 8:12, and Wisdom 14:22–26.

[52] See, for example, Foxe, *A&M*, 8:497–503; I discuss the metaphor of the stranger in the narrative of Prest's wife in Chapter 2.

[53] Kaula, "Othello Possessed," p. 127.

Moor. He uses the exotic stranger to examine the seductive power of his own art and the forces at work in reform culture that threaten to reduce and contain that power.

Just as it is Iago who fuels the racial prejudices of the Venetians, it is Iago who is contemptuous of magic and erotic love. Declaring the magical handkerchief a trifle and Othello's romantic narratives "fantastical lies," he dismisses the love between Desdemona and Othello as nothing more than "a frail vow betwixt an erring barbarian and a supersubtle Venetian" (1.3.352–53). But though it is tempting to see Iago in the role of the iconoclast and to read *Othello* as a simple protest against the iconophobia and antitheatricality of the Protestant reformers, such a reading would have to ignore the way Iago is himself an actor and a manipulator of images. Iago's plain and open manner is a pose, one that he cynically adopts in order to circulate false narratives and stages fraudulent scenes. His is a deceptive, dangerous, and demonic theater, and he is a master at blearing the eyes of unsuspecting, innocent people, tricking them into believing what is patently false, all the while letting the audience in on his malicious intent: to damn the Moor. Whereas Othello's theatricality draws the audience in, arouses desire, and gives pleasure, Iago's disgusts and unsettles. Shakespeare thus uses his villain to create distrust of the theatrical, a distrust that eventually extends even to the Moor's alluring and exotic theatricality. As Iago maliciously plays the honest friend and spins his lies about the handkerchief, he confides in the audience that he is not what he appears to be, exposing and utterly demystifying his theatrical strategies. However seductive the magic of his own theater, Shakespeare thus never allows the audiences of *Othello* to lose themselves in it. Rather, he engages them in an exploration of their own responses to erotic and magical images and forces them to confront their vulnerability both to Iago's fraudulent and Othello's enchanting theatricality.

Inasmuch as his play deconstructs its own romantic assumptions, exposing the dark side of eros, the erring ways of the imagination, and the fraudulent nature of magic, it participates in a process of demystification that ultimately results in Enlightenment critiques such as Rymer's. As Desdemona's handkerchief circulates among various characters in the play, it moves farther and farther from its magical and mysterious origins. Like the sacred images of the Roman Catholic Church in Germany that R. W. Scribner describes being taken from the churches, paraded in the streets, interrogated in taverns, and ultimately desacralized, and like the sacred images that Keith Thomas describes being removed from holy places and converted to domestic use as kitchen utensils, building materials, and dolls, the handkerchief undergoes a process of demystification.[54] It passes from the strange and wonderful realm of Egyptian magic and romantic passion into the domestic world of marital love, then into the clutches of a malicious villain, and finally into the hands of an ordinary prostitute. But if *Othello* enacts early Protestant culture's rituals of desacralization, subduing its spectators as well as its protagonist, it also works its own magic, seducing and enchanting audiences who, horrified by the skeptic Iago's relentless assaults on the imagination, earnestly wish to be beguiled by Othello's narratives "of most disastrous chances, / Of moving accidents by flood and field, / Of hairbreadth scapes i 'th'imminent deadly breach" (1.3.134–36).

We flatten out both the dynamic nature of this provocative drama and the cultural conflicts that energize and complicate it if we, as post-Enlightenment readers, acknowledge only one side of the dialectic between belief and doubt, magic and empiricism, that informs the play and the culture that produces it. In the open-ended exploration of the napkin's meaning, in Iago's cruel manipulation of an unsuspecting man's sight, in the dramatist's manipulation, by means of dramatic irony, of the audience's own seeing, and in the fatal and tragic consequences of Othello's faulty seeing, Shakespeare explores a deep and pervasive cultural anxiety. We can appreciate this anxiety and its capacity to disturb and disrupt more fully if we recognize the ways in which Shakespeare's play reflects upon the devastating iconoclastic violence unleashed by the reformation.

[54] R. W. Scribner, *Popular Culture and Popular Movements in Reformation Germany* (1987), p. 114; Thomas, *Religion and the Decline of Magic*, p. 75.

CHAPTER SIX

Iconophobia and Gynophobia:
The Stuart Love Tragedies

> We rede in the histories of the greekes, that a certain image of Venus
> was so cunningly made, and so gorgeously trimmed, that many yong
> men were inflamed and set on fire with a love of it, so that many tymes
> the idol was founde in the morning polluted & defyled with the sede
> of man. And do they not nowe a daies, where papistry doth yet raigne,
> set out the ymages of their holy women, as very brothels, strompets and
> whores?
>
> —John Veron, *A stronge battery against the*
> *idolatrous invocation of the dead Saintes*

"So sweet was ne'er so fatal"

When Othello enters the room where Desdemona sleeps,
intent on killing the woman he has loved as his "soul's
joy," he marvels at her beauty.[1] Likening her body to a
well-made statue, he admires it as one might a magnificent work of art:
her skin, he observes, is "as smooth as monumental alabaster"; she,
the "cunning'st pattern of excelling nature." The awe that Othello
feels when he looks at Desdemona, however, only intensifies his resolve
to kill her, for her beauty, so exquisite that "the sense aches at" the
sight of her, reinforces his conviction that she is "a strumpet" and
"whore." Imagining the murder he is about to commit as a sacrifice,
he feels compelled to kill the woman he loves so intensely because he
is convinced her beauty is a danger to the community: "Yet she must
die, else she'll betray more men," he laments, "So sweet was ne'er so
fatal" (5.2.6, 20).

For those of us in Shakespeare's audience who gaze in horror at

---

[1] All citations of *Othello* refer to Shakespeare, *The Complete Plays*, ed. Alfred Harbage
(1969); the scene discussed here is 5.2.

Othello as he gazes in murderous wonder at his sleeping wife, this scene is excruciating, for it simultaneously arouses and thwarts erotic desire, displays and destroys the female body, idealizes and demeans a woman character. Othello, we feel with Emilia, "hath so bewhored" the woman he has loved—by his own admission "not wisely, but too well"—that "true hearts cannot bear." From our privileged perspective, we have watched Iago manipulate what Othello sees, including, especially, the handkerchief that the Moor misinterprets as the "ocular proof" of Desdemona's adultery. Now, looking into the most private of places, the marriage bed, positioned in a sense as voyeurs, we witness a murderer who longs to embrace his victim, a killing that is prefaced with a kiss, a death that originates in desire.

Why, we might well ask, is Othello so quick to assume that his lovely wife is an adulterous whore, her beauty too dangerous and threatening to tolerate? How can he possibly construct his violent act—surely a crime of passion—as a deliberate, honorable, and necessary sacrifice based on "just grounds"? How are we to understand his objectification of Desdemona when he vows not to "scar" the beautiful body he is prepared to kill; how to interpret his perverse fantasy that he might preserve and go on loving this body after the woman herself is dead? And how does this scene, so attentive to Othello's erotic gaze, and later to the powerful and disturbing sight of Desdemona's smothered body, "pale as [her] smock," engage our own seeing?

Answers to such questions have traditionally been sought within the dramatic text itself or in psychoanalytic theory rather than in the culture that produced and consumed the stage plays of Tudor and Stuart London.[2] Recently feminist and new historicist critics have begun as well to examine Shakespeare's play in the context of seventeenth-century discursive practices and sociocultural issues. Their readings of *Othello* have tended to focus on the social, legal, and economic status of women in the early modern era, on the relation of race to gender, and on the enduring conventions of a misogynist tradition that the Renaissance inherited from classical and medieval Christian cultures.[3]

---

[2] See, for example, James Calderwood, "Appealing Property in *Othello*" (1988); Peter Erickson, *Patriarchal Structures in Shakespeare's Drama* (1984); Arthur Kirsch, *Shakespeare and the Experience of Love* (1980); Richard Wheeler, "Since First We Were Discovered" (1980).

[3] See Catherine Belsey, *The Subject of Tragedy* (1985); Stephen Greenblatt, *Renaissance Self-Fashioning* (1980); Karen Newman, *Fashioning Femininity and English Renaissance Drama*

I wish to locate the misogyny of *Othello* and other Stuart tragedies about love and marriage in the historical moment of the Protestant Reformation. This chapter addresses what textual, psychoanalytical, and most historicist and feminist critics tend to ignore: the religious dimension of erotic love and the erotic dimension of religion in the seventeenth century. The violence against beautiful and beloved women that is repeatedly enacted in these tragedies may in fact be informed by the iconoclastic violence against beautiful and beloved images that was such a significant, and disruptive, dimension of the English Reformation.

Bewhored Images

In their rhetorical and physical attacks on the sacred images of the Roman Catholic Church, Protestant iconoclasts manifest a keenly felt and deeply troubling ambivalence toward the beautiful. Distressed by what they perceive to be a pervasive, indeed almost universal iconophilia among the devout, Protestant reformers and reform-minded Roman Catholics alike express concern because so many lay worshipers treat images "as if they were alive; that people should bow their heads, fall on the ground, or crawl on their knees before them; and that worshippers should kiss or fondle the carvings."[4] However critical they are of such devotion, many of the reformers who advocate the removal and even the violent destruction of sacred art cite their own deep attachment to images as a justification for iconoclasm. Admitting "how firmly and deeply images are rooted in my heart," the German reformer Karlstadt, for example, urges their immediate destruction because images exert such a powerful hold over him.[5] For many early Protestants, images are "snares and traps," dangerous precisely because they are inherently so alluring and appealing.[6]

Although they renounce sacred images and attempt to disrupt their powerful appeal, the reformers thus reveal, in the very metaphors they

---

(1991); Mary Beth Rose, *"The Expense of Spirit": Love and Sexuality in English Renaissance Drama* (1988); Peter Stallybrass, "Patriarchal Territories" (1986); and Valerie Wayne, "Historical Differences" (1991).

[4] Erasmus, paraphrased by Carl C. Christensen, *Art and Reformation in Germany* (1979), p. 22; see also John Foxe, *A&M* 6:29; Charles Garside, *Zwingli and the Arts* (1966), p. 134.

[5] Qtd. in Margaret Miles, *Image as Insight* (1985), p. 108; see also Foxe, *A&M*, 6:29.

[6] Nicholas Ridley, "A Treatise . . . Concerning Images" (1843), 39:86.

choose, their own intensely felt attraction to them. Images are "in-chantments" which the Roman Church, another "Circe," uses to "in-toxicate the earth, that the inhabitants *are drunken with the wine of her fornication.*" Ecclesiastical ornaments are dangerous because of the "sweetness of [their] deceit." The devout are "ravish[ed]" when they gaze upon images. Seduced by their beauty and "bewitched" by their promise of magical powers, people "pant after" images, finding them-selves powerless to resist their allure. Wary of the "outward glittering bewtie" of the Church of Rome, "guilded with gold and precious stones and pearles," Protestant polemics warn that "the abundance of her pleasures" beguiles the unsuspecting layperson.[7] Fearing the power of images to intoxicate and bewitch, many iconoclasts repudiate what threatens to enthrall them. Their urgent sense that the beautiful must be eradicated because it cannot be resisted manifests an intensified, not a diminished, pleasure in the visible and beautiful, a pleasure too seductive to be either contained, as in medieval asceticism, or tran-scended, as in medieval mysticism.

In their efforts to disrupt popular devotional practices that centered on sacred images, the reformers thus associate the devotional gaze with the erotic gaze, and they liken sacred images to the sexualized woman who, although beautiful, is dangerously seductive. Many of these images were idealized representations of holy women, and they especially are singled out. Protestant polemicists rage against representations of the Virgin Mary, Mary Magdalene, and the female saints because, they as-sert, such images portray the female body in such a way as to arouse carnal desire.

If they borrow from Italian Renaissance art theory a well-known and widely used trope in which "the portrayal of a beautiful woman" serves "as a synecdoche for the beauty of painting itself," the polemicists undermine rather than enhance the appeal of art by arousing misog-ynist hostility toward feminine beauty.[8] Woman in their construction is

---

[7] Henry Ainsworth, *An Arrow Against Idolatrie* (1624), pp. 113, 33; John Calvin, *Institutes of the Christian Religion*, 1.11.1; an English visitor to a Jesuit Church in 1620, qtd. in Miles, *Image as Insight* , p. 109; Henry Ainsworth and Francis Johnson, *An Apologie or Defense of . . . Brownists* (1604), sig. iv^v.

[8] Elizabeth Cropper, "The Beauty of Woman" (1986), p. 176; see also Frances E. Dolan, "Taking the Pencil Out of God's Hand" (1993); Shirley Nelson Garner, " 'Let Her Paint an Inch Thick' " (1989); Jacqueline Lichtenstein, "Making Up Representa-tions" (1987).

not natural but artful and artificial: she is painted, ornamented, adorned; her beauty glistens and glitters; and her attractiveness, calculated for its rhetorical effect, is a terrible kind of cunning, something to be feared.

Invoking scriptural passages that declare images whores (e.g., Wisdom 14:11), the Protestant reformers thus attempt to incite iconophobia through appeals to gynophobia. Images of saints are "examples of the most abandoned lust and obscenity," complains Calvin, who notes "how wickedly and indecently the greater part of them have been fashioned, how licentiously the painters and sculptors have played the wanton here."[9] Similarly, "an image with a nice and wanton apparell and countenance," a sixteenth-century Anglican homily asserts, is "more like to *Venus* or *Flora*, then Mary Magdalen, or if like to Mary Magadalen, it is when she played the harlot, rather then when shee wept for her sinnes."[10] Asserting that "A painted . . . Image" is nothing more than "a wanton harlot," "a strumpet with a painted face," the reformers denounce images because they "bring in a certaine whorish bravery into the service of God: the worship wherof they make to be Carnal."[11] Iconoclastic discourse transforms the most sacred images of the Roman Catholic Church—and most especially the revered and adored images of the Virgin Mary—into harlots whose betrayal is inevitable and whose allure is fatal.

Fearful that images draw the devout away from a god who they insist is invisible, Protestants—to borrow Shakespeare's term—"bewhore" images. They play upon widespread fears of female promiscuity and infidelity in order to foster doubt, arouse contempt, and elicit disgust toward images in the very people who had most passionately loved them. Although they tend to focus on sacred images of holy women, the reformers thus systematically assign all sacred images—including images of Christ's body and the cross—a female gender. Invoking a symbolic order that aligns the masculine with the spirit, the feminine with the body, they identify all images with women and therefore denounce them because they are of the flesh and not the spirit. In their repudiation of a late medieval incarnational theology that focused on

[9] Calvin, *Institutes* 1.11.7; 1.11.12.

[10] "An Homily Against perill of Idolatrie and superfluous decking of Churches in the time of Queen Elizabeth I" (1623), p. 72.

[11] "Homily," p. 61; Robert Parker, *A scholasticall discourse* (1607), sig. X3ᵛ.

the body of Christ and even feminized that holy body, the reformers assert that the image seduces and deceives, drawing believers away from an invisible God rather than giving access to the divine.[12]

To substantiate their claims that devotion to images is carnal rather than spiritual, they cite Scripture. John Knewstub, for instance, reminds his English readers that Isaiah associates images with the polluted (menstruating) female body, and he repeats Isaiah's call to "cast" the offending images "away as a menstruous cloth," with the words of repudiation: " 'Get thee hence.' "[13] Other reformers cite as their authority biblical texts from Hosea, Wisdom, Romans, and Revelation to convince their readers that the devotional gaze is a manifestation of sexual desire, rather than of godliness. "As the looking upon an harlot will infest one with bodily uncleannesse," John Dod warns, "so also the looking upon an Idoll will pollute an ignorant and blind heart with Idolatry, and bring it to confusion."[14] Even as they seek to arouse distrust of images by provoking disgust and fear of sexual women, however, the reformers attribute to images an enormous amount of power: as glittering whores and wanton women, images arouse passion, promise pleasure, offer sanctuary, and lure the devout away from God.

The Protestant iconoclasts thus do not indifferently rid themselves of meaningless and trivial objects; they seek to destroy what they fear they cannot resist, what they experience as seductive and powerful. To counter the seductive power of images, they justify the removal and even the violent destruction of sacred images by comparing iconoclasm to legitimate civic actions undertaken to control prostitution, actions that are deemed necessary in order to purify and maintain the community. Like the secular authorities who drive out whores, the iconoclasts see themselves as ridding their community of what is filthy, polluting, and offensive. "As good magistrates, who intend to banish all whoredom, do drive away all naughty persons, especially out of such places as be suspected," writes the English reformer Nicholas Ridley, "even so images, being 'Meretrices,' *id est,* 'Whores'—for that the worshipping of them is called in the prophets fornication and adultery—

---

[12] For discussions of the incarnational focus of late medieval piety, including the role of the feminine in popular piety, see Carolyn Walker Bynum, *Holy Feast and Holy Fast* (1987) and *Jesus as Mother* (1982); Gail Gibson, *The Theater of Devotion* (1989).

[13] Isaiah 30:22, cited in Knewstub, *Lectures of John Knewstub* (1577), sig. C5^r.

[14] John Dod and Richard Cleaver, *A Plaine and Familiar Exposition of the Ten Commandments* (1606), sig. G3^r.

ought to be banished."[15] Counter to the view of many modern scholars who see iconoclasts as frenzied and irrational, motivated by hatred or economic grievances, Ridley imagines them as sober governors, "good magistrates" intent on upholding the divine law that forbids idolatry, that spiritual whoredom of the heart.[16]

How typical is Ridley's view that iconoclasm is a just and necessary act of purification? What does his trope of the whore reveal about the symbolic dimension of acts of violence against images? What ritual function did iconoclasm serve?[17] The evidence suggests that Protestant iconoclasm often took the form of a symbolic or ritual killing. Iconoclasts almost never looted the images for material gain, instead preferring to deface or desecrate them in certain highly symbolic ways, gouging out their eyes, for instance, or piercing their sides.[18] They decapitate, dismember, torture, disfigure, and even crucify the offending images.[19] Because they have constructed those images as seductive women, they symbolically kill women they believe are polluted in ritual acts of purification.

Although the reformers frequently accuse Roman Catholics of believing that images "live and breathe," they thus act out just such a belief, finding it necessary to "kill" what threatens to seduce them. And although they ridicule Roman Catholics for mourning the destruction of their beloved images as if living beings had been, quite literally, murdered or martyred, they nevertheless repeatedly, perhaps obsessively, pronounce images "dead and insensible" things, "dead stocks

---

[15] Ridley, "Treatise Concerning Images," 39:87; see also Foxe, *A&M*, 8:166, 500, 648, 702–3; Parker, *Scholasticall discourse*, sig. F3ʳ·ᵛ.

[16] This argument corroborates the thesis of Natalie Zemon Davis, who considers the issue of religious violence in sixteenth-century France in *Society and Culture in Early Modern France* (1975), pp. 152–87.

[17] Davis, *Society and Culture*, p. 170.

[18] Phyllis Mack Crew writes that "it was more satisfying to urinate in the Communion wine-cup than to pawn it," *Calvinist Preaching and Iconoclasm* (1978), p. 26.

[19] See, for example, John Phillips, *The Reformation of Images* (1973), p. 90, who describes an image with "one eye bored out and the side pierced"; John Stowe, *Survey of London* (1908), pp. 266–67, who describes an act of iconoclasm carried out on December 24, 1600, against the cross in West Cheape in which "the Image of our Lady was again defaced, by plucking off her crowne, and almost her head, taking from her her naked child, & stabbing her in the breast." David Freedberg writes in *Iconoclasts and Their Motives* (1985), p. 35, that "we fear the image which appears to be alive, because it cannot be so; and so people may evince their fear, or demonstrate mastery over the consequences of elision, by breaking or mutilating the image."

and stones," "mute, dumb, blind, and dead."[20] In their rhetorical as well as their literal acts, then, the iconoclasts symbolically "kill" images. Inasmuch as they had formerly attached themselves to images, gazing upon them, "kiss[ing] and fondl[ing]" them, projecting their desires onto them, the iconoclasts may enact in shocking ways the reformers' call to "root" and "tear" images out of their hearts, sacrificing what they love in order to purify the community and themselves.[21]

For the iconoclasts, sacred images may well function like those "symbolic devices" Kenneth Burke identifies in his discussion of the symbolic act he calls "dying dialectically." By means of such devices, Burke argues, "a man can 'substantially' slay himself through the sacrifice of another who is cosubstantial with him," and thus effect a transformation.[22] If iconoclastic violence is sacrificial—if the iconoclasts kill what they love—it may represent a symbolic attempt to transcend the physical, to escape the body by smashing clay and stone. By "killing" (female) images and pronouncing them dead, the iconoclasts may be attempting to liberate themselves from all that the image has come to represent for them: the fallen world and its illusory surfaces, the sinful body and its dangerous desires, the corrupt imagination and its falsifying fantasies. Implicit in iconoclastic acts, I would therefore suggest, is a profound recognition of the world's luminous beauty, the body's sensual pleasures, the imagination's splendid creations: the iconoclasts fear what they love, destroy what they desire. Read as symbolic action, iconoclastic violence may paradoxically express the depth of attachment its perpetrators feel toward the beautiful and imaginary. Their rage as they smash statues and deface painted images surely derives from the intensity of their original desire for these sacred images, a desire their religion requires them to repress.

[20] For examples of accusations that papists believed images were alive, see Calvin, *Institutes* 1.11.13; John Veron, *A stronge battery against the idolatrous invocation of the dead Saints* (1562), sig. Oviii^v–Pi^r. For assertions that papists treated images that were destroyed by iconoclasts as martyrs, see Foxe, *A&M*, who quotes the Lord Protector during the reign of Edward IV as complaining, "Let one image . . . be burnt or abolished, by and by some men are in an exceeding rage, as though not a stock or a stone, but a true saint of flesh and blood should be cast into the fire" (6:29). I quote from "Homily," p. 49; John Calvin, *A very profitable treatise* (1561), sig. A5^v; Phillips, *Reformation of Images*, p. 86; see also Foxe, *A&M*, 4:175; 7:108; 8:143, 340–41.

[21] Quoted in Miles, *Image as Insight*, pp. 99, 112.

[22] Kenneth Burke, *A Rhetoric of Motives* (1950), p. 266.

Imagined Whores

I have shown how the reformers incite fear of sacred images by invoking the figure of the seductive, sexualized woman. In their polemics against idolatry, they also tend to collapse images of adoration—figured as seductive women—with women themselves. In doing so, they arouse in men a fear of women, particularly the eroticized women of male desire. Such women, they warn, are potential idols who lure men from God. Protestant polemics thus appeal to Christian culture's deeply ingrained suspicion of women in order to instill a fear of images and, simultaneously, to the newly aroused fear of images to reinforce and intensify a suspicion of women.

Actual women are identified as potential idols because the reformers teach that whatever entices the eyes, beguiles or enchants the mind, fires the imagination, or captivates the heart is idolatrous, and according to Renaissance theories of eros, women do all these things. The neoplatonic theory of phantasmic infection, for instance, grants to the beloved—particularly the beautiful female beloved—an extraordinary power over her lover, for when he gazes upon her, her image enters through his eye and in a sense possesses him, driving him to "reestablish contact with the object that was converted into the obsessing phantasm: the woman."[23] Whereas neoplatonic philosophers and Petrarchan sonneteers, among others, nurture the perceived relation between woman and image and between eros and imagination, linking desire with sight, poetic inspiration with female beauty, and magic with the artful manipulation of images, the Protestant reformers use these very associations to arouse suspicion of art, women, and erotic phantasms—those interior images of the beloved that so charm, captivate, and obsess the lover.

The distrust of eros evident in the Protestant attacks on images is magnified in England by an increasing attention to the "inner" idols of the mind and heart. By the beginning of the seventeenth century, the iconoclastic project of many English reformers targets not only ecclesiastical images but any person, object, or thought upon which man "setteth his whole felicitie."[24] English Calvinists warn especially of the danger of "erect[ing] unto themselves Idols within their own hearts,

---

[23] Ioan Couliano, *Eros and Magic in the Renaissance* (1987), p. 21; see also pp. 29–31.

[24] John Calvin, *The Sermons of M. John Calvin upon the Epistle of S. Paule too the Ephesians* (1577), fol. 246ᵛ; see also Margaret Aston, *England's Iconoclasts*, 1:458–60.

and commit[ting] a most secret and spirituall idolatrie, which the world cannot discerne."[25] Arousing fears of an idolatry of the heart, they urge the faithful to practice a kind of inner iconoclasm. "Everyone was therefore under the obligation to deal with his own imagery," Margaret Aston explains, "to act the iconoclast on the idol-processes of his mind. It was not enough to turn away from the objects made by cunning craftsmen set up in popish places. The destroying must burn within, in the 'house' of the imagination."[26]

When the English reformers insist that "it is not sufficient that we cast off the worship and service of the Idols and Images of stone, wood, and painting, which are without us: but that wee must also quite discharge the Idols which are within us," they identify as inner idols any loved one who is so passionately loved and cherished that she displaces God in the heart of the lover.[27] In fact, because "man is the living image of God, made by the very hand of God: and in this respect a thousand fold more excellent than all Images made by the hand of man," William Perkins warns that people are even more inclined to misplace the devotion due to God onto a fellow human being—a lover or a spouse or a child—than a sacred image. He therefore emphasizes that excessive love of a human being is idolatry: "Now if any meere man shal be worshipped with any worship that is more then politicke or civill, he is made more then a man, and by this meanes he is transformed into an Idol."[28] So fearful of this possibility are some radical Protestants that they even object to the traditional marital vows of the English Church in which the wife promises to "worship" her husband, claiming that these words turn marital love into idolatry.[29] Although such a position may seem extreme, it illustrates the very real concern of early Protestants that passionate love, even of one's spouse, may be idolatrous because humans are so prone to "setting the heart inordinately upon any creature, by fearing, loving, trusting in it, more than in God, and above him."[30]

[25] William Perkins, *A Warning Against the idolatry of the last times* (1601), p. 5.

[26] Aston, *England's Iconoclasts*, 1:460.

[27] Abraham Scultetus, *A Short Information, but agreeable unto Scripture: of Idol-Images* (1620), sig. D3ᵛ; William Bradshaw explains that anything that a man "giveth . . . interne confidence which is due unto God . . . is truely called his Idoll," *A Short Treatise, of the Crosse in baptism* (1604), p. 11.

[28] Perkins, *Warning*, pp. 46, 31.

[29] Aston quotes John Reynolds, who argues that the use of the word *worship* "make[s] the new married man . . . an idol of his wife" (*England's Iconoclasts*, 1:467).

[30] Thomas Wilson, *Christian Dictionarie* (1612), taken from his definition of idolatry;

Early modern writers who embrace Protestantism frequently dramatize the dire consequences of loving "not wisely but too well." Narratives like *Paradise Lost*, which explores the idolatrous potential of Adam's love for Eve, manifest a pronounced ambivalence toward the beautiful female beloved, an ambivalence that we can better understand if we recognize how the eroticized woman not only figures the religious idol in reform culture, but is herself considered a potential idol, her beauty a temptation so great she imperils the soul of her lover. A Protestant-induced anxiety that the passionate love of a beautiful women may be a form of idolatry pervades the love tragedies of Shakespeare, Middleton, Webster, and Ford, tragedies that dramatize the powerful allure of beauty, the disruptive energy of eros, and the tragic fallibility of the imagination.[31] The tragedies I discuss here all focus on marital, familial, and sexual relationships and dramatize the conflicts of private life: adultery, sexual jealousy, passionate desire. In contrast to the domestic tragedies set in England, however, all are set in Roman Catholic countries (*The Changeling* in Spain, the others in Italy) and all exploit English fears of—and fascination with—the Roman Catholic other.[32]

The romantic protagonists in these tragedies describe the women they desire in the language of religious devotion, many pronouncing their beloveds "divine."[33] Desdemona appears to Othello as "a young and rose-lipped cherubin." Bianca in *Women Beware Women* seems a "Saint" to her husband, who likens his love for her to "a Religion." Annabella is a woman whose beauty, according to her adoring and incestuous brother, "if framed anew, the gods / Would make a god of, if they had it there, / And kneel to it, as I do kneel to them" (*'Tis Pity*

---

see also John Dod and Richard Cleaver, who caution that idols are "creatures that God hath made for our use, whereunto men through his folly so tyeth himself, and is so snared with one affection or other of them, that the Lord is . . . thrust out of place," *Exposition of the Ten Commandments*, sigs. B8ᵛ–Cʳ.

[31] Citations to the plays I discuss below are to the following editions: John Ford, *'Tis Pity She's a Whore*, in *Drama of the English Renaissance*, ed. Russell A. Fraser and Norman Rabkin (1976); Thomas Middleton and William Rowley, *The Changeling*, ed. George Walton Williams (1966); Thomas Middleton, *Women Beware Women*, ed. Charles Barber (1969); John Webster, *The Duchess of Malfi*, ed. John Russell Brown (1964); Webster, *The White Devil*, ed. John Russell Brown (1960).

[32] For a discussion of domestic tragedy and Othello see Lena Cowen Orlin, *Private Matters and Public Culture in Post-Reformation England* (1994), pp. 246–52.

[33] See, for example, *The Changeling* 1.1.1–12; *The Duchess of Malfi* 1.1.199; *'Tis Pity She's a Whore* 2.5.36.

She's a Whore 1.1.21–23). Although the male lovers use what is a commonplace image, their adoration of women they call divine, angelic, and saintly is literalized and made hyperbolic: they do not seem to figure their beloveds as gods so much as literally to substitute them for God. Rather than functioning to celebrate the desirability of the beloved, the imagery of angels and saints thus constructs erotic passion as a kind of idolatry that endangers the very soul of the lover. The perceived danger inherent in such adoration is an explicit concern of the playwrights: Desdemona, Beatrice-Joanna, Bianca, and Annabella all die violent deaths, either betrayed by or the betrayers of the men who love them "not wisely, but too well."

The instability of the erotic relationships in the Stuart love tragedies can surely be attributed in part to early Protestant culture's anxiety that erotic love may be idolatrous, putting the lover's soul at risk. Iago recognizes this risk and exploits this cultural fear. When he claims that Othello's "soul" is "enfettered" to Desdemona's love so completely that the Moor would "renounce his baptism. / All seals and symbols of redeemed sin" rather than deny her, and when he accuses Othello of allowing "her appetite" to "play the god / With his weak function" (2.3.330–31), he implies that Othello idolizes his wife. Othello may be especially vulnerable to Iago's insinuations because, as a converted Christian who once believed in a "pagan" god, his capacity to sustain faith in the "one" God may be in doubt. He himself fears his love is idolatrous. "I fear / My soul hath her content so absolute," he confesses, "That not another comfort like to this / Succeeds in unknown fate." Anxious about the intensity of his feelings, he chides himself, saying, "I dote, / In mine own comforts" (2.1.188–91, 204–5).[34]

If his fear undermines Othello's trust in the woman he loves, arousing unfounded suspicions of her, it also provides an explanatory key to the destructive love affairs in many later love tragedies. In *The Changeling* Alsemero notes that he had made Beatrice-Joanna his "absolute

[34] Others have suggested that the love between Othello and Desdemona is a form of idolatry. In a brief footnote in his *Tragedy of Othello* (1941), George Kittredge suggests that Desdemona alludes "to the idea that to idolize a mortal is a sin against God" when she says "They are loves I bear to you." R. N. Hallstead argues in "Idolatrous Love" (1968) that Othello's love for Desdemona is a form of idolatry, but he makes no attempt to locate his argument in the Reformation or its iconoclastic impulse. Arthur Kirsch contests Hallstead's thesis in "The Polarization of Erotic Love in *Othello*" (1978). Shakespeare, of course, frequently explores this cultural fear, writing in sonnet 105, for example, "Let not my love be called idolatry / Nor my beloved as an idol show."

treasure", and recalls with deep regret his first sight of her in "the temple / Where blood and beauty first unlawfully / Fir'd their devotion and quench'd the right one" (5.3.74–76). In *Women Beware Women* Leantio revises his opinion of his wife, Bianca, denouncing the woman he had once called his saint as a "Court-Saint" who consorts with a "Devil," and he threatens "to play a hot religious bout" with her. And in *'Tis Pity She's A Whore* Giovanni readily admits that he worships his sister but refuses to relinquish the woman the Friar describes as "this idol thou adore'st," while Soranzo confesses to Annabella that "in my heart / I did too superstitiously adore thee" (4.3.121–22). Erotic passion, originating as it does in the eye, is explicitly identified as an impediment to faith in many of these plays: "our very eyes / Are far more poysonous to Religion," laments Isabella to her incestuous lover, "Then Basilisks to them" (*Women Beware Women* 4.2.147–49).

If the Stuart love tragedies address reform culture's fears that the beautiful woman has the power to displace God in a man's affections, they also address, and in some cases even arouse, Protestant iconophobia.[35] In *Women Beware Women*, for example, Thomas Middleton insists on the relation between looking and lust and between idolatry and adultery, a relation that the reformers repeatedly sought to establish. He combines a chilling portrayal of the destructive male passions unleashed by the beauty of Bianca with a sinister depiction of Bianca's seduction by means of erotic art.

In this play the Duke falls "in a rapture" upon spying Bianca at her window, and he immediately seeks to lure "this absolute Creature"— who has been "Cas'd up from all men's eyes" by her adoring but possessive husband—to his palace. Overcome by Bianca's beauty, he relies on visual images to turn this virtuous woman into an adulterous whore. His pander arranges to have Bianca tour a gallery of erotic paintings, where he "prepare[s] her stomach by degrees / To *Cupids* feast" by showing her "naked pictures . . . to stay the appetite" (2.2.471–74). Marveling that "mine eye nev'r met with fairer Ornaments" (2.2.361), Bianca is enticed by the promise that she will be shown "the Monument too, and that's a thing / Every one sees not" (2.2.318–19). She finds herself suddenly alone with the lecherous Duke, who alternately at-

---

[35] For discussions of the relation between idolatry and adultery, see Scultetus, *Short Information*, sig. C2ʳ, and the commentary on the book of Hosea in *The Geneva Bible* (1560), chaps. 1–3.

tempts to seduce her and threatens to rape her. Although she protests and resists, vainly trying to fend off the Duke by invoking "Religion," Bianca cannot escape his advances (or, presumably, resist the lure of his erotic pictures). Having submitted to him, she joins in the courtiers' licentious double entendre, telling her mother-in-law that she has seen "the Monument and all . . . Faith, I have seen that I little thought to see" (2.2.527–32).

Although he clearly depicts Bianca as a victim of male lust and aristocratic power, Middleton nevertheless locates the source of the Duke's illicit passion in her beauty, a beauty described as a "wonder" powerful enough "to draw a State from serious business" (2.2.18). In his play Bianca's beauty is repeatedly aestheticized and deified, compared, for instance, to "such as bless the faces / Of figures that are drawn for Goddesses, / And makes Art proud to look upon her work" (2.2.400–402). Identifying the beautiful woman with the exquisite work of art, Middleton shows how the eroticized woman and the erotic image are dangerously seductive. In his play women serve as a stimulus for idolatry, and images as a stimulus for adultery.

The tendency to blur the distinction between woman and image, idolatry and adultery, is evident in other love tragedies of the Stuart period. In them the female beloveds are repeatedly figured as objects of art—painted images, carved statues, elaborate temples, ornamented shrines—their bodies identified with the materials of the artist—alabaster, marble, chrysolite, crystal. The metaphors of art, however, are contaminated by a dread of the artful and artificial that is everywhere present in the plays as well as in the culture. A woman's "beautifi'd body," for instance, is compared in *Women Beware Women* to a "goodly Temple" not because it is holy but because it is both outwardly dazzling and inwardly corrupt, "built on Vaults where Carkasses lie rotting." The analogy serves to reinforce a disciplined repression of male desire: because he recognizes the similarity between a woman's beautiful body and a rotting Temple, Leantio finds himself able to repress his sexual appetite: "And so by little and little I shrink back again, / And quench desire with a cool Meditation" (3.1.98–104).

The connection between women and art that these tragedies establish thus undermines the credibility of the female beloved. Because her extraordinary beauty reminds her lover of a finely wrought statue, she is perceived as "cunning." In both the fictional world of the play and the actual world of the original audience, however, *cunning* connotes

the kind of deceptive, dangerous, and fraudulent artifice that the reformers condemn and attempt to eradicate.[36] Such beauty inspires misogynist tirades against cosmetics or "painting" and against what is
perceived to be the inherent theatricality of women.[37] It may therefore
be because Othello considers Desdemona a perfect work of art that he
doubts the sincerity of her protestations of innocence, dismissing her
weeping as mere artifice, a "well-painted passion." It is, I suggest, the
identification of women and art—present in Renaissance culture but
greatly problematized by a Calvinist distrust of the imagination—that
fuels the anxiety about erotic desire in the years after the Reformation.

At the heart of this anxiety is the reformers' radical disruption of the
Roman Catholic categories of virgin and whore, and the Protestant-
induced fear that the virgin is a whore. When they condemn the beloved images of medieval popular piety, the iconoclasts call attention
to the erotic dimension of late medieval sacred art, sexualizing the
Virgin Mary and the chaste female saints. "I often had base thoughts
when I looked at the female images on the altars," confesses a peasant
in a sixteenth-century Lutheran dialogue. "For no courtesan can dress
or adorn herself more sumptuously and shamelessly than they nowa-
days fashion the Mother of God, Saint Barbara, Katherine and other
saints."[38] In such attacks on images the reformers transform one of the
most powerful and beloved images of the Middle Ages—the idealized,
holy woman—into a whore. Might not Othello's denunciation of "the
divine Desdemona" as "that cunning whore of Venice" rehearse this
same terrible transformation?

I have shown how the most venerated images of the Roman Church
undergo a radical reevaluation during the Reformation, their holiness
recast as "filthines," their beauty reappraised as mere trumpery, "all
shining and glittering," and their power reinterpreted as the seduction

---

[36] For example, see *Othello* 5.2.11; Middleton and Rowley, *The Changeling* 4.2.138,
5.3.47; Webster, *White Devil* 3.2.124. The OED records how, in the sixteenth and seventeenth centuries, the word *cunning* came to have the negative connotation of "crafty,
artful, guileful" that it retains today; its original meaning of "learned, skillful" was positive.

[37] See, for example, Webster, *The Duchess of Malfi* 2.1.1–62. For an interesting discussion of the connection between women and theater, see Timothy Murray, "*Othello*, An
Index and Obscure Prologue to the History of Foul Generic Thoughts" (1988), pp. 213–
43.

[38] Qtd. in Michael Baxandall, *The Limewood Sculptors of Renaissance Germany* (1980), p.
88.

of a "grosse or dirtie harlot"[39] The female characters in the love tragedies undergo an equally radical reassessment of their value. Although
they had initially inspired intense devotion in their male admirers, they
are ultimately denounced as "glorious dangerous Strumpet[s] / Spar-
kling in Beauty and Destruction too" (*Women Beware Women* 3.1.98–99).
Their beauty, earlier praised as holy, blessed, saintly, divine, and chaste,
is ultimately declared to be duplicitous, superficial, untrustworthy, and
dangerous. "Here's beauty chang'd / To ugly whoredom," Alsemero
laments after renaming his wife "a whore" (*The Changeling* 5.3.198–
199). Leantio likewise reevaluates the woman he had called his "Saint"
and proclaims his "matchless Jewel" to be instead "that glistring
Whore, shines like a Serpent" (*Women Beware Women* 4.2.21).

The very categories of virgin and whore are openly interrogated in
the love tragedies. Through the use of dramatic irony, audiences observe how easily characters can confuse the two. When, for example,
Othello hears Cassio tell Iago about his amorous relationship with the
whore Bianca, the Moor erroneously assumes that Cassio is speaking
about Desdemona, and thus mentally substitutes his chaste wife for the
prostitute. In *The Changeling*, a suspicious Alsemero resorts to a virginity
test to ascertain whether his new wife is a virgin, but Beatrice-Joanna
cunningly imitates the physiological reactions of the virgin she is not,
and then substitutes her virgin maid for herself on her wedding night
to cover up her ruse.

The easy interchangeability of the virgin and the whore indicate just
how unstable these constructions are in a culture traumatized by the
reformers' revelations that the beloved images of the holy virgin and
the virgin saints are nothing more than whores. Alsemero's anguish
when he discovers that his beloved is unfaithful prompts a question
that haunts not only the love tragedies but seventeenth-century Protestant culture as well: "Oh, cunning devils! / How should blind men
know you from fair-fac'd saints?" (*The Changeling* 5.3.109–10). Alsemero's bewilderment, I suggest, expresses a larger, cultural confusion
in the face of an epistemological crisis originating in the Protestant
Reformation. When the reformers declare virgins whores, saints devils,
sacred images seductresses, and beloved women idols, they call into
question the assumed relations between the spiritual and the erotic,

[39] Parker, *Scholasticall discourse*, sig. N4ᵛ; "Homily," p. 72; Parker, *Scholasticall discourse*,
N4ᵛ.

the holy and the demonic, the divine and the feminine, the cherished and the idolatrous.

Killing the Beloved (Woman/Image/Theater)

Although historians of the Reformation frequently refer to Protestantism's "masculinization of piety," literary scholars have, to my knowledge, not examined the way the reformers' successful suppression of the "richly symbolic feminine aspects" of the Roman Catholic religion, "represented by the Virgin Mary as 'Mother of God,' and by other female saints," might inform the presentation of women—and especially the killing of women—on the stages of early modern London.[40] And yet the Stuart love tragedies could be said to participate in Protestant culture's suppression of the feminine. Their display of beautiful women repeatedly ends in violence against the female beloved that its perpetrators justify as necessary to purify their society. Desdemona, Beatrice-Joanna, Bianca, Vittoria, Annabella: all are eroticized and aestheticized, proclaimed to be whores, and renounced or killed by male lovers who believe them to be too powerful to control, too bewitching to resist, and too promiscuous to tolerate.

Inasmuch as the male lovers rage against what they desire and kill what they love, they resemble the Protestant iconoclasts who "bewhore" and "kill" sacred images they had once adored. Their actions, represented on the stages of the Stuart theaters, may rehearse the trauma of iconoclasm and reflect upon the losses incurred when the cherished female images of popular medieval piety were systematically removed from the churches and destroyed. If the iconoclastic impulses of early Protestantism are in fact played out on the body of the beautiful female beloved, the violence perpetrated against women in the love tragedies may thus enact on a symbolic level the kind of radical, inner purification that the reformers call for when they urge believers to tear images out of their hearts.[41] In the course of each of these plays, the-

---

[40] Eire, *War against the Idols* (1986), p. 315.

[41] See Miles, *Image as Insight*, p. 112, *England's Iconoclasts*, 1: 460, who quotes Luther: "I seek to tear [images] out of the hearts of all and want them despised and destroyed." See also Aston, who quotes a Puritan definition of reformation as a kind of killing. Leonard Tennenhouse, "Violence Done to Women on the Renaissance Stage" (1989), offers a different thesis. He argues that violence against the aristocratic woman in Jacobean

atrical images of eroticized women are displayed, demystified, and destroyed, their power to enchant exhausted, their capacity to enthrall contained.

But if these tragedies seek to master the very eroticized images they display, they also self-reflexively explore their own idolatrous potential. Because they manifest the same theatricality, spectacle, and artifice as the female characters they bewhore—and exhibit the same seductive power—they are implicated in the very problem of idolatry they examine.[42] In the remaining portion of this chapter I argue that the theatrical representation of violence against beautiful women is an antitheatrical gesture, one that may even anticipate and prepare the way for the closing of the theaters in 1642.

I have shown in Chapter 3 how the antitheatrical tracts written in the late sixteenth and early seventeenth century echo the reformers' attacks on images and the imagination and even condemn the stage as a form of idolatry. Repeatedly identifying stage plays with the idolatrous pagan and Roman Catholic cultures, they declare any supporter of the stage to be an "accessary to idolatry" and condemn playwrights as "open professors of Idolatrie."[43] And they are especially concerned about the power of the theater's "wicked spectacles," complaining that they pull their spectators "from discipline, to libertie; from vertue, to pleasure; from God, to Mammon."[44]

Despite the often-expressed Protestant anxieties about the idolatrous potential of the Renaissance stage, most studies of antitheatricality tend to focus on the complaints—about the licentious sexual behavior of audiences, the erotic dimension of the plays themselves, and the transgressive behavior of men playing women—without examining closely

---

tragedies was political: "She was the site on which to stage an assault on the monarch. As a source of pollution, she empowered the monarch," for her ritual subjugation "purified the community" (p. 79). In a feminist reading of three domestic tragedies, "Painting Women: Images of Femininity in Jacobean Tragedy" (1984), pp. 361–62, Laurie Finke argues that the male characters in these plays, like the sixteenth-century lyric poets, kill these women "into art," achieving "immortality . . . at the price of her vitality."

[42] Although she does not address the problem of idolatry or religious discourse, Katherine Eisaman Maus makes a related argument in "Horns of Dilemma" (1987), p. 563: "The dynamic of sexual jealousy provides a complex analogy to theatrical performance and response in a culture that tends to conceive of theatrical experience in erotic terms, and of certain sexual impulses as highly theatrical in character."

[43] Stephen Gosson, *Plays Confuted in Five Actes* (1582), sigs. B8ᵛ, C3ʳ.

[44] Ibid., sig. E2ʳ⁻ᵛ.

their theological grounds. One exception is Jean Howard, who acknowledges "a rhetoric of idolatry" in the antitheatrical tracts and recognizes "the iconoclastic potential of the stage," a potential she believes the antitheatricalists do not perceive. Another is Laura Levine, who addresses some of the central issues surrounding the charge that the theater is idolatrous, including early modern beliefs in magic and theories of representation. Both Howard and Levine, however, locate the antitheatrical impulse in anxieties about gender identity and social change. Howard primarily reads these tracts as "a discursive site where the anxiety about social change was both created . . . and awkwardly managed." Levine focuses on the cross-dressed male actor, finding the cultural fear "that there is no such thing as a masculine self" at the heart of Renaissance antitheatricality.[45]

In his exhaustive study of antitheatricality Jonas Barish, in contrast, dismisses as "hardly . . . germane" a Lollard charge that plays are idolatrous. He concludes that it "empties the word *maumetry*—idolatry—of all precision, converting it into little more than a loose synonym for 'immorality.' " Ignoring the bond Protestantism forges between the idolatrous and the carnal, he argues that the "antitheatrical prejudice" is a transhistorical phenomenon that "seems too deep-rooted, too widespread, too resistant to changes of place and time to be ascribed entirely, or even mainly, to social, political, or economic factors."[46] When he asserts the continuity of a deeply conservative, classical, and Christian antitheatrical tradition, Barish de-emphasizes the particular theological beliefs that provoke the eruption of antitheatricality in late sixteenth-century England. His thesis ignores the way Protestant critiques of the stage, although deeply indebted to the Bible and certain Church fathers, serve a radical cause, challenging and disrupting traditional—that is, late medieval—beliefs. Instead, he attributes antitheatricality to puritanical prudery, and he positions himself in enlightened opposition to puritans like Prynne whose obsessive atten-

[45] Jean Howard, *The Stage and Social Struggle in Early Modern England* (1994), pp. 37, 31, 44. Corroborating my argument, Howard observes that "the painted woman and the Catholic Church—itself personified as a painted woman—are interchangeably constructed" (p. 38). Laura Levine, *Men in Women's Clothing* (1994), p. 24. See also Jonathan V. Crewe, "The Theatre of the Idols: Marlowe, Rankins, and Theatrical Images" (1984) (see chap. 3, n. 5).

[46] Jonas Barish, *The Antitheatrical Prejudice* (1981), pp. 78–79, 116–17.

tion to "feminine sexuality" appear to him "morbidly fixated," "lunatic," "obstinate and insane."[47]

Colin MacCabe likewise focuses on complaints about the erotic nature of the stage without considering how such complaints might derive from a religious discourse that sexualizes images and arouses fears of their seductive power. "What Gosson finds so disturbing," he writes, "is a public display of sexuality both on the stage and . . . in the audience." MacCabe encourages his readers to imagine "how important sexuality was to the Shakespearean theatre," but his analysis of hostility toward the stage does not identify the intense fear of women and of sexuality that the antitheatrical tracts associate with Protestant culture's iconophobia.[48] MacCabe and Barish are too quick to assume that the primary concern of the antitheatricalists was sexuality. Although the impulse to censor erotic display and to control sexual behavior is a distinguishing feature of Tudor and Stuart attacks on the stage, it originates in a Calvinist-induced fear of idolatry.

Idolatry is, in fact, frequently condemned as a cause of sexual promiscuity and perversity. "When the Israelites fell from God to idols," explains William Perkins, "oftentimes they fell to Sodomie. In Italie for their Idolatries are left to themselves to permit the Stewes and to abound (as the fame is) in whoredoms and fornications."[49] In Perkins's interpretation, image worship among Israelites who stray from the Hebrew God is the source for unnatural sex acts, and the widespread abuse of images in Roman Catholic Italy is the source of the reputed sexual promiscuity of the Italians. Physical lust and sexual license are thus understood to be a consequence of idolatry, indeed sometimes even a divine punishment for it. According to an official Anglican Homily, God decreed that "they which fell to Idolatry, which is spirituall fornication, should also fall into carnall fornication, and all uncleannesse . . . delivering them over to abominable concupiscenses."[50] Idolatry and sexual promiscuity, this sermon suggests, are related acts, and any pollution of the spirit leads to the defilement of the body. Fear of idolatry is therefore inextricably connected to fear of sexuality in the

---

[47] Ibid., pp. 115, 87, 115.

[48] Colin MacCabe, "Abusing Self and Others" (1988), pp. 3, 6.

[49] Perkins, *Warning*, p. 91.

[50] "Homily," p. 49; this homily was read on a regular basis in English churches of the Elizabethan and Jacobean period. See also Perkins, *Warning*, p. 91.

minds of the reformers, and Protestant attempts to suppress erotic narratives and advance puritanical attitudes toward sexuality are inseparable from their attempts to break images, suppress plays, and censor
the imagination.

When the antitheatricalists attack the eroticism of the stage, they
appropriate the language and arguments of the Protestant iconoclasts.
Like the reformers, the antitheatricalists condemn what they acknowledge delights them, railing against the pleasures of the stage. They
warn that plays "enchant," "bewitch," "charm," "beguile," "entice,"
"seduce," and "ravish."[51] Constructing an opposition between imaginative art and Protestantism, Stephen Gosson laments that "a greate
number of my gay countrymen, which beare a sharper smacke of Italian
devises in their heades, then of English religion in their heartes . . . are
so asotted with these delightes, so blinded with the love, and drunken
with the sweetnes of these vanities, that greedely we flocke together"
to the theaters.[52] Rankins, too, cautions his readers about the seduc-
tions of the stage, lamenting how easily men are "seduced with col-
oured pretences" and warning that the players "present before theyr
[audience's] eyes . . . such inchaunting Charmes, and bewitched wyles,
to alienate their mindes from vertue."[53]

Like the reformers, too, the antitheatricalists feminize the art form
they seek to discredit, invoking the trope of the whore, for instance, to
warn their readers about the seductive nature of the stage. Condemned
as "the very markets of bawdry"—the site of rape and prostitution—
the theaters are attacked not only for contributing to moral vices and
social ills, but, more centrally, for resembling whores.[54] The theater's
critics warn that "filthy Playes rehearsed . . . are the bellowes to blowe
the coales of lust, soften the minde, and make it flexible to evil incli-
nations," and they claim that "the lustful theaters" seduce their audiences into whoredom, using their "Sirens charme" to "turne a
modest audience / To brazen-fac'et profession of a whore."[55]

[51] See William Rankins, *A Mirrour of Monsters* (1587), sigs. B2ᵛ, B3ᵛ, C4ʳ, D2ʳ; Stephen
Gosson, *Ephemerides of Phialo* (1579), sig. L5ʳ; Gosson, *Plays Confuted*, sig. D1ʳ; Gosson, *The
School of Abuse* (1579), sig. A6ʳ.

[52] Gosson, *Plays Confuted*, sigs. B4ᵛ–B5ᵛ.

[53] Rankins, *Mirrour*, sigs. D2ʳ, E1ᵛ.

[54] Gosson, *Plays Confuted*, sig. G5ᵛ.

[55] Henry Cross, *Vertues Common-wealth* (1603), sig. Q3ʳ⁻ᵛ; Robert Anton, *The Philosophers
Satyrs* (1616), sig. I4r.

By invoking the metaphor of whoredom and arousing fears of female sexuality's emasculation of men, the antitheatricalists attempt to disrupt the playgoer's pleasure. "The divel is not ignorant how mightely these outward spectacles effeminate, & soften the hearts of men," Gosson warns, "vice is learned with beholding, sense is tickled, desire pricked." Stage plays, he rails, present "straunge consortes of melody, to tickle the eare; costly apparel, to flatter the sight; effeminite gesture, to ravish the sence; and wanton speache, to whet desire too inordinate lust."[56] Gynophobia thus fuels antitheatricality, as well as iconophobia, in early modern England.

Appeals to gynophobia also serve to align the theater with a negative kind of artifice in the antitheatrical literature of this era. Just as the reformers use the metaphor of whoredom to associate sacred images with a false beauty, so antitheatrical writers use it to portray the stage as fraudulent and unnatural. Advising his readers to "Beware of beautifull boyes transformed into women by putting on their raiment, their feature, lookes, and facions," John Rainolds, for example, warns that "men may be ravished with love of Stones, of dead stuffe, framed by cunning gravers to beautifull women's likenes."[57] Explicitly linking the theater to the image and playwrights to visual artists, Rainolds identifies players, and specifically the boys who play female parts, with the artifice and cunning of a beautiful woman. The language he uses to arouse suspicion of the stage—"love of stones," "dead stuffe," "cunning gravers," "ravished"—appears to be borrowed directly from Protestant polemics that attack sacred images, and it comes laden with Calvinist fears of art, imagination, and idolatry.

Like most of the antitheatricalists, Rainolds objects to male actors playing female parts not simply because this practice violates religious and social sanctions against cross-dressing, but more importantly because the female likenesses the boy actors create are fraudulent, cunning, and artificial and yet, nevertheless, have the capacity to "ravish" their spectators. Players, complains William Perkins, "doe devise artificiall formes and favours, to set upon their bodies and faces, by painting and colouring; thereby making themselves seeme that which indeede they are not." Gosson likewise condemns them because they

---

[56] Gosson, *Plays Confuted*, sigs. G4ʳ; Gosson, *School of Abuse*, sig. B6ᵛ; see also *School of Abuse*, sigs. B8ᵛ, C5ᵛ, D7ʳ, G5ᵛ.

[57] Rainolds, *The Overthrow of Stage-playes* (1599), p. 34.

"falsifie, forge, and adulterate" nature.[58] The convention of cross-dressing thus reinforces fears of the actor's cunning, linking players to women, who are assumed to be theatrical by nature. In a sense, then, the very skill of the actor causes the antitheatrical writers to brand plays and players effeminate and whorish. The fear that the theater "besotteth the senses and bewitcheth the myndes of menne" is integrally connected to the charge that the players, having grown so "singular in these subtill sleights," flaunt their "cunning" and "delude" their spectators.[59]

The Stuart love tragedies express Protestant culture's deep antipathy for images and theatricality even as they self-consciously explore their own idolatrous potential. In them certain female characters, played by boy actors whose very ability to mimic the feminine calls attention to their artifice, figure the theater itself. Identified with spectacle and art, linked to eros and bewitchment, accused of cunning, deceit, and fraud, and denounced for polluting their societies, the female characters confront the plays' spectators with both the power and the duplicity of theatrical representation. By making them the object of the spectators' gaze, then, the love tragedies reflexively address their own capacity to seduce and delude their audiences.

In John Webster's *The White Devil*, to take one noteworthy example, Vittoria Corombona is deeply disturbing, for she is charismatic and rhetorically sophisticated, and yet cunning and morally repulsive. Those who gaze upon her, both in the fictional world of the play and in the playhouse as well, cannot help but admire her even as they recognize the need to repudiate her. A dazzling beauty and a consummate actress, Webster's Vittoria exemplifies the seductive duplicity of the theater. Even after she is openly denounced as a whore and "the most corrupted of women" (spoken in Latin) at her arraignment in act 3, scene 2, Vittoria performs the role of the wronged innocent so brilliantly that the audience is tempted to forget that the prosecutor's case against her is essentially accurate. Her riveting theatrical performance is so seductive, and so effective, that the English Ambassador remarks in admiration, "She hath a brave spirit" (3.2.140). Webster both celebrates the theater and contains its power. Considered in the context

[58] Perkins, *The Whole Treatise of the Cases of Conscience* (1608), sig. 2G7ʳ; Gosson, *Plays Confuted*, sig. E3ᵛ.

[59] Rankins, *Mirrour*, sigs. C4ʳ, C3ʳ, F1ʳ.

of Protestant polemics that seek to discredit the power of image and theater, Vittoria's trial might even be said to foreground the relation between gynophobia and antitheatricality in early Protestant culture.

No one to my knowledge has pointed out that Webster's play is marked by a pronounced iconophobia, an iconophobia that is inseparable from the gynophobia that pervades it. And yet *The White Devil* repeatedly calls attention to images that are abused, broken, fraudulent, and deadly. Many of these images clearly allude to the religious controversies about image worship and iconoclasm that raged in sixteenth- and seventeenth-century England. A poisoned portrait kills the woman who comes daily to kiss and adore it. A crucifix is broken by a baby in his mother's arms, an iconoclastic act that family members interpret as a foreboding sign. Another crucifix comforts a dying man even though it is a fraudulent object, brandished by murderers in clerical disguises who wish to torment him.

References to religious images also abound in *The White Devil,* and they are frequently linked to the epithet of whore. When Monticelso attempts to discredit Vittoria, likening her to a "guilty conterfeited coin" and mocking the time when "This whore, forsooth, was holy," Vittoria dismisses his construction of her as nothing more than those "painted devils" and "feigned shadows" that superstitious men use to "Terrify babes" (3.2.77, 146–47). When Bracciano renounces his mistress Vittoria, he not only declares her to be "a stately and advanced whore" but also compares her to the figure of a saint contained in a small crystal shrine of the type popular among lay Catholics. "Your beauty!" he laments, "O ten thousand curses on't / How long have I beheld the devil in crystal?" (4.2.87–88). Having transformed his saint into a common whore, he compares her to "an heathen sacrifice" that has imperiled his soul and led him "to [his] eternal ruin." Webster thus associates the theatrical Vittoria with the images of Roman Catholic saints and pagan gods, and he gives Bracciano a recognition scene in which the adulterous Duke recasts his saint as a whore and a devil and identifies his lust for her with idolatry.

The White Devil engages its audiences in many of the most compelling issues of early Protestant culture. It raises disturbing questions about the nature and legitimacy of its own theatrical representations and about the appropriateness of the responses it elicits in its audiences. Surely, Webster's "white devil" refers as much to the religious and aesthetic images as to Vittoria, whose beauty and cunning figure both image and theater. The play participates in the iconoclastic and anti-theatrical project of the reformers more fully than recent criticism has recognized. The violence committed against eroticized women may thus resonate for a contemporary audience in an especially powerful way. By symbolically linking women and images, it addresses the darker consequences of the iconoclasts' efforts to tear images out of the hearts of men.

According to Ioan Couliano, the burning of images and the burning of women are related symbolic activities in early Protestant culture. "One can assert without any doubt," he maintains, "that there is an immediate connection between the witch craze and the European Reformation. In a sense, the witch craze was the social counterpart of the destruction of religious images: in both cases, the victim was human fantasy."[60] Women accused of witchcraft are, in Couliano's view, not so much victims of misogyny per se as victims of a reformed theology that mistrusts the imaginative capacity of the human mind and identifies women with the artificial, the spectacular, the theatrical, and the phantasmic.

If, as Couliano argues, violence against women accused of witchcraft can be understood in symbolic terms as a zealous repudiation of the imagination, then the representation of violence against beautiful women in the Stuart love tragedies may in fact be a symbolic form of iconoclasm, a repudiation not only of the imagination but of the theater itself. By staging violence against the eroticized women it puts on display, these plays—like Cranach's painting *Lucretia*, discussed in Chapter 2—act to suppress the very images they produce and to curb the very imaginations they excite. The playwrights who create them and the actors who stage them may thus perform a sacrificial (and some might say a suicidal) act of their own. By enacting such violence, they impose constraints on their own power to enchant and enthrall. Othello's "sacrifice" is therefore also Shakespeare's: the victim, Couliano would say, "is human fantasy."

Although Shakespeare's *Othello* protests against a world that has come to identify eros with witchcraft, virgins with whores, and the imagination with a corrupting and false fancy, it is nevertheless also implicated in the iconoclastic project of the reformers, for it disrupts the erotic gaze of its spectators, destabilizes the medieval categories of virgin and

---

[60] Couliano, *Eros and Magic*, p. 191.

whore, and undermines its audiences' trust in the imaginative art that is the theater. However much its audiences concur with Desdemona's protest, "That death's unnatural that kills for loving" (5.2.42), the play requires them to replicate that killing by relinquishing the powerful and erotic images it displays. Like other love tragedies written for the Stuart stage, *Othello* makes its spectators acutely aware of its own power to seduce and enthrall, thereby distancing them from the immediacy of the theater.

If they weep with Othello when he looks "with subdued eyes" upon the body of the woman he has loved and killed, they do so in part because they have identified with his earlier idealization of Desdemona. The viewers' chastened eyes—along with the deification and aestheticization of the female beloved, the abuse of the beautiful female body, the manipulation of the ocular proof—resonate more fully when we read this and other Stuart love tragedies in the context of a Reformation English culture traumatized by violent iconophobic and iconoclastic reactions to a deeply ingrained iconophilia. Othello's play ends with Lodovico issuing contradictory orders: "Look," he commands Iago, "on the tragic loading of this bed." And then, "The object poisons sight; / Let it be hid" (5.2.363–65). Like so many other plays written during the years of the English Reformation, Shakespeare's *Othello* demands our attention only to poison our sight, arouses our gaze only to subdue our eyes.

CHAPTER SEVEN

The Rhetoric of Witnessing:
The Duchess of Malfi

Martyrdom (bearing witness) is so essentially rhetorical,
it even gets its name from the law courts.
                              —Kenneth Burke, *A Rhetoric of Motives*

Plagued in Art

Perhaps more than any other play written for the Elizabethan and Jacobean commercial theaters, *The Duchess of Malfi* (1612) is deeply informed by English Calvinism.[1] It explores Calvinist notions of predestination through the character of Bosola, an alienated malcontent who is unable "to do good when" he has "a mind to it."[2] It raises the issue, prominent in Calvin, of the conflict between a corrupt ruler and the individual conscience. It draws on early Protestant satires of the Roman clergy, depicting the Cardinal as a hypocritical, sexually promiscuous, and morally corrupt man who spies on loved ones, betrays servants, and kills mistresses without compunction.[3] And in its final act, the ruins of an ancient abbey elicit an elegiac

---

[1] A number of other scholars have pointed out the Calvinist elements of Webster's play. See Dennis Klinck, "Calvinism and Jacobean Tragedy" (1978); Dena Goldberg, *Between Worlds* (1987), pp. 106–7; John S. Wilks, *The Idea of Conscience in Renaissance Tragedy* (1990), pp. 194–220; and Bryan Crockett, *The Play of Paradox* (1996).

[2] Webster, *The Duchess of Malfi*, ed. John Russell Brown (1964), 4.2.360; all subsequent citations of this play are given within the text.

[3] Orazio Busino, Venetian envoy in England, calls attention to how Roman Catholics were being satirized on the English stage in *Anglopatrida* (1618). He complains that "the English scoff at our religion as disgusting and merely superstitious; they never put on any public show whatever, be it tragedy or satire or comedy, into which they do not insert some Catholic churchmen's vices and wickednesses, making mock and scorn of him, according to their taste," and he goes on to describe what appears to be Webster's portrayal of the Cardinal in *The Duchess of Malfi*. Qtd. in G. K. Hunter and S. K Hunter, eds. *John Webster* (1969), p. 31.

meditation on the temporality and corruption of the traditional Church.

Like Calvin, Webster is essentially pessimistic about the human capacity to see or know correctly. He dramatizes the flawed sight of characters who equate their tragic errors with a universal blindness and, echoing Calvin, declare themselves to be in "a labyrinth," "a mist," "a shadow," and "a deep pit of darkness."[4] Nevertheless, his play features many memorable stage images that engage its spectators in crucial acts of seeing. Especially striking, because they are so cruel, are the disturbing images that Ferdinand uses to torture his sister after he has imprisoned her: a dead man's hand, wax figures fashioned to look like the corpses of her husband and children, and a perverse masque of distracted madmen. In displaying such images, Webster arouses in his spectators an anxiety about art and theater. His play is thus both intensely visual and profoundly iconoclastic.

When the Duchess looks upon "the artificial figures" of her husband and children, she believes they are the very corpses of her loved ones. Having just been tricked into kissing a dead man's hand by her sadistic brother, Ferdinand, a hand he tells her belongs to her husband, Antonio, she discovers the figures of her family "appearing as if they were dead." "Look you," Bosola instructs her, "here's the piece from which 't [the hand] was ta'en." He explains to the shocked Duchess that her brother "doth present you this sad spectacle / That now you know directly they are dead" (4.1.56–58). Horrified by the cold reality of the severed hand and overwhelmed by her apparent loss, the Duchess identifies Ferdinand's cruelty with witchcraft and, curiously, likens her reaction of horror to the deadly pain aroused by the magical manipulation of an effigy:

> it wastes me more
> Than were't my picture, fashion'd out of wax,
> Stuck with a magical needle and then buried
> In some foul dunghill.
>
> (4.1.62–65)

---

[4] Calvin, for example, speaks of humankind as being "compassed with many mistes of errors" (*The Institution of Christian Religion* [1562], 3.2.4); he dwells on men's "blindness of heart" and "darkened" understanding, calling them "utterly blind," and deriding

Unbeknown to her, however, what she gazes upon is itself only a picture fashioned out of wax, and its power to harm her lies in its capacity to deceive her into confusing the representation for the reality. Far from providing direct knowledge of her husband's death, Bosola deludes her eyes. The figures she takes to be the "true substantial bodies" of her family "are but fram'd in wax" by a clever artist, and the pain, loss, and desperation she feels is caused by artifice. The Duchess, Ferdinand gloats triumphantly, is "plagued in art."

Ferdinand's fiendish trick raises troubling questions for Webster's audiences who gaze with the Duchess upon the corpse-like wax figures. These questions go to the very heart of the Reformation controversy over images and Protestant antagonism toward the stage. In tempting the Duchess to believe a man-made image is the "true substantial body" that it represents, Ferdinand abuses her in precisely the way that the reformers claim priests abuse the worshipers at the Roman Mass.[5] But in presenting the counterfeit as the real, the cruel Ferdinand imitates the playwright as well as the priest. When he torments his sister with the grotesque tableau of her family and, later, with the frenzied masque of singing and dancing madmen, he practices forms of the theatrical arts. And Ferdinand's morbid theater is part of Webster's own theater, a disturbing series of spectacles within a play featuring many other striking stage images that seem calculated to horrify and unsettle: the strangulation of the Duchess, the murder—in full view of the audience—of her young children and her maid, the final disintegration of Ferdinand, who, believing he is a wolf, haunts graveyards and digs up the bodies of the dead, and the accumulation of dead bodies in the final, bloody act. Like the imprisoned Duchess, the playwright's captive audiences are thus forced to watch powerful and disturbing spectacles, spectacles that are by definition artificial and illusory. Does Webster intentionally torment his audiences with theatrical representations of dismembered limbs, dead bodies, and mad actors? Are the play's spectators, like the Duchess, plagued in art? And if not, why not?

"the greatest geniuses" as "blinder than moles!" (*Institutes of the Christian Religion* [1960] 2.3.2; 2.2.19; 2.2.18); and he declares that man's mind "cannot hold to the right path, but wanders through various errors and stumbles repeatedly, as if it were groping in darkness" (*Institutes* 2.2.12).

[5] For a discussion of the English reformers' polemical attacks on the Roman Mass, see Chapter 4.

In this chapter I argue that Webster carefully distinguishes the perverted theater of the mad Duke from his own art. Although he repudiates Ferdinand's theater, with its display of grotesque images and its cunning and counterfeit theatrics, he insists on the validity of his own drama, a drama that pointedly disavows the kind of rhetorical strategies Ferdinand employs. Even as he rejects art that conceals the gap between the literal and the figurative and pretends to enact what it represents, he creates theatrical spectacles that have the power to elicit pity and stir the conscience. His play shifts attention from the spectacle to the spectator and thus reflexively explores the very act of seeing required of his own audiences. By constructing his own spectators as witnesses and making them aware of themselves as watchers, Webster employs a Protestant rhetoric of martyrdom, a rhetoric that draws on the Calvinist notion of the conscience as an internalized spectator. Exposing Ferdinand's theatricality as manipulative and fraudulent, Webster thus seeks to create a new kind of theater, one I wish to associate with an emerging Protestant aesthetics of the stage in early modern England.

Witnessing Martyrdom

Despite his iconoclastic agenda, John Foxe enthusiastically endorses a particular kind of image, one he calls "the sorrowful spectacle."[6] Most of the illustrations in *Actes and Monuments* depict Protestant martyrs being reviled, tortured, and mercilessly executed. These images of martyrdom—in all their spectacular and theatrical detail—are powerful weapons in the reformers' war against the papists because, as graphic evidence of the cruelty and tyranny of the Roman Church, they arouse pity for the victims and their cause. For the student of Renaissance tragedy, they thus provide valuable insights into the uses of violent spectacle in early modern English culture.

Violence against the Protestant faithful is, for Foxe, a "pitiful sight," the martyrdom of a reformer, a "lamentable and most pitifull spectacle."[7] Such spectacles clearly serve Foxe's purposes because pity is an emotion of identification, linking the witness to the victim and requir-

[6] John Foxe, *A&M*, 8:84.
[7] Ibid., 7:359–60; *A&M* (1563), p. 1544.

ing him or her to mourn with the victim. "We must not be too delicate, not too tender in shrinking away from shewing pitie and compassion towards such as are in adversitie," Calvin counsels in his sermons on Job, "but we must bee touched with grief of our neighbors, to mourne with them."[8] *Actes and Monuments,* I suggest, seeks to elicit a communal mourning for the Protestant martyrs in order to forge a Protestant community among its readers.

In a preface addressing "The Persecutors of God's Truth, Commonly Called Papists," Foxe attempts to elicit outrage in his Protestant readers by demanding that his antagonists look upon the spectacles of death they have caused and confront their guilt. Directly addressing the papists he is attacking, he writes: "See, I say, and behold, here present before your eyes, the heaps of slain bodies, of so many men and women, both old, young, children, infants, new born, married, unmarried, wives, widows, maids, blind men, lame men, whole men; of all sorts, of all ages, of all degrees; . . . whose wounds, yet bleeding before the face of God, cry vengeance! . . . See, therefore, I say—read, and behold your acts and facts; and when you have seen, then judge what you have deserved."[9] Foxe thus invites his readers to look upon the bodies of the slain martyrs, to imagine their "wounds, yet bleeding before the face of God," and to judge the perpetrators from the perspective of an angry and all-seeing God. The act of looking upon the "heaps of slain bodies" is therefore not an idolatrous act but an ethical one.

Throughout his monumental book Foxe similarly urges his readers to see—visualize—the suffering of the martyrs whose history he records. Accompanying one illustration, for instance, is an aside to the reader emphasizing that "the grevous afflictions and sorrowful tormentes" of God's martyrs have been deliberately "set forth and exhibited before thine eies."[10] Foxe even expresses the hope that monarchs reading his book "would paint" images of the martyrs "upon their walls, cups, rings, and gates," reproducing spectacles of martyrdom so that they could have them "always in sight."[11]

Particularly significant, for my purposes, is the way Foxe constructs

---

[8] John Calvin, *Sermons of Maister John Calvin, upon the Book of Job* (1584), 519.b.38.

[9] Foxe, *A&M*, 1:508.

[10] Foxe, *A&M* (1570), p. 925.

[11] Foxe, *A&M*, 1:522.

FIGURE 11. "A Table describyng the burning of Byshop Ridley and Father Latymer at Oxford, Doct. Smith there preachyng at the tyme of theyr Martyrdome." John Foxe, *Actes and Monuments* (London, 1570), p. 1938. By permission of the University of Iowa Libraries (Iowa City).

Protestant martyrdoms as spectacular theater that is observed by witnesses. Many of the illustrations in *Actes and Monuments* show martyrs at the moment of death, surrounded by spectators who stand or sit around the scaffold, watching the proceedings like the audiences of a stage play (Figure 11). Displays of power, gestures of defiance, spectacles of suffering and death: all are recorded as high drama, played out on public stages, watched by crowds of spectators. Their gazes mark the spectators as witnesses (Figure 12). Some appear to be unmoved by the sight of the suffering martyrs. They avert their eyes, turn their attention away from the dying martyrs, engage in conversation with their neighbors, actively try to keep away the crowds that press toward the condemned, and stare impassively at the scaffold. But others are shown to be compassionate and sympathetic observers. They watch intently, react in horror, weep, and even offer gestures of sympathy and solidarity. In an illustration of the martyrdom of John Hooper, Bishop

❡The burnyng of Iohn Frith,and Andrew Hewet.

Iohn Frith, and Andrew Hewet, Martyr.

FIGURE 12. "The burnyng of John Frith, and Andrew Hewet." John Foxe, *Actes and Monuments* (London, 1570), p. 1179. By permission of the University of Iowa Libraries (Iowa City).

of Gloucester, for example, a woman in the crowd openly mourns the bishop's fate, another man rubs a tear from his eye, and two more spectators express pity for the condemned man by lowering their eyes in sorrow (Figure 13).

The images of martyrdom in *Actes and Monuments* differ in significant ways from Counter-Reformation images of martyrdom. Whereas Foxe calls attention to the crowd that gathers to witness the executions of Protestants, Counter-Reformation artists typically ignore this dimension of martyrdom, preferring instead to depict only the martyrs and their oppressors. Working within a well-developed late medieval pictorial tradition, Antonio Gallonio, for example, features images of heroic martyrs of the Roman Church in his *De S.S. Martyrum Cruciatibus*, a book published in the 1590s that achieved a wide readership in the seventeenth century. His illustrations focus the viewer's attention on the barbarous torture and miraculous strength of the holy saints.

¶The burnyng of Maiſter Iohn Hoper Byſhop at Glouceſter.
Anno. 1555. February. 9.

¶In clariſſimi Doɛtrina & Pietate viri Iohannis
Hoperi Martyrium,Conrardi Geſneri carmen.

FIGURE 13. "The burnyng of Maister John Hoper Byshop at Gloucester. Anno. 1555. February. 9." John Foxe, *Actes and Monuments* (London, 1570), p. 1684. By permission of the University of Iowa Libraries (Iowa City).

Although many depict the violent perpetrators of torture as well as the suffering martyrs, none of them constructs martyrdom as a theater or represents spectators who witness the event (Figure 14). Gallonio's emphasis on the bodily presence of the martyrs and the technology of persecution is typical of Roman Catholic representations of martyrdom in northern Europe during the early Counter-Reformation.[12] Foxe's illustrations, in striking contrast, tend to deflect attention from the persecutors, the instruments of torture, and even the bodies of

[12] For a detailed discussion of Counter-Reformation images of martyrdom, see David Freedberg, "The Representation of Martyrdoms During the Early Counter-Reformation in Antwerp" (1976).

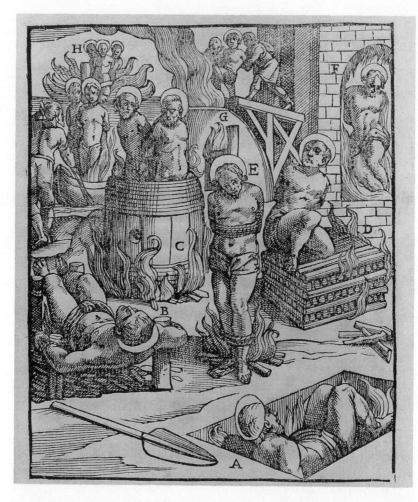

FIGURE 14. "Martyrs burned in various ways." Antonio Gallonio, *De S.S. Martyrum Cruciatibus* (Rome, 1594), p. 179. By permission of the Getty Center, Resource Collections, Santa Monica, California.

the martyrs to the witnesses who gather to watch the martyrdoms. Foxe thus adds a metatextual dimension to his images, thereby nurturing in his readers a self-consciousness about their own seeing. Martyrdom, Foxe implies, is a rhetorical act; it requires witnesses; it must be seen.

In his text, too, Foxe emphasizes the rhetorical effect of martyrdom on those who witness it. He tells, for example, how the condemned Cranmer, standing on the scaffold awaiting execution, presents a "sorrowful spectacle to all christian eyes that beheld him." He invites his readers to imagine the power of that "lamentable . . . sight," and he likens the experience of this spectacle to the aesthetic experience of tragic drama, pointedly asking "who would not pity his case, and bewail his fortune, and might not fear his own chance, to *see* such a prelate . . . descend to such vile and ragged apparel?" (emphasis mine).[13] Foxe thus insists that his readers confront the visual image of Cranmer and respond emotionally to it (Figure 15). He asks them to imagine themselves present at the site of martyrdom and to accept the role of witness.

In another narrative, Foxe recounts how a Dr. Taylor, wondering why so many people have gathered at the place where he is to be executed, is told "the people are come to look upon you." Indeed, the very sight of this martyr aroused great sorrow in those who gathered to watch his execution: "when the people saw his reverend and ancient face, with a long white beard," Foxe tells us, "they burst out with weeping tears."[14] The outpouring of compassion among the onlookers helped to construct Taylor's execution as a martyrdom, rather than a just execution, for the people's tearful presence served as evidence of Taylor's goodness: "Such witness had the servant of God [Taylor] of his virtuous and charitable alms given in his lifetime," Foxe writes, "for God would now the poor should testify of his good deeds, to his singular comfort, to the example of others, and confusion of his persecutors and tyrannous adversaries."[15] The ordinary men and women who gathered to witness Taylor's execution thus played an important role in constructing the meaning of that event. Witnessing, then, is a crucial element in Foxe's drama of reform, situating the readers at the

[13] Foxe, *A&M*, 8:84.
[14] Ibid., 6:698.
[15] Ibid., 6:697.

¶The burning of the Archbithop of Cant. D.Tho.Cranmer, in the Towndich at Oxford, with his
hand firſt thruſt into the fire, wherewith he fubfcribed before.

FIGURE 15. "The burning of the Archbishop of Cant. D. Tho. Cranmer, in the Towndich at Oxford, with his hand first thrust into the fire, wherewith he subscribed before." John Foxe, *Actes and Monuments* (London, 1570), p. 2067. By permission of the University of Iowa Libraries (Iowa City).

very sites of execution and providing a way of experiencing suffering and death.

Playing on the etymology of the word "martyr," Foxe identifies martyrdom itself with witnessing. "In these men we have an assured and plain witness of God," he explains in the preface of his book, and he refers again and again to the martyrs as "faithful witnesses of the truth" and "assured and plain witness[es] of God."[16] If the martyrs occupy center stage in Foxe's divine theater, providing "a lively testimony of God's mighty working in the life of man," however, their martyrdom must be witnessed in order to be meaningful.[17] Because martyrdom

---

[16] Ibid., 1:519, 521; see also 1:517–18.
[17] Ibid., 1:521.

provides a kind of proof of God's truth, the tortured bodies of the martyrs serve as marks or signs that require visual observation and examination. Foxe therefore stresses the presence of the historical witnesses, and he constructs his own readers as witnesses. His representations of martyrdom are calculated both to elicit outrage and pity and assign to his readers the responsibility of keeping the memory of the martyrs alive.

But the Protestant drama of martyrdom is not seen only by human eyes. God is also watching, Foxe reminds his readers.[18] He is the ultimate witness—the "true Judge"—of the drama that unfolds in the theater of the world.[19] A few of the illustrations in *The Book of Martyrs* even encourage viewers to imagine the drama of martyrdom from God's perspective. A picture of the martyrdom of Anne Askew, for example, gives a bird's-eye view of the scene (Figure 16). Such a view from above reveals that the anonymous onlookers, as well as the suffering martyr, are visible, and it suggests that seeing itself is an act that will be judged by an all-seeing and all-knowing God.

Rather than suppress the role of sight in the practice of faith, Foxe thus invites his readers to look upon horrifying spectacles of martyrdom, and he carefully structures their responses to what they see. His illustrations encourage his readers to seek Christ in the acts of the faithful throughout history rather than in visual representations of God. They also forge identifications with the eyewitnesses who by their active and sympathetic presence validate the spectacle of suffering they observe. By emphasizing the response—and responsibility—of the spectators, he fosters in his readers a self-conscious attention to their own seeing. Witnessing is, for Foxe, a reflexive act. He depicts the martyr as both a spectacle—the object of everyone's gaze—and a witness whose actions affirm God's truth; and he portrays the onlooker as an eyewitness whose own watching—hostile or compassionate—is itself an action with spiritual consequences. In addition, he reminds his reader that God is a divine spectator, who watches and judges both the actors and the human spectators in the theater of the world.

[18] In his discussion of martyrdom Kenneth Burke notes that "mortifications *must* be witnessed; they are evidence, presented to an invisible divine audience. . . . Martyrdom would be but a severe kind of 'epideictic oratory,' were it not for the supernatural witness which it postulates" (*A Rhetoric of Motives* [1950], p. 222).

[19] Foxe, *A&M*, 1:522.

FIGURE 16. "The order and manner of the burning of Anne Askew, John Lacelles, and others, with certayne of the Counsell sitting in Smithfield." John Foxe, *Actes and Monuments* (London, 1570), p. 1420. By permission of the University of Iowa Libraries (Iowa City).

"Fix Your Eye Here"

A reflexive attention to the acts of seeing and being seen also characterizes *The Duchess of Malfi*. Webster employs a rhetorical strategy similar to Foxe's by repeatedly positioning his characters as on-stage spectators who observe the main action. As a result, his audiences watch characters who look, spy, witness, and sometimes even watch others watch. In the course of this play: Antonio and Delio stand outside the main action and observe the Italian court; Cariola hides behind an arras and witnesses the Duchess's secret marriage; Antonio and Cariola peer from their hiding place and watch the confrontation between Ferdinand and his sister; Bosola joins the Duchess's household and observes her every move as a spy for her brothers; two pilgrims visit the shrine of our Lady of Loretto and watch the Cardinal exchange the robes of the Church for military armor; Bosola and Ferdinand torture the Duchess and carefully monitor her responses to their cruelty; Pescara withdraws and observes the Doctor examining the mad Ferdinand; and Bosola hides in a closet and witnesses the murder of Julia.

Critical commentary has tended to ignore the distinctive way Webster structures the audience's sight through the repeated use of on-stage spectators.[20] I would like to suggest that the presence of these fictional spectators is a metadramatic technique that constructs the real audience as participants, active witnesses to the action performed on stage. Engaged in watching characters watch, as well as act, Webster's audiences cannot help but attend to their own roles as watchers, spectators. As a result, they become aware of how their watching implicates them in the action.

When Cariola withdraws behind the arras to watch the Duchess woo Antonio, for instance, her watching becomes an important aspect of this fascinating scene, first, because she witnesses the private marriage of the couple and can therefore testify to its existence, and second, because she serves as both a moral commentator who evaluates the unusual event she witnesses and a sympathetic onlooker who responds with pity to what she sees:

> Whether the spirit of greatness or of woman
> Reign most in her, I know not, but it shows
> A fearful madness; I owe her much of pity.
>
> (1.1.504–06)

Like Cariola, the play's spectators peer into the private world of the Duchess, observing her secret, and like her, too, they are constructed as witnesses to the marriage, so that they are inclined to accept its legitimacy even if they are troubled by its secrecy. Through an identification with the maid, who hides and watches, they also are encouraged to evaluate what they see enacted before them and to feel both fear and pity. In grappling with the issues raised by the Duchess's ac-

---

[20] See Ralph Berry, *The Art of John Webster* (1972); Lee Bliss, *The World's Perspective: John Webster and the Jacobean Drama* (1983); Charles Forker, *The Skull beneath the Skin* (1986); Dena Goldberg, *Between Worlds* (1987); Christina Luckyj, *A Winter's Snake* (1989).

tion, they become aware of the moral dimension of their own seeing. Such an awareness is reinforced by repeated references in the marriage scene to sight and blindness: bloodshot eyes, efforts to improve another's eyesight, declarations of blindness, a playful imitation of blind Fortune. Wordplay and stage images increase the pressure on Webster's audience to pay attention to their own watching, to become aware of themselves as spectators.

In a later scene at the Roman Catholic Shrine of our Lady of Loretto, unidentified pilgrims watch as the Cardinal exchanges his holy apparel ("cross, hat, robes, and ring") for a soldier's armor and banishes the Duchess and her family who have "feign[ed] a pilgrimage" to the holy site. The audience thus watches bystanders watching a quasi-religious ceremony, in which the Cardinal brazenly uses a holy shrine to assert and display his political power and the Duchess fraudulently poses as a holy pilgrim. All this action is presented as a dumb show—a dramatic convention that displays images divorced from words and thereby calls attention to itself as spectacle. Webster uses the dumb show to arouse suspicion of both spectacle and theatricality. An accompanying song, sung by churchmen to heighten the awe of the beholders at the Cardinal's display of ecclesiastical power, uses repeated references to artifice and adornment ("deck," "arts," "beautify," "adorn'd"), further reinforcing a distrust of the ecclesiastical spectacle by invoking the language of the reformers to associate it with the man-made and ungodly. Identified with the bystanders who watch from the margins, expressing skepticism about the Cardinal's orchestrated spectacle, Webster's spectators become aware of themselves as witnesses, actively interpreting what they see.

Such an awareness is particularly acute in act 4, when Bosola carries out Ferdinand's orders to torture and kill the Duchess. Forced to look upon images of death and madness, while she herself is watched intently by both her tormentors and Webster's audiences, the Duchess functions here as both spectator and spectacle. As a spectator, she finds herself "plagued in art": her eyes are deceived, her emotions manipulated, her reason assaulted. Although she is initially tricked into believing the wax figures are the corpses of her family, and suffers accordingly, her watching becomes more and more self-reflexive. Forced by her mad brother to look upon a series of images and shows concocted to horrify and terrorize her, and ultimately "to bring her to despair," the Duchess uses her brother's perverted art, paradoxically, to thwart his sadistic desires. Rather than fixing her eyes on the bodies of her loved ones or becoming transfixed by the theater of madmen, she uses spectacle to turn away from the visible things of the world—her wealth, titles, status, even her husband and children—and to intensify her desire for God. The corpse-like bodies in the morbid theatrical tableau, the anguished speeches and chaotic dances in the madmen's theater, and the satirical descriptions of the aristocrats' tomb sculpture do not crush the Duchess, as Ferdinand intends, but rather strengthen her, for in confronting them—looking upon them—she begins to acknowledge, and then to relinquish, her love of the world.

By casting the Duchess as a spectator who is tricked and tormented by representations of death and madness, Webster makes the act of viewing representational art visible. Rather than fool the eye, as Ferdinand (and Foxe's papists) do, he instructs it, showing his spectators how to view scenes of bodily torture and death. By encouraging them to consider their own watching, he prevents them from being tricked into believing that the image of the thing is the thing itself and makes them less vulnerable to being "plagued in art."

If the Duchess is a spectator of art and theater, she herself is closely observed by both on-stage spectators and those who watch from their seats in the theater. Her suffering is presented as a sorrowful spectacle, a martyrdom that, much like Foxe's martyrdoms, constructs its viewers as witnesses with moral responsibility. Webster's appropriation of the rhetoric of martyrdom is quite explicit. He calls the Duchess "a wretch that's broke upon the wheel," "one / Of the miracles of pity," and one who "gives a majesty to adversity." He depicts his heroine as a woman who openly identifies with religious martyrs, one who asks heaven to "cease crowning martyrs," acknowledges to her tormentor that she is "chain'd to endure all [his] tyranny," and bravely faces death, declaring, "I long to bleed" (4.1, 4.2). And he depicts her responses to torture as essentially those of the Protestant martyr: exemplary patience, remarkable fortitude, and extraordinary faith in an unseen God. She stands up to the tyranny of her brothers, the powerful representatives of church and state, and, like Foxe's martyrs who "neither struggled nor stirred, but only lifted up [their] hands towards heaven," she calmly and heroically anticipates heaven.[21]

---

[21] Foxe, *A&M*, 8:404. For a discussion of Christian martyrs as "mirrors of patience," see William J. Bouwsma, *John Calvin* (1988), pp. 170–71. For a discussion of Calvin's

Although it may seem unlikely that Webster would cast an Italian duchess as a Protestant martyr, he aligns the Duchess with the reformed religion in a number of ways. First, by locating her conflict with her brothers in the issue over whether a private vow of marriage is a legitimate one, he links her to some of the more radical Protestant positions on rituals and authority. Second, by depicting her as a rebel against powerful agents of the Roman Church and Italian aristocracy, he appeals to English prejudices against the Roman clergy and implicitly associates her with English Protestantism. Finally, in portraying her responses to her torture, he emphasizes her renunciation of earthly things and her faith in an invisible God, precisely the qualities celebrated in the Protestant martyrs. If at the beginning of the play the Duchess is a problematic character, willful and defiant and determined to realize her desires, she becomes in act 4 the very mirror of patience, tested and purified by suffering, her calm acceptance of death contrasting dramatically with the fury of her persecutors. Because her tormentors are a duke and a cardinal, her capacity to endure their cruelty functions as John Knott believes the Protestant martyrs' response to suffering does, revealing "the limitations of the power of church or state to control the subversive spirit."[22]

In constructing the Duchess's death as a martyrdom, Webster, like Foxe, emphasizes the act of watching. However riveting the theatrical display of her persecution and strangulation, Webster's audiences view it, at least in part, through the eyes of others who are present on stage with her and witness her pain, anguish, and death. Cariola, Ferdinand, and especially Bosola all serve as on-stage spectators who observe the Duchess as she watches Ferdinand's cruel theater. Webster's audiences, like Foxe's readers, are thus engaged simultaneously in watching the torture of a heroic figure (a torture that takes the form of theater and art) and in watching witnesses watch this event. As witnesses, however, they find themselves uncomfortably aligned with Bosola who, as Ferdinand's spy, makes his living as a watcher and observer. Webster's spectators occupy a position that is very similar to Bosola's: marginali-

---

theory of suffering, see ibid., pp. 183–84, and John Calvin, *Four godlye sermons agaynst the pollution of idolatries* (1561), sermon no. 3, sig. D7ʳ–C2ᵛ. For a discussion of Foxe's construction of Protestant heroism and martyrdom, see John R. Knott, *Discourses of Martyrdom* (1993), pp. 2–9.

[22] Knott, *Discourses of Martyrdom*, p. 8.

zed and disempowered, they are onlookers who keenly observe the behavior of others from a distance. Like Bosola, they gain access to the private world of the Duchess as observers who spy, eavesdrop, and interpret what they see and hear. And like Bosola, too, they assume they can do nothing about the corruption, hypocrisy, and evil they discover, constrained as they are by their status as audience members.

Bosola, however, takes on the role of the player as well as the spectator. To carry out his duties as Ferdinand's spy, Bosola must be a skillful actor as well as an astute observer, deviously playing the part of a loyal servant in order to carry out his espionage. In the torture scenes he continues to play roles, wearing a series of masks—old man, tomb-maker, bellman—as he torments the Duchess. But the last of these roles makes Bosola an actor in the other sense of the word: when he orders the executioners to kill the Duchess, his act causes the death of the woman he has been watching so intently. Although he tries to distance himself from his evil acts by adopting fictional masks, refusing at one point to appear before the Duchess "in my own shape," Bosola discovers that he cannot maintain the gap he would preserve between self and mask, acting and playacting. Bosola's eventual complicity in the Duchess's death thus raises disturbing questions about the audience's own watching.[23]

In the immediate aftermath of the Duchess's execution, Ferdinand rebukes Bosola both for playing the role of villain and failing to be a sympathetic spectator. Although he masterminded the torture of his sister, Ferdinand castigates Bosola for his failure to feel compassion for the woman he watched being tortured. "Why," he asks as he gazes upon his dead sister, "didst not thou pity her?" And, although he assigned Bosola the role of torturer and executioner, he both likens his servant to a stage actor who plays a villain and holds him responsible for the role he has played: "as we observe in tragedies / That a good actor many times is curs'd, / For playing a villain's part," he tells Bosola, "I hate thee for 't" (4.2.288–90). Having been positioned repeatedly as onlooker and actor, Bosola finds himself being held accountable for actions he performed both as a spectator and a player. Through the character of Bosola, Webster thus explores the relation

---

[23] For an interesting discussion of the way Renaissance plays implicate their audiences in the action, see Marjorie Garber, " 'Vassal Actors': The Role of the Audience in Shakespearean Tragedy" (1979).

between looking and acting (in both senses of the word). How, he asks, is playacting akin to acting in the world? In what way does watching a representation of a violent act implicate the spectator in that act of violence? How is watching a play an action with moral consequences? What are the consequences of witnessing acts of cruelty and feeling no pity? And what difference does pity make?

Webster forces his spectators to reflect upon the very act they engage in when they watch a play. By positioning the Duchess as *both* the spectator of Ferdinand's morbid art and mad theater *and* the object of Bosola's and the audience's gaze, he encourages them to see themselves seeing and being seen. And by positioning Bosola as *both* the observer of the Duchess *and* the actor who dutifully plays his part in Ferdinand's sadistic theater, he invites them to consider the ways in which they are implicated in the actions they witness. By reflexively engaging his spectators in acts of looking, spying, and judging, he turns their powers of observation upon themselves.

Significantly, both Ferdinand and Bosola are deeply affected by the sight of the woman they have tortured and executed. When Bosola presents Ferdinand with the spectacle of the dead Duchess and her children, telling him to "Fix your eye here," Ferdinand initially resists looking. He orders Bosola to "Cover her face," and he complains "mine eyes dazzle." Almost immediately, however, he demands to look upon her, saying "Let me see her face again." The sight of her uncovered corpse apparently breaks down his defenses, for it is then that he berates his servant for failing to feel pity and following his orders. Declaring his sister's murder to be "a deed of darkness," he abruptly exits, only to appear in the final act a deranged man totally unable to confront his own dark deed. "I have cruel sore eyes," he laments.

When Bosola looks upon the body of the Duchess, however, the sight of it arouses the pity that Ferdinand had found so notably absent in him. Although he had willingly tormented her and mercilessly overseen her execution, the sight of the dead Duchess profoundly moves Bosola, who, quite out of character, weeps with compassion, admits his own wrongdoing, and vows to make amends. Alone in the room with the corpses of the Duchess and her children, he speaks of pity, mercy, sorrow, tears, and penitence. Feeling keenly the pangs of conscience, he envisions himself in hell. "A guilty conscience," he declares remorsefully as he gazes upon the corpse, "is a black register, wherein is writ / All our good deed and bad, a perspective / That shows us hell!"

(4.2.356–59). What Bosola sees when he looks on the strangled Duchess, in other words, is his own depravity. In marked contrast to Ferdinand's dazzled and "cruel sore eyes," Bosola's eyes are directed inward, to his own sinfulness, and beyond to a final reckoning. The sorrowful spectacle of the dead Duchess arouses Bosola's conscience, enabling him to see himself in an internal "court of conscience," arraigned, judged, and condemned.

Conscience: A Thousand Witnesses

Bosola can only read the "black register" of his deeds and look through the optic glass that shows him himself damned in hell by taking up a position outside himself and witnessing his own actions as if he were a spectator of them. In Webster's construction, the conscience acts as an independent, though interior, witness that shows the self to the self. This is precisely how Calvin defines the conscience. The conscience, he writes—and I quote from Thomas Norton's 1562 English translation of *The Institutes*—is "a feling of God's judgement as a witnesse adjoyned with [men], whiche doth not suffer them to hyde theyr synnes." It "doth together witnesse with men, when theyr thoughtes do accuse or acquite them in the judgement of God." It is "a keper joyned to man, to marke and watch all hys secretes, that nothing should remaine buried in darkenesse. Whereupon also cometh that old proverbe, conscience is a thousand witnesses."[24] In defining the conscience, Calvin thus focuses on the act of witnessing, an act he associates with seeing and judging. He imagines the conscience an interior spectator "joyned to man, to marke and watch all hys secretes," and therefore a faculty that enables the self to see itself fully, without suppressing knowledge of its evil ways or rationalizing its sins. The conscience, then, enables man to see himself as God sees him. "By it," the English Calvinist William Perkins writes, "man knowes that thing of himselfe, which God also knowes of him. Man hath two witnesses of his thoughtes, God, and his owne conscience . . . [which bears] witnes unto God either with the man or against him."[25] Both Perkins and Calvin thus identify the conscience with the reflexive act of seeing oneself being seen.

---

[24] Calvin, *Institution of Christian Religion* 4.10.3.
[25] William Perkins, *The Whole Treatise of the Cases of Conscience* (1608), sig. C6ᵛ.

The reflexivity of the conscience is a central concern of the English Calvinists who write in the late sixteenth and early seventeenth centuries. Devoting whole tracts to the subject of the conscience, they repeatedly use metaphors of sight and spectatorship to convey the inner workings of the conscience. Some even associate the interior act of witnessing one's own actions with espionage, calling the conscience a spy who informs the self about the self. "Conscience," writes Jeremiah Dyke," "is placed in the soule as God's spy, and man's superiour and overseer." It is "exact and punctual in setting down the particulars of a mans whole life, that it may bee a faithful witnesse either for him, or against him . . . The office it is ready to doe at all times . . . and most of all at the last day."[26] John Woolton also describes the conscience as a spy, "fashioned in man by almighty God, to be a witnesse and an informer of mankinde." He stresses the judgmental function of the conscience, noting that the conscience "summoneth us as it were before the tribunall seat of God, sometime accusing, sometime excusing."[27] Spy, overseer, informer, judge: according to the early English Protestants, God placed the conscience in humans "to prescribe, prohibit, absolve and condemne *de jure.*" Defining the conscience as " 'a man's judgment of himself, according to the judgment of God of him,' " William Ames describes the process by which the conscience examines the self as a " 'reflex act' " that gives one "a power . . . to enter into and perceive what is in himself."[28] Reflexivity characterizes all these Protestant constructions of the conscience. By stressing the central role of the conscience in faith, the reformers therefore nurture in the Protestant believer the development of a self-conscious, self-regulating inner spectator who, split off from its own willful self, spies on itself, witnessing its own actions from the perspective of an all-seeing and all-knowing God and judging them accordingly.

Calvin's notion of the conscience as an internalized witness who marks and watches the self's secrets fosters a heightened attention to the gaze that I find operating in both Foxe and Webster. Foxe, who

[26] Jeremiah Dyke, *Good Conscience* (1624), sigs. B6ᵛ–B7, B8.

[27] John Woolton, *Of the Conscience* (1576), sig. A1ᵛ.

[28] Richard Carpenter, *The Conscionable Christian* (1623), sig. K1ᵛ; and William Ames, *Conscience with the Power and Cases Thereof* (1639), 2.5.9–10. For a discussion of early Protestant notions of the conscience, see David Foxgraver, "Self-Examination in John Calvin and William Ames" (1994); John S. Wilks, *The Idea of Conscience in Renaissance Tragedy* (1990).

expresses the hope that his narratives of martyrdom will help his readers establish "a good conscience," believes that his verbal and visual representations of martyrdom will function as mirrors, enabling his readers to see and judge themselves: "For what man, reading the misery of these godly persons may not therein, as in a glass, behold his own case, whether he be godly or godless?"[29] Foxe assumes that his spectacles of martyrdom will elicit self-examination. He asks his readers to consider whether they, like the martyrs he celebrates, could sustain faith in an invisible God in the face of sustained persecution, bodily torture, and extreme psychological pressure. For Foxe, the historical act of witnessing (observing, testifying, giving evidence) is integrally connected to an internal kind of witnessing (seeing oneself being seen by God, providing evidence for or against oneself). To observe the martyrdom of heroic Protestants is also to observe—look into and judge—oneself.

Webster presents Bosola as a character whose conscience, once aroused, condemns his evil acts and motivates him to make amends. He also depicts the Cardinal as a man who is, in the end, tormented by "a guilty conscience." Both Bosola and the Cardinal associate the awakened conscience with spectatorship. Bosola experiences the conscience as an optical instrument, "a perspective" powerful enough for him to see himself in hell. The Cardinal finds that his conscience is a punitive mirror, reminding him of his inevitable damnation and tormenting him with threatening images of retribution. When he looks at his own reflection in water, he sees not the reflection of his face but a terrifying image of judgment:

> When I look into the fish-ponds, in my garden,
> Methinks I see a thing, arm'd with a rake
> That seems to strike at me.
>
> (5.5.5–7)

Both the Cardinal and Bosola turn their eyes inward, internalizing the act of seeing. Both come to see their evil deeds from the perspectives of an informer, a witness, and a judge. Both imagine themselves damned in hell for acts they committed in secret.

Webster does not simply thematize the awakening of conscience,

---

[29] Foxe, *A&M*, 1:521–22.

however. Through such metadramatic devices as the singing and dancing madmen, he explores the capacity of theater to arouse the consciences of its spectators. Ferdinand hopes that the lunatics' disturbing
performance will bring his sister to despair, and he tempts her to see
herself reflected in the mad actors' disorienting antics. He hopes, in
other words, that she will identify with the lost souls whose inner torment he stages and, as a consequence, believe herself to be one of the
damned. Webster here addresses one of the most controversial aspects
of the reformers' relentless attention to the conscience: religious despair. Opponents of reform frequently accused the Protestant religion,
with its emphasis on internal surveillance and judgment, of endanger-
ing souls by leading the faithful to despair of their salvation. Madness,
suicide, and other self-destructive behavior, they claimed, were the dangerous consequences of an overactive, keenly sensitive, and unneces-
sarily harsh conscience.[30]

The madmen sent by Ferdinand to terrorize his sister appear to be
victims of their own overactive consciences. Anticipating the hellish interior images that later haunt Bosola and the Cardinal, they describe
their personal, terrifying visions of Doomsday and hell. Furthermore,
their visions feature the metaphor of glass and its multiple associations
with seeing and spectatorship. They imagine themselves drawing nearer
to Doomsday by peering at it through a telescope, setting the world on
fire with a magnifying glass and thus bringing on the Judgment Day,
surveying hell—a glass house where devils are glassblowers, "continually blowing up women's souls"—and using a glass to project shocking
pornographic images. Their obsession with different kinds of lenses
that magnify, bring into focus, and make visible terrifying visions of
Judgment Day, hell, and sexual perversions suggests that madness, for
Webster, is closely associated with an extreme form of the seeing pro-
moted by an activated conscience.

Although the theatrical madmen prompt the Duchess to ask, "Who
am I?" they do not succeed in driving her to despair. Instead of overwhelming her with their copious images of sexuality, judgment, and
damnation, and thus burdening her conscience with guilt, the theatrical spectacles that Ferdinand employs to drive her to despair have a

---

[30] For an excellent discussion of early Protestantism and despair, see John Stachniewski, *The Persecutory Imagination* (1991); see also D. C. Gunby, "*The Duchess of Malfi*: A
Theological Approach" (1970).

salutary effect. After watching the chaotic dancing and listening to the bizarre songs and crazed speeches of the madmen, she declares she is now "well awake," and she accepts her impending death as a "gift." The Duchess thus uses the theatrical display of madmen in a way that defeats her brother. Turning her eyes inward, she acknowledges her sinfulness, confronts her mortality, and yet, contrary to Ferdinand's expectations, anticipates heaven. Ferdinand's disruptive and frightening theater backfires; though it awakens her conscience, the Duchess does not despair but instead arrives at a new awareness of herself and a strengthened faith in God.

The belief that theater can awaken the conscience of a spectator motivates Hamlet's production of "The Murder of Gonzago," as I have shown in Chapter 3. It is perhaps most fully articulated by Thomas Heywood in his defense of the stage, *An Apology for Actors*, published just a year before *The Duchess*, in 1612, along with a commendatory verse by John Webster. Answering vitriolic attacks on the stage, Heywood asserts that dramatic representations of vicious acts, far from encouraging vice, attack "the consciences of the spectators."[31] He relates specific incidents in which audience members watching theatrical representations of crimes they have secretly committed, are, like Shakespeare's Claudius, overcome with guilt. Influenced, perhaps, by *Hamlet*, Heywood defends the stage in part because it fosters precisely that sense of a split self that Shakespeare's play so effectively cultivates. Drama thus enables guilty audience members to observe their own evil acts from a position outside themselves, to, in effect, see themselves being seen.

In all of Heywood's examples, spectators who see their crimes reenacted on the stage can no longer repress their guilt and confess. One woman, "finding her conscience (at this presentment) extremely troubled, suddenly skritched and cryd out, 'O my husband, my husband,' " thus revealing her complicity in her husband's murder. Another, "out of the trouble of her afflicted conscience," confessed a murder she had committed many years earlier. Although scholars doubt that these stories are true, Heywood vehemently asserts their veracity, claiming in one instance that "many eye-witnesses of this accident yet living, vocally do confirm it."[32] Surely Protestant notions of the conscience inform

---

[31] Thomas Heywood, *An Apology for Actors* (1612), sig. F3ᵛ.
[32] Ibid., sigs. G1ᵛ, G2ᵛ, G2ʳ.

both Heywood's belief that theater has the power to awaken the conscience and Webster's keen interest in theatricality and spectatorship.
Nurturing the development of an internalized spectator—a witness—
who both spies on the self and judges its behavior, Protestantism may
also help to account for the intensely reflexive nature of so many Elizabethan and Jacobean plays.

According to Heywood, stage plays invite their spectators to adopt
the perspective of an omniscient and judging God, and thus to internalize the divine spectator in the theater of the world. Drawing on the
conventional *theatrum mundi* trope, he explicitly calls attention to God
as a divine spectator who watches—and judges—the human theater
from a privileged seat in the heavens:

> If then the world a Theater present,
> As by the roundnesse it appears most fit,
> Built with starre-galleries of hye ascent,
> In which *Jehove* doth as spectator sit.
> And chiefe determiner to applaud the best,
> And their indevours crowne with more then merit.
> But by their evill actions doomes the rest,
> To end disgrac't whilst others praise inherit.[33]

By emphasizing the seeing, knowing, and judging functions of God in
the larger theater of the world, Heywood encourages his readers to
think of the audiences in a theater as both powerful spectators—their
position analogous to an all-seeing God—and as powerless actors—objects of the divine gaze, their roles scripted:

> This a true subject acts, and that a Traytor,
> The first applauded, and the last confin'd
> This plaies an honest man, and that a knave
> .   .   .   .
>
> All men have parts, and each man acts his owne
> .   .   .   .
>
>   then our play's begun,

---

[33] Ibid., sig. A4ᵛ.

When we are borne, and to the world first enter,
And all finde Exits when their parts are done.[34]

Imagining a world divided into the elect and the reprobate—"a true subject" and "a Traytor," "an honest man and a knave"—Heywood interprets the *theatrum mundi* trope in a distinctly Calvinist way.

Like Heywood, Webster uses the trope to raise questions about human agency, free will, and moral action. Confounded by his inability to do good, Bosola draws an analogy between himself and an actor in a play. When asked to explain how he mistakenly killed the man he set out to save, he replies:

> In a mist: I know not how—
> Such a mistake as I have often seen
> In a play . . .
>
> (5.5.94–96)

In dramatizing the tragic predicament of characters like Bosola, who "cannot be suffer'd / To do good" even when they "have a mind to it!" (4.2.359–60), Webster thus calls attention to the way a dramatic script can serve as a metaphor for predestination. His metadramatic gestures invite his audiences to imagine themselves playing scripted parts in a larger theater of the world. "I account this world a tedious theatre," sighs the Duchess during her torture, "For I do play a part in't 'gainst my will" (4.1.84–85).

Watching is, for Webster, not only an act of observation, but an observable act. Furthermore, *not* watching can be fatal. In an episode that seems to parody and invert the counterfeit corpses that Ferdinand shows his sister, Webster depicts "real" death and violence being mistaken for pretend violence. Having assured his men that any noises they might hear emanating from his chamber will be the result of "counterfeiting" and should therefore be ignored, the Cardinal cannot convince his men that his anguished cries for help are authentic. In obeying his instructions, they fail to maintain their watch, fail to interpret the desperate cries for help as genuine, and fail to distinguish between literal violence and a staged representation of violence. Webster presents their inattention to the drama unfolding in the Cardinal's

[34] Ibid., sigs. A4–A4^v.

chambers, their stubborn refusal to believe that the Cardinal's terror is real, as a faulty kind of witnessing, no less contemptible than Ferdinand's pitiless gaze.

Like the Protestant artists and polemicists I discuss in Chapter 2, Webster presents two rival theaters, the one (Ferdinand's) demonic and dangerous, the other (the Duchess's) godly and potentially redemptive. The theatricality associated with Ferdinand, his brother the Cardinal, and, by extension, the Roman Catholic Church, involves an abuse of images, but the sorrowful spectacle of the Duchess's martyrdom, appropriated from Protestant martyrologies, arouses pity and awakens the conscience. The former collapses the distinction between sign and thing signified, deceiving and confusing the spectator. The latter induces self-examination.

Webster thus fosters in his audiences a self-consciousness about the nature of theater, a self-consciousness that derives from two competing kinds of theater. The one, polluted and perverse, cozens the eye; the other, pure and heroic, arouses the conscience and nurtures its audience's capacity for judgment, compassion, self-knowledge, and moral action. Through this juxtaposition, Webster articulates a Protestant aesthetics of the stage and explores the crucial distinctions between false and true, artificial and natural, duplicitous and honest, cunning and plain. A long critical tradition that celebrates the character of the Duchess as a true, essential, and authentic self suggests how fully he succeeded in naturalizing a Protestant form of theatricality.

"Never See Her More"

Webster's deliberate juxtaposition of a pure and a polluted theater continues in the final act of *The Duchess.* In striking contrast to the final scenes of intrigue set in the decadent court, scenes that feature cunning and misperception, the churchyard scene dramatizes and elicits an inward or spiritual kind of sight. Walking in the ruins of a medieval cloister, Antonio experiences a moment of profound illumination. Unaware of his wife's death, he hears an echo that sounds like her voice, but he dismisses it as a "dead thing" until it declares that he will "never see her more." Shaken by the possibility that he will be forever denied the sight of her, he sees a vision of her. At the very moment he hears the echo repeat the words "*never see her more,*" he explains to his companion Delio that "on the sudden, a clear light / Presented me a face folded in sorrow" (5.3.39–45). The dead Duchess seems to him to be present in the ruins, her voice speaking to him in the echo, her face appearing to him in a sorrowful vision.

Antonio's transcendent vision is in marked contrast to the rest of act 5, which features Machiavellian intrigue, deadly espionage, covert acts, tragic errors, accidental deaths, and faulty interpretations. Concealed in the dark, Bosola overhears the Cardinal's secret confession that he ordered the murder of the Duchess and then observes the Cardinal poison his mistress. A violent confrontation between Bosola and Antonio—potential allies who mistake each other for enemies—results in Antonio's death. And a bloody melee in which Ferdinand stabs the Cardinal and Bosola before Bosola kills Ferdinand is ignored by the Cardinal's men, convinced that the commotion is a theatrical act.

Juxtaposed to all this confusion, the scene in the ruins explores the possibility of a startlingly different mode of seeing, one understood to be either an interior or a supernatural kind of vision. Antonio's vision is anticipated in the scene immediately preceding it, where a guilty Bosola thinks he sees the ghost of the Duchess—"still methinks the duchess / Haunts me; there, there!"—then dismisses it as a product of his "melancholy" (5.2.345–47). But Antonio does not rationalize his experience, nor does he accept Delio's explanation that it is merely the workings of his "fancy." Instead, his vision of the Duchess's illuminated face, folded in sorrow, inspires him to act.

The spirit of the Duchess seems to inhabit and enliven the ruined abbey, stirring in a receptive Antonio the memory of her. And it is as an internal memory image—divorced from her material presence, aroused by language, seen with the mind's eye—that her sorrowful face moves her husband, and, I suggest, the play's spectators. Although many critics have fretted over the absence of the Duchess in the fifth act, complaining of "the dangerously disrupted, broken-backed structure" of the play,[35] her physical absence, I suggest, is precisely the point. Removed from the sight of the audience, transformed into a voice or echo, manifested in Bosola's haunting vision and Antonio's clear vision, the Duchess does not disappear in the final act but rather reappears in the spirit. Her absent presence forces Webster's audiences, as well as Antonio, to look beyond the material stage. Only by relin-

[35] Bliss, *World's Perspective*, p. 140.

quishing the body of the player can they successfully internalize the image of the Duchess. Having witnessed her death in act 4, a death depicted as a martyrdom, they are confronted here with its implications. How are they to understand Antonio's vision? How to interpret the echo that resembles the voice of the dead Duchess?

Antonio confronts his personal loss in a place that evokes for him— as it surely would for many members of the Stuart audience—a deep sense of cultural loss as well: the ruins of a medieval cloister. In his elegiac response to the "ancient ruins" he surveys in sadness, he laments the transience of all earthly structures and ponders the fallacy of believing in the external trappings of the church. Standing among the skeletal remains of monasticism, near a "piece of a cloister," Antonio associates the physical ruins of the abbey with death and disease, not only of the body but also of the church:

> I do love these ancient ruins:
> We never tread upon them but we set
> Our foot upon some reverend history.
> And questionless, here in this open court,
> Which now lies naked to the injuries
> Of stormy weather, some men lie interr'd
> Lov'd the church so well, and gave so largely to't,
> They thought it should have canopy'd their bones
> Till doomsday; but all things have their end:
> Churches and cities, which have diseases like to men,
> Must have like death that we have.
>
> (5.3.9-19)

Surely for most of Webster's original audiences, the ancient ruins— the broken walls of a Roman Catholic abbey—are emblematic of the medieval church and all it had come to represent in seventeenth-century England: artifice, ostentation, corruption, and carnality. At the time Webster was writing, of course, medieval abbeys and cloisters lay in physical ruins throughout England, the sites of iconoclastic violence. They must have served as powerful reminders to Webster and his contemporaries of the wholesale destruction of the old religion, visual proof of the success of the Reformation. "Temples stande now forlorne," Robert Parker comments with some sadness, then adds, "yet must they be razed because in time they may recover credit againe."[36]

Webster uses the ruins to evoke feelings of loss and to mourn the passing of the medieval church, remembering its beauty, comfort, and stability. But he also turns his spectators eyes away from its artifice and worldliness. Although Antonio laments the death of the church in whose open courtyard he stands, he also accepts the inevitability of its demise and moralizes on the delusion of men who "gave so largely to't," thinking it would house their bodies until the end of time. Despite his deep sense of loss, he does not try to hold on to the past or celebrate the material splendor of the older church; instead, in the spirit of an emerging Protestantism, he renounces the beautiful. Stripped of their original grandeur, the ruins no longer inspire awe or admiration, but instead elicit inner reflection.

The physical ruins where Antonio sees the vision of "a face folded in sorrow" echo a figure of speech applied to the Duchess during the torture scenes. In a conversation with her maid, the Duchess describes her suffering and then asks Cariola, "who do I look like now?" After likening her to a portrait of herself—"a deal of life in show, but none in practice"—Cariola compares her to "some reverent monument / Whose ruins are even pitied." The Duchess assents to this analogy and then adds, "And Fortune seems only to have her eyesight / To behold my tragedy" (4.2.30–36). Portrait, ruined monument, tragic spectacle: the Duchess is constructed here in terms of art, and Webster's audiences are encouraged both to view her and to view themselves viewing her. Surely it is relevant that earlier in the play the Duchess struggles against her brothers' attempts to encase her "like a holy relic" and protests to Antonio that she is not a "figure cut in alabaster" but rather "flesh and blood." Her attempt to escape the aestheticized and fetishized images men construct of her—to shatter their images, play the iconoclast—culminates, ironically, with the theatrical display of her strangled body. But Webster does not end his play with the display of the Duchess's body, nor does he perpetuate an idealizing/idolizing view of the Duchess. Rather, in portraying her death as a martyrdom, he explores the ways in which her murder—her physical annihilation— affects the spectators who witness it. And in the scene set in the ancient ruins, he entertains the possibility that her spirit—liberated from the

---

[36] Robert Parker, *A scholasticall discourse* (1607), sig. I4^r.

prison of the body—can communicate to the living, that her death need not be experienced as either silence or absence.

Although Bosola dies lamenting that "We are only like dead walls, or vaulted graves, / That ruin'd, yields no echo" (5.5.97–98), Webster's deeply ironic play questions Bosola's conclusion: the audience, along with Antonio and Delio, has heard the echo in the ruins and grappled with its meaning. Surveying the bodies of Bosola, Ferdinand, and the Cardinal, Delio likens "these wretched eminent things" to prints made in snow that evaporate with the sun, but he also holds out the possibility that the bodies have a use, can be put to some higher purpose. Speaking to the play's spectators, as well as the men gathered on stage, he instructs, "Let us make noble use / Of this great ruin" (5.5.110–11). Having constructed his audiences as witnesses, Webster here charges them with making "noble use" of his play's spectacles. What might the noble use of the spectacle of death entail?

The ruined body of the Duchess, the hollow ruins of the Roman Catholic abbey, the devastating, general ruin of the final scene are powerful theatrical images that probe their viewers' capacity for pity, self-examination, and ethical choice. Unlike the ostentatious images of the decadent Cardinal and the demonic images of the mad Duke, they deflect the eyes of their spectators away from the physical world and direct them inward and, perhaps, heavenward.

Epilogue

The dedicatory verses appended to the 1612 edition of Thomas Heywood's *An Apology for Actors* are remarkable for their gestures toward an explicitly "Protestant" aesthetics. Their embrace of "plainnesse," their distrust of any "florish of Eloquence," their disavowal of "glosse" and "painting," their distinction between "us'd" and "abus'd" art, their construction of the antitheatrical antagonist as an "open Saint, and secret varlet": all these expressions are appropriated from Protestant discourse.[1] Like the *Apology* itself, these poems carefully align the theater with Protestantism, deriving their defense of plays from the very theology that inspires their antitheatrical opponents.

Similarly coded language appears in a poem by Thomas Middleton praising *The Duchess of Malfi* and its author. Middleton claims that Webster's art is superior to the most magnificent monuments of medieval culture, "express[ing] more art," he writes, "than Death's cathedral palaces." And he explicitly identifies Webster's aesthetics with the Protestant aesthetic of plainness: "Thy note / Be ever plainness, 'tis the richest coat."[2] On what grounds does Middleton declare a play like *The Duchess*, with its intricate and highly contrived plot and its richly figurative language, plain? More to my point, how can Webster's play be said to achieve an aesthetic of plainness when it so unabashedly displays elaborate spectacles of horror, madness, and death, including such sen-

---

[1] Heywood, *An Apology for Actors*, (1612), sigs. A3ʳ, a3ʳ.

[2] Thomas Middleton, "Commendatory Verses," in *The Duchess of Malfi*, by John Webster (1964), p. 4; I am struck by Middleton's use of a theatrical metaphor here, speaking of plainness as a costume, "the richest coat."

sational images as a dead man's hand? The answer, I submit, has less to do with the spectacular content of the play—which can hardly be understood as plain—than with the aesthetic experience of the spectators.

As early as Foxe, English reformers identify Protestantism with plainness, which they understand as both an ethos—a way of being—and an aesthetics. Basing their notion of plainness on the character of Christ, they privilege the ethical qualities of authenticity, openness (guilelessness), humility, inwardness, and truthfulness. Plainness in art therefore expresses what is natural, authentic, heartfelt, and true. Instead of calling attention to the author's artfulness and cunning through the use of fanciful ornaments and unnecessary rhetorical embellishments, it seeks to stir the emotions, move the soul, and reveal inner truths. Predictably, the English reformers contrast plainness to an ethos and aesthetics of worldliness they associate with the Roman Church, its ceremonies, rituals, and devotional practices. Roman Catholicism, they insist, fosters worldly sophistication, encouraging a perverse love of artifice and an excessive attention to externals and also promoting worldly desires, duplicity, arrogance, and cunning.[3]

The Duchess of Malfi is in many ways *about* worldly desires, duplicity, arrogance, and cunning, all of which Webster locates in the Italian court and Roman Church. But, as I show in Chapter 7, it exposes the worldliness of court and church as dangerous and deadly, arousing distrust of artifice and cunning, not awe or admiration. Instead of affirming the ostentatious theatricality of the Duke and the Cardinal, it nurtures in its audiences a self-consciousness about their own act of watching a play, thus enabling them to see how images can be cynically manipulated, identities fraudulently constructed, externals deceptively employed. Rather than celebrate human achievement, it elicits pity for human vulnerabilities and insists that its own spectators confront their flaws and fallibilities. For these reasons Middleton can, I think, justifiably claim for Webster the "note" of "plainness."

How viable is Middleton's notion of a plain theater? To what degree did other Renaissance dramatists embrace an aesthetic of plainness, to what degree did they oppose it? And what were the consequences of

---

[3] For discussions of the aesthetic of plainness, see Kenneth J. E. Graham, *The Performance of Conviction* (1994); N. H. Keeble, *The Literary Culture of Non-conformity* (1987), pp. 247–60; John R. Knott, *Discourses of Martyrdom* (1993), pp. 69–74.

dramatists embracing a Protestant aesthetics that, on some level, was profoundly antitheatrical? In exploring these questions, I have shown how plays with strong antitheatrical biases can nevertheless be powerful theater. Indeed, the tragedies of the English Renaissance stage—plays I have identified with the iconoclasm and antitheatricality of early English Protestantism—are generally regarded as the finest drama England has ever produced, their capacity to move and speak to audiences continuing to this day.

If, as I have argued, these plays are the products of the Protestant Reformation, they are also, in the end, the victims of the reformed religion's iconoclastic impulses. Or perhaps it would be more accurate to say they participate in their own demise. By adopting the iconoclastic motives and appropriating the revolutionary rhetorical strategies of the Protestant reformers, they not only reform the stage, they actively engage in suppressing it. Inasmuch as they successfully demystify and contain their own dazzling spectacles and flamboyant theatricality, they purge the theater of much of its most alluring elements. Displays of magic, haunting visions, enchanted images, seductive women, exotic strangers: eventually all are anatomized, exposed as fraudulent, rendered impotent, and discarded, their power to enthrall exhausted. The closing of the theaters, I am suggesting, occurs not just because of pressures from the outside, but also because of pressures from within. However powerful, however moving and true, an iconoclastic theater eventually consumes itself.

More than twenty years after the closing of the London theaters in 1642, the best known puritan poet of England, John Milton, wrote *Samson Agonistes,* a closet drama in the form of a classical tragedy and, fittingly, perhaps the last English play to rehearse the central dialectics of Reformation culture.[4] In his profoundly antitheatrical poem, Milton appears to be fully aware of the conventions of English Protestant tragedy I have been examining here. Like Webster and his contemporary playwrights—and before them, John Bale—Milton juxtaposes two kinds of theaters: a godly with an ungodly one. He depicts the Philistine temple—the house of the pagan god Dagon and thus, for the Hebrews, a place of idolatry—not as a religious temple but as "a spacious theatre" (1605), and he characterizes the celebrations honoring Dagon as the kind of theatrics the reformers associate with the Roman Church,

---

[4] John Milton, "Samson Agonistes," *The Complete Poetry,* ed. Merritt Hughes (1957).

that is, nothing but "triumph, pomp, and games" (1312). In striking contrast to the idolatrous theatricality of the Philistines, Milton imagines that stunning moment when Samson liberates his people by pulling down the pagan temple as divine theater. Samson's iconoclastic act is, for Milton, spectacular theater, both terrifying and triumphant. He constructs the struggle between the idolatrous heathens (aligned with Roman Catholics) and the iconoclastic Israelites (aligned with Protestants) as a struggle between competing modes of theater. In writing what one scholar has called "an antitheatrical text about the theatricality of an iconoclastic act," he in fact works within an established tradition of English Protestant drama, a tradition that includes Kyd and Marlowe, Shakespeare, Middleton, and Webster.[5]

Like the plays of these Renaissance dramatists, Milton's poem is highly attentive to the gaze. It examines and contrasts various modes of seeing: the idolatrous gaze of the Philistine worshipers of Dagon, the erotic gaze of Samson before his fall, when he cannot resist the allure of the beautiful women who repeatedly seduce and trick him, and the inward sight that Samson achieves only after he has been cruelly blinded. Appropriating the Reformation trope of the beautiful woman to figure the idol, Milton portrays Dalila as both a ravishing seductress and a seductive spectacle. By making the biblical whore Samson's legitimate wife, he intensifies the Protestant-induced fear that uxoriousness is a form of idolatry. And by depicting her as a captivating theatrical spectacle, he reinforces fears that the stage itself is a dangerous enchantress. Samson is able to resist Dalila only after he is blind, and it is the blind man's interior gaze—oblivious to externals, judgmental, self-reflective, and aroused by a guilty conscience—that Milton affirms, finding it to be the kind of looking that activates faith. Though the Philistines attempt to display the defeated Samson at their festival, Samson thwarts them, discovering in his defeat the power of God working through him. Instead of becoming the passive and humiliated object of the Philistine's gaze, Samson—"with inward eyes illuminated" (1689)—becomes an actor in a different kind of drama, a divine drama. By allowing God to work through him, he attains martyrdom, becoming the iconoclast through which God achieves his victory over Dagon, a victory that is presented as powerful, spectacular theater.

---

[5] David Loewenstein, *Milton and the Drama of History* (1990), p. 137; I am indebted to Loewenstein's perceptive reading of *Samson Agonistes*.

If Milton appropriates the conventions and strategies of an established tradition of Protestant tragedy, he nevertheless writes at the end of that tradition, after the Renaissance theaters have been closed, their energies spent. His play was never intended to be produced or to be watched, but to be read silently. Its violent iconoclastic spectacle is reported by a messenger, in the tradition of the classical but not the English theater, and is thus even further removed from the bloody spectacles presented on the stages of the Elizabethan and Jacobean theaters. It is a spectacle only in the imagination, a spectacle evoked entirely through language. If its blind hero, like the blinded Gloucester in *King Lear*, learns to "see feelingly," he has no need, as Gloucester has, for some kind of external proof—some miracle—of God's love, but is able to intuit "some rousing motions" (1382) within him, to know without seeing. And although Samson, like Othello, has loved his beautiful wife "not wisely but too well," he is not, as Othello is, tragically mistaken in his assessment of her. Milton's Dalila is the unfaithful temptress that Othello only imagines Desdemona to be, and Samson's fierce, clear-eyed rejection of her is presented as a crucial moment in his spiritual regeneration, not an error that will destroy him.

Closer in time to the disruptive energies of the Reformation, Shakespeare and his contemporaries are far more attentive than Milton to the allure of the old images, the power of the old mysteries, the magic of the old theater. They explore what is lost when the medieval world breaks apart, and they dramatize the fear and confusion that ensue, even as they adopt the demystifying and revolutionary strategies of the reformers. If, for them, iconoclasm is liberating and exhilarating, it is also disturbing and even terrifying. I see them as killing what they love—sumptuous spectacle, awesome ceremony, wondrous magic, and the older, miraculous forms of theatricality. Although Milton depicts a sacrificial act, one committed by a character who surely represents himself, his attitude toward images and theater has hardened. Unlike the earlier dramatists, the blind poet, like his blind hero, does not appear any longer to be tempted by the theatricality he seeks to destroy; he holds it in contempt. One of the great achievements of Renaissance tragedy, in contrast, is surely its capacity to capture the mystery of what it would demystify, the allure of what it would master and contain.

Bibliography

Primary Texts

Ainsworth, Henry. *An Arrow against Idolatrie.* London, 1624.

Ainsworth, Henry, and Francis Johnson. *An Apologie or Defense of . . . Brownists.* London, 1604.

Ames, William. *Conscience with the Power and Cases Thereof.* London, 1639.

Anton, Robert. *The Philosopher's Satyrs.* London, 1616.

Beza, Theodore. *A Book of Christian Questions and Answers.* Trans. Arthur Golding. London, 1586.

Bradshaw, William. *A Short Treatise, of the Crosse in baptisme.* London, 1604.

Browne, Thomas. "Pseudodoxia Epidemica." In *The Works of Sir Thomas Browne,* ed. Charles Sayle. 3 vols. Edinburgh: J. Grant, 1927.

Bucer, Martin. *A treatise declaryng and shewing dyvers causes that pyctures and other ymages ar in no wise to be suffred in churches.* London, [1535?].

Calvin, John. *The Catechisme, or Manner to teache children the Christian religion.* London, 1582.

———. "The Epistle of Paul the Apostle to the Hebrews." C. 's Commentaries. Trans. William B. Johnston. Grand Rapids, Mich.: Wm. B. Eerdmans, 1963.

———. *Four godlye sermons agaynst the pollution of idolatries.* London, 1561.

———. *Institutes of the Christian Religion.* Trans. Ford Lewis Battles. Ed. John T. McNeill. 2 vols. Philadelphia: Westminster, 1960.

———. *The Institution of Christian Religion.* Trans. Thomas Norton. London, 1562.

———. *Sermons of Maister John Calvin, upon the Book of Job.* Trans. Arthur Golding. London, 1584.

———. *The sermons of M. John Calvin upon the Epistle of S. Paule too the Ephesians.* Trans. Arthur Golding. London, 1577.

———. *Sermons of M. John Calvin upon the Epistle of Saincte Paule to the Galathians.* Trans. Arthur Golding. London, 1574.

———. *A very profitable treatise, made by M. John Calvyne, declaryinge what great profit might come to al christendome, yf there were a regester made of all Saintes bodies and other reliques.* Trans. Steven Wythers. London, 1561.

Cardwell, Edward H. J. *Documentary Annals of the Reformed Church of England 1546–1716.* 2 vols. Oxford, 1844.

Carpenter, Richard. *The Conscionable Christian, or the Indevour of Saint Paul.* London, 1623.

Crosse, Henry. *Vertues Common-wealth.* London, 1603.

Dod, John, and Richard Cleaver. *A Plaine and Familiar Exposition on the Ten commandments with a . . . Catechisme.* 3d ed. London, 1606.

Donne, John. *The Sermons.* Ed. George R. Potter and Evelyn Simpson. 10 vols. Berkeley: University of California Press, 1953–1962.

Du Jon, François, the Younger. *The painting of the ancients in three books.* London, 1638.

Dyke, Jeremiah. *Good Conscience: Or a Treatise shewing the Nature, Meanes, Marks, Benefit and Necessity Thereof.* London, 1624.

F., P. *The Historie of the damnable life, and deserved death of Doctor John Faustus.* London, 1592.

Ford, John. *'Tis Pity She's a Whore.* In *Drama of the English Renaissance: The Stuart Period,* ed. Russell A. Fraser and Norman Rabkin. New York: Macmillan, 1976.

Foxe, John. *Actes and Monuments.* London, 1563.

——. *Actes and Monuments.* London, 1570.

——. *Actes and Monuments of John Foxe.* Ed. Stephen Reed Cattley. With an introduction by George Townsend. 8 vols. London, 1837–1841.

Gallonio, Antonio. *De S.S. Martyrum Cruciatibus.* Rome, 1594.

The Geneva Bible. Geneva, 1560.

Gosson, Stephen. *The Ephemerides of Phialo.* London, 1579.

——. *Plays Confuted in Five Actes.* London, 1582.

——. *The School of Abuse.* London, 1579.

Heywood, Thomas. *An Apology for Actors.* London, 1612.

"An Homily Against perill of Idolatrie and superfluous decking of Churches in the time of Queen Elizabeth." In *Certain Sermons or Homilies appointed to be read in Churches in the Time of Queen Elizabeth I.* London, 1623.

Jenner, Thomas. *The Soules Solace; or Thirtie and one Spiritual Emblems.* London, 1631.

Knewstub, John. *Lectures of John Knewstub Upon the Twentieth Chapter of Exodus.* London, 1577.

Kyd, Thomas. *The Spanish Tragedy.* In *Drama of the English Renaissance: The Tudor Period,* ed. Russell A. Fraser and Norman Rabkin. New York: Macmillan, 1976.

Machyn, Henry. *The Diary of Henry Machyn.* Ed. John Gough Nichols. London, 1848.

Marlowe, Christopher. *Doctor Faustus: A- and B-texts (1604, 1616).* Ed. David Bevington and Eric Rasmussen. Manchester: Manchester University Press, 1993.

Melanchthon, Philip. *A newe work concerning both partes of the sacrament to be receyved of the lay people.* [Zurich], 1543.

Middleton, Thomas. *The Revenger's Tragedy.* In *Drama of the English Renaissance:*

The Stuart Period, ed. Russell A. Fraser and Norman Rabkin. New York: Macmillan, 1976.

———. *Women Beware Women.* Ed. Charles Barber. Berkeley: University of California Press, 1969.

Middleton, Thomas, and William Rowley. *The Changeling.* Ed. George Walton Williams. Lincoln: University of Nebraska Press, 1966.

Milton, John. "Samson Agonistes." In *The Complete Poetry and Selected Prose of John Milton,* ed. Merritt Hughes. Indianapolis: Odyssey Press, 1957.

Nashe, Thomas. *Pierce Penniless his Supplication to the Devil.* Ed. Stanley Wells. London: Edward Arnold, 1964.

Parker, Robert. *A scholasticall discourse against symbolizing with Antichrist in ceremonies.* Amsterdam, 1607.

Perkins, William. *A Discourse of the Damned Art of Witchcraft.* N. p., 1608.

———. *A Warning against the idolatrie of the last times.* Cambridge, 1601.

———. *The Whole Treatise of the Cases of Conscience.* Cambridge, 1608.

Porder, Richard. *A sermon of Gods fearefull threatnings for idolatrye mixing of religion, retayning of Idolatrous remnaunts, and other wickedness.* London, 1570.

Rainolds, John. *The Overthrow of Stage-playes.* London, 1599.

Rankins, William. *A Mirrour of Monsters.* London, 1587.

Ridley, Nicholas. "A Brief Declaration of the Lord's Supper, or A Treatise against the Error of Transubstantiation." In *The Works of Bishop Ridley,* ed. Henry Christmas, vol. 39. Cambridge, 1843.

———. *A friendly farewell.* London, 1559.

———. "A Treatise of Dr. Nicholas Ridley . . . Concerning Images, that they are not to be set up nor worshipp'd in Churches." In *The Works of Bishop Ridley,* ed. Henry Christmas, vol. 39. Cambridge, 1843.

Rymer, Thomas. "A Short View of English Tragedy" (1693). In *Critical Essays of the Seventeenth-Century,* ed. J. E. Spingarn, 2:208–55. Bloomington: Indiana University Press, 1957.

Scultetus, Abraham. *A Short Information, but agreeable unto Scripture: of Idol-Images.* Trans. Gotthard Voegehu. London, 1620.

Shakespeare, William. *The Complete Works.* Ed. Alfred Harbage. Baltimore: Penguin Books, 1969.

Sidney, Sir Philip. *An Apology for Poetry.* Ed. Forrest G. Robinson. Indianapolis: Bobbs-Merrill, 1970.

Stowe, John. *Survey of London* (1603). Oxford: Clarendon Press, 1908.

Tourneur, Cyril. *The Atheist's Tragedy.* Ed. Irving Ribner. Cambridge: Harvard University Press, 1964.

Tyndale, William. *An Answer to Sir Thomas More's Dialogue.* Ed. Henry Walter. Cambridge, 1850.

Veron, John. *A stronge battery against the idolatrous invocation of the dead Saintes, and against the having or Setting by of Images in the house of prayer.* London, 1562.

Webster, John. *The Duchess of Malfi.* Ed. John Russell Brown. Cambridge: Harvard University Press, 1964.

———. *The White Devil.* Ed. John Russell Brown. Cambridge: Harvard University Press, 1960.

Wilson, Thomas. *A Christian Dictionarie.* London, 1612.
Wood, William. *A Fourme of Cathechizing in true religion.* London, 1581.
Woolton, John. *Of the Conscience.* London, 1576.
Wriothesley, Charles. *A Chronicle of England During the Reigns of the Tudors.* Ed. William Douglas Hamilton. 2 vols. London, 1877.

Secondary Texts

Alexander, Gina. "Bonner and the Marian Persecutions." In *The English Reformation Revised,* ed. Christopher Haigh, pp. 157–75. Cambridge: Cambridge University Press, 1987.
Alpers, Svetlana. *The Art of Describing: Dutch Art in the Seventeenth Century.* Chicago: University of Chicago Press, 1983.
Andrews, Michael C. "Honest Othello: The Handkerchief Once More." *Studies in English Literature 1500–1900* 13 (1973): 273–84.
Ardolino, Frank. "The Hangman's Noose and the Empty Box: Kyd's Use of Dramatic and Mythological Sources in *The Spanish Tragedy* (III. iv-vii)." *Renaissance Quarterly* 30 (1977): 334–40.
——. " 'In Paris? Mass, and Well Remembered!': Kyd's *The Spanish Tragedy* and the English Reaction to the St. Bartholomew's Day's Massacre." *The Sixteenth-Century Journal* 21 (1990): 401–9.
Aston, Margaret. *England's Iconoclasts.* Vol. 1, *Laws against Images.* Oxford: Oxford University Press, 1988.
Baines, Barbara J. "Kyd's Silenus Box and the Limits of Perception." *Journal of Medieval and Renaissance Studies* 10 (1980): 41–51.
Baker, Steven. "Sight and a Sight in *Othello.*" *Iowa State Journal of Research* 61 (1987): 301–9.
Barber, C. L. *Creating Elizabethan Tragedy: The Theater of Marlowe and Kyd.* Ed. Richard P. Wheeler. Chicago: University of Chicago Press, 1988.
Barish, Jonas. *The Antitheatrical Prejudice.* Berkeley: University of California Press, 1981.
Battenhouse, Roy W. *Shakespearean Tragedy: Its Art and Its Christian Premises.* Bloomington: Indiana University Press, 1969.
Baxandall, Michael. *The Limewood Sculptors of Renaissance Germany.* New Haven: Yale University Press, 1980.
Belsey, Catherine. *The Subject of Tragedy: Identity and Difference in Renaissance Drama.* London: Methuen, 1985.
Berger, John. *Ways of Seeing.* London: Penguin, 1972.
Berry, Ralph. *The Art of John Webster.* Oxford: Clarendon Press, 1972.
Bliss, Lee. *The World's Perspective: John Webster and the Jacobean Drama.* New Brunswick, N.J.: Rutgers University Press, 1983.
Bloom, Harold. Introduction to *Christopher Marlowe's* Doctor Faustus, ed. Harold Bloom, pp. 1–11. New York: Chelsea House, 1988.
Boose, Lynda B. "Othello's Handkerchief: 'The Recognizance and Pledge of Love.' " *English Literary Renaissance* 5 (1975): 360–74.

Bouwsma, William J. *John Calvin: A Sixteenth-Century Portrait.* Oxford: Oxford University Press, 1988.

Breitenberg, Mark. "The Flesh Made Word: Foxe's *Acts and Monuments.*" *Renaissance and Reformation* 25 (1989): 381–407.

——. "Reading Elizabethan Iconicity: *Gorboduc* and the Semiotics of Reform." *English Literary Renaissance* 18 (1988): 194–217.

Broude, Ronald. "Time, Truth, and Right in *The Spanish Tragedy.*" *Studies in Philology* 68 (1971): 130–45.

Bryant, James. *Tudor Drama and Religious Controversy.* Macon, Ga.: Mercer University Press, 1984.

Burke, Kenneth. "Revolutionary Symbolism in America." In *The Legacy of Kenneth Burke,* ed. Herbert W. Simons and Tevor Melia, pp. 292–95. Madison: University of Wisconsin Press, 1989.

——. *A Rhetoric of Motives.* Berkeley: University of California Press, 1950.

Bynum, Caroline Walker. "The Body of Christ in the Later Middle Ages: A Reply to Leo Steinberg," *Renaissance Quarterly* 30 (1986): 399–439.

——. *Holy Feast and Holy Fast: The Religious Significance of Food to Medieval Women.* Berkeley: University of California Press, 1987.

——. *Jesus as Mother: Studies in the Spirituality of the High Middle Ages.* Berkeley: University of California Press, 1982.

Calderwood, James L. "Appealing Property in *Othello.*" *University of Toronto Quarterly* 57 (1988): 353–75.

——. *To Be or Not to Be: Negation and Metadrama in* Hamlet. New York: Columbia University Press, 1983.

Cannon, Charles K. " 'As in a Theater': *Hamlet* in the Light of Calvin's Doctrine of Predestination." *Studies in English Literature* 11 (1971): 203–22.

Charney, Maurice. *Style in* Hamlet. Princeton: Princeton University Press, 1969.

Christensen, Carl C. *Art and the Reformation in Germany.* Athens: Ohio University Press, 1979.

Coats, Catharine. *(Em)bodying the Word: Textual Resurrections in the Martyrological Narratives of Foxe, Crespin, de Beze, and d'Aubigné.* New York: Peter Lang, 1992.

Cohen, Walter. "The Reformation and Elizabethan Drama." *Shakespeare Jahrbuch* 120 (1984): 45–52.

Collinson, Patrick. *The Birthpangs of Protestant England.* New York: St. Martin's, 1988.

——. *From Iconoclasm to Iconophobia: The Cultural Impact of the Second English Reformation.* Reading: University of Reading Press, 1986.

——. *Godly People: Essays on English Protestantism and Puritanism.* London: Hambledon, 1983.

——. *The Religion of Protestants.* Oxford: Oxford University Press, 1982.

Couliano, Ioan P. *Eros and Magic in the Renaissance.* Trans. Margaret Cook. Chicago: University of Chicago Press, 1987.

Coursen, Herbert R., Jr. *Christian Ritual and the World of Shakespeare's Tragedies.* Lewisburg, Pa.: Bucknell University Press, 1976.

Crew, Phyllis Mack. *Calvinist Preaching and Iconoclasm in the Netherlands, 1544–1569.* Cambridge: Cambridge University Press, 1978.

Crewe, Jonathan V. "The Theatre of the Idols: Marlowe, Rankins, and Theatrical Images." *Theatre Journal* 36 (1984): 321–33.

Crockett, Bryan. *The Play of Paradox: Stage and Sermon in Renaissance England.* Philadelphia: University of Pennsylvania Press, 1996.

Cropper, Elizabeth. "The Beauty of Woman: Problems in the Rhetoric of Renaissance Portraiture." In *Rewriting the Renaissance*, ed. Margaret W. Ferguson, Maureen Quilligan, and Nancy J. Vickers, pp. 175–90. Chicago: University of Chicago Press, 1986.

Daston, Lorraine. "Marvelous Facts and Miraculous Evidence in Early Modern Europe." *Critical Inquiry* 18 (1991): 93–124.

Davidson, Clifford. "The Anti-Visual Prejudice." In *Iconoclasm vs. Art and Drama*, ed. Clifford Davidson and Ann Eljenholm Nichols, pp. 33–46. Kalamazoo, Mich.: Medieval Institute, 1988.

Davies, Horton. *Worship and Theology in England from Cranmer to Hooker, 1534–1604.* Princeton: Princeton University Press, 1970.

Davis, Natalie Z. *Society and Culture in Early Modern France.* Palo Alto: Stanford University Press, 1975.

Dawson, Anthony B. "Performance and Participation: Desdemona, Foucault, and the Actor's Body." In *Shakespeare, Theory and Performance*, ed. James Bulman, pp. 29–45. New York: Routledge, 1996.

Dickens, A. G. *The English Reformation.* New York: Schocken, 1964.

Diehl, Huston. "Parody, Irony, and Inversion: The Visual Rhetoric of Renaissance English Tragedy." *Studies in English Literature 1500–1900* 22 (1982): 197–209.

——. " 'Reduce Thy Understanding to Thine Eye': Seeing and Interpreting in *The Atheist's Tragedy*." *Studies in Philology* 78 (1981): 47–60.

Dolan, Frances E. *Dangerous Familiars: Representations of Domestic Crime in England, 1550–1700.* Ithaca: Cornell University Press, 1994.

——. "Taking the Pencil Out of God's Hand: Art, Nature, and the Face-Painting Debate in Early Modern England." *PMLA* 108 (1993): 224–39.

Dollimore, Jonathan. "*Doctor Faustus* (ca. 1589–1592): Subversion Through Transgression." In *Christopher Marlowe's* Doctor Faustus, ed. Harold Bloom, pp. 105–14. New York: Chelsea, 1988.

Donaldson, Ian. *The Rapes of Lucretia.* Oxford: Clarendon Press, 1982.

Dowling, Maria, and Peter Lake, eds. *Protestantism and the National Church in Sixteenth-Century England.* London: Croom Helm, 1987.

Duffy, Eamon. *The Stripping of the Altars: Traditional Religion in England, c. 1400–c.1580.* New Haven: Yale University Press, 1992.

Egan, Robert. *Drama within Drama.* New York: Columbia University Press, 1975.

Eire, Carlos M. N. *War against the Idols: The Reformation of Worship from Erasmus to Calvin.* Cambridge: Cambridge University Press, 1986.

Erickson, Peter. *Patriarchal Structures in Shakespeare's Drama.* Berkeley: University of California Press, 1984.

Finke, Laurie A. "Painting Women: Images of Femininity in Jacobean Tragedy." *Theatre Journal* 36 (1984): 357–70.

Forker, Charles R. *The Skull beneath the Skin: The Achievement of John Webster.* Carbondale: Southern Illinois University Press, 1986.

Foxgraver, David. "Self-Examination in John Calvin and William Ames." In *Sixteenth-Century Essays and Studies: Later Calvinism* 22 (1994): 451–69.

Freedberg, David. *Iconoclasts and Their Motives.* Maarssen, Netherlands: Gary Schwartz, 1985.

———. *The Power of Images: Studies in the History and Theory of Response.* Chicago: University of Chicago Press, 1989.

———. "The Representation of Martyrdoms During the Early Counter-Reformation in Antwerp." *Burlington Magazine* 118 (1976): 128–38.

Friedlander, Max J., and Jakob Rosenberg. *The Paintings of Lucas Cranach.* Rev. ed. London: Sotheby Parke Burret, 1978.

Frye, Roland Mushat. *The Renaissance Hamlet.* Princeton: Princeton University Press, 1984.

Garber, Marjorie. " 'Vassal Actors': The Role of the Audience in Shakespearean Tragedy." *Renaissance Drama* 9 (1979): 71–89.

Gardiner, Harold C. *Mysteries' End: An Investigation of the Last Days of the Medieval Religious Stage.* New Haven: Yale University Press, 1946.

Garner, Shirley Nelson. " 'Let Her Paint an Inch Thick': Painted Ladies in Renaissance Drama and Society." *Renaissance Drama* 20 (1989): 123–39.

Garrard, Mary D. "Artemisia and Susanna." In *Feminism and Art History: Questioning the Litany,* ed. Norman Broude and Mary D. Garrard, pp. 147–71. New York: Harper & Row, 1982.

Garside, Charles. *Zwingli and the Arts.* New Haven: Yale University Press, 1966.

Gasper, Julia. *The Dragon and the Dove: The Plays of Thomas Dekker.* Oxford: Clarendon Press, 1990.

Gatti, Hilary. *The Renaissance Drama of Knowledge: Giordano Bruno in England.* New York: Routledge, 1989.

Geertz, Clifford. *The Interpretation of Cultures.* New York: Basic Books, 1973.

Gibson, Gail McMurray. *The Theater of Devotion: East Anglican Drama and Society in the Late Middle Ages.* Chicago: University of Chicago Press, 1989.

Gillies, John. *Shakespeare and the Geography of Difference.* Cambridge: Cambridge University Press, 1994.

Gilman, Ernest B. *Iconoclasm and Poetry in the English Reformation: Down Went Dagon.* Chicago: University of Chicago Press, 1986.

Goldberg, Dena. *Between Worlds: A Study of the Plays of John Webster.* Waterloo, Ont.: Wilfrid Laurier University Press, 1987.

Graham, Kenneth J. E. *The Performance of Conviction: Plainness and Rhetoric in the Early English Renaissance.* Ithaca: Cornell University Press, 1994.

Grant, Patrick. "Imagination in the Renaissance." In *Religious Imagination,* ed. James Mackey, pp. 86–101. Edinburgh: Edinburgh University Press, 1986.

Greenblatt, Stephen. *Renaissance Self-Fashioning.* Chicago: University of Chicago Press, 1980.

———. *Shakespearean Negotiations.* Berkeley: University of California Press, 1988.

Gregerson, Linda. *The Reformation of the Subject: Spenser, Milton, and the English Protestant Epic.* Cambridge: Cambridge University Press, 1995.

Gunby, D. C. "*The Duchess of Malfi*: A Theological Approach." In *John Webster*, ed. Brian Morris, pp. 181–204. London: Benn, 1970.

Haigh, Christopher, ed. *The English Reformation Revised*. Cambridge: Cambridge University Press, 1987.

Haller, William. *The Rise of Puritanism*. 2d ed. Philadelphia: University of Pennsylvania Press, 1984.

Hallstead, R. N. "Idolatrous Love: A New Approach to *Othello*." *Shakespeare Quarterly* 19 (1968): 107–24.

Hamilton, Donna B. *Shakespeare and the Politics of Protestant England*. Lexington: University Press of Kentucky, 1992.

——. "*The Spanish Tragedy*: A Speaking Picture." *English Literary Renaissance* 4 (1974): 203–17.

Harris, Anthony. *Night's Black Agents: Witchcraft and Magic in Seventeenth-Century English Drama*. Totowa, N.J.: Rowman and Littlefield, 1980.

Hattaway, Michael. *Elizabethan Popular Theater*. London: Routledge and Kegan Paul, 1982.

Heinemann, Margot. *Puritanism and Theatre: Thomas Middleton and Opposition Drama under the Early Stuarts*. Cambridge: Cambridge University Press, 1980.

Helgerson, Richard. *Forms of Nationhood*. Chicago: University of Chicago Press, 1992.

Holborn, Hajo. *A History of Modern Germany: The Reformation*. New York: Alfred A. Knopf, 1959.

Howard, Jean E. *The Stage and Social Struggle in Early Modern England*. New York: Routledge, 1994.

Hunter, G. K., and S. K. Hunter. *John Webster: A Critical Anthology*. Baltimore: Penguin, 1969.

Jones, Eldred. *Othello's Countrymen: The African in English Renaissasnce Drama*. London: Oxford University Press, 1965.

Justice, Steven. "Spain, Tragedy, and *The Spanish Tragedy*." *Studies in English Literature 1500–1900* 25 (1985): 271–86.

Kaula, David. "*Hamlet* and the Image of Both Churches." *Studies in English Literature 1500–1900* 24 (1984): 241–55.

——. "Othello Possessed: Notes on Shakespeare's Use of Magic and Witchcraft." *Shakespeare Studies* 2 (1966): 112–32.

Kay, Carol McGinnis. "Deception through Words: A Reading of *The Spanish Tragedy*." *Studies in Philology* 74 (1977): 20–38.

Keeble, N. H. *The Literary Culture of Non-conformity in Later Seventeenth-Century England*. Leicester: Leicester University Press, 1987.

Kemp, Anthony. *The Estrangement of the Past: A Study in the Origins of Modern Historical Consciousness*. New York: Oxford University Press, 1991.

Kendall, R. T. *Calvin and English Calvinism to 1649*. Oxford: Oxford University Press, 1979.

Kendall, Ritchie D. *The Drama of Dissent: The Radical Poetics of Nonconformity, 1380–1590*. Chapel Hill: University of North Carolina Press, 1986.

King, John N. *English Reformation Literature: The Tudor Origins of the Protestant Tradition*. Princeton: Princeton University Press, 1982.

Kirsch, Arthur. "The Polarization of Erotic Love in *Othello*." *Modern Language Review* 73 (1978): 721–40.

——. *Shakespeare and the Experience of Love*. Cambridge: Cambridge University Press, 1980.

Kirschbaum, Leo. "Religious Values in *Doctor Faustus*." In *The Plays of Christopher Marlowe*, Cleveland: World Publishing, 1962. In *Twentieth-Century Interpretations of* Doctor Faustus, ed. Willard Farnham, pp. 77–87. Englewood Cliffs, N.J.: Prentice-Hall, 1969.

Kittredge, George Lyman. "Notes." In *The Tragedy of Othello*, ed. George Lyman Kittredge. Boston: Ginn, 1941.

Klinck, Dennis R. "Calvinism and Jacobean Tragedy." *Genre* 11 (1978): 333–58.

Koch, Robert A. "Venus and Amor by Lucas Cranach the Elder," *Record of the Art Musuem of Princeton University* 28, no. 1 (1969): 54.

Knapp, Jeffrey. "Preachers and Players in Shakespeare's England." *Representations* 44 (1993): 29–59.

Knapp, Robert S. *Shakespeare—The Theater and the Book*. Princeton: Princeton University Press, 1989.

Knights, L. C. *Further Explorations*. London: Chatto and Windus, 1965.

Knott, John R. *Discourses of Martyrdom in English Literature, 1563–1694*. Cambridge: Cambridge University Press, 1993.

Lake, Peter. *Moderate Puritans and the Elizabethan Church*. Cambridge: Cambridge University Press, 1982.

Lentricchia, Frank. "An Analysis of Burke's Speech." In *The Legacy of Kenneth Burke*, ed. Herbert W. Simons and Trevor Melia, pp. 292–95. Madison: University of Wisconsin Press, 1989.

Levine, Laura. *Men in Women's Clothing: Anti-theatricality and Effeminization, 1579–1642*. Cambridge: Cambridge University Press, 1994.

Lewalski, Barbara. *Protestant Poetics and the Seventeenth-Century Religious Lyric*. Princeton: Princeton University Press, 1979.

Lichtenstein, Jacqueline. "Making Up Representations: The Risks of Femininity." *Representations* 20 (1987): 77–87.

Loewenstein, David. *Milton and the Drama of History: Historical Vision, Iconoclasm, and the Literary Imagination*. Cambridge: Cambridge University Press, 1990.

Loomba, Ania. *Gender, Race, Renaissance Drama*. Manchester: Manchester University Press, 1989.

Luckyj, Christina. *A Winter's Snake: Dramatic Form in the Tragedies of John Webster*. Athens: University of Georgia Press, 1989.

MacCabe, Colin. "Abusing Self and Others: Puritan Accounts of the Shakespearean Stage." *Critical Quarterly* 30 (1988): 3–17.

Marcus, Leah S. "Textual Indeterminacy and Ideological Difference: The Case of *Doctor Faustus*." *Renaissance Drama*, n.s. 20 (1989): 1–29.

Maus, Katherine Eisaman. "Horns of Dilemma: Jealousy, Gender, and Spectatorship in English Renaissance Drama." *ELH* 54 (1987): 561–83.

——. *Inwardness and Theater in the English Renaissance*. Chicago: University of Chicago Press, 1995.

McGee, Arthur. *The Elizabethan Hamlet.* New Haven: Yale University Press, 1987.

Mebane, John. *Renaissance Magic and the Return of the Golden Age.* Lincoln: University of Nebraska Press, 1989.

Miles, Margaret. *Image as Insight: Visual Understanding in Western Christianity and Secular Culture.* Boston: Beacon Press, 1985.

Milward, Peter. *Shakespeare's Religious Background.* Bloomington: Indiana University Press, 1973.

Montrose, Louis Adrian. "The Purpose of Playing: Reflections on a Shakespearean Anthropology." *Helios* 7 (1980): 51–74.

Mullaney, Steven. *The Place of the Stage: License, Play, and Power in Renaissance England.* Chicago: University of Chicago Press, 1988.

Murray, Timothy. "*Othello*'s Foul Generic Thoughts and Methods." In *Persons in Groups; Social Behavior as Identity Formation in Medieval and Renaissance Europe,* ed. Richard C. Trexler, pp. 67–77. Binghamton, N.Y.: Medieval and Renaissance Texts and Studies, 1985. Expanded in "*Othello*, An Index and Obscure Prologue to the History of Foul Generic Thoughts." In *Shakespeare and Deconstruction,* ed. Douglas G. Atkins and David M. Bergeron, pp. 213–43. New York: Peter Lang, 1988.

Neill, Michael. "Unproper Beds: Race, Adultery, and the Hideous in *Othello.*" *Shakespeare Quarterly* 40 (1989): 383–412.

Newman, Karen. *Fashioning Femininity and English Renaissance Drama.* Chicago: University of Chicago Press, 1991.

Nicholl, Charles. *The Reckoning: The Murder of Christopher Marlowe.* Chicago: University of Chicago Press, 1992.

O'Connell, Michael. "The Idolatrous Eye: Iconoclasm, Anti-Theatricalism, and the Image of the Elizabethan Theater." *ELH* 52 (1985): 279–310.

Orkin, Martin. "Othello and the 'plain face' of Racism." *Shakespeare Quarterly* 38 (1987): 166–88.

Orlin, Lena Cowen. *Private Matters and Public Culture in Post-Reformation England.* Ithaca: Cornell University Press, 1994.

Ozment, Steven. *The Reformation in the Cities.* New Haven: Yale University Press, 1975.

Panofsky, Erwin. *The Life and Art of Albrecht Dürer.* Princeton: Princeton University Press, 1943.

Patterson, Annabel M. *Censorship and Interpretation.* Madison: University of Wisconsin Press, 1984.

——. *Shakespeare and the Popular Voice.* Cambridge, Mass.: Basil Blackwell, 1989.

Phillips, John. *The Reformation of Images: Destruction of Art in England, 1535–1660.* Berkeley: University of California Press, 1973.

Rose, Mark. "Conjuring Caesar: Ceremony, History, and Authority in 1559." In *True Rites and Maimed Rites: Ritual and Anti-Ritual in Shakespeare and His Age,* ed. Linda Woodbridge and Edward Berry, pp. 256–69. Urbana: University of Illinois, 1992.

Rose, Mary Beth. *"The Expense of Spirit": Love and Sexuality in English Renaissance Drama.* Ithaca: Cornell University Press, 1988.

Rosenberg, Jakob. "Lucas Cranach the Elder: A Critical Appreciation." *Record of the Art Musueum of Princeton University* 28, no. 1 (1969): 27–53.

Ross, Lawrence J. "The Meaning of Strawberries in Shakespeare." *Studies in the Renaissance* 7 (1960): 225–40.

Rothwell, Kenneth S. "Hamlet's 'Glass of Fashion': Power, Self, and the Reformation." In *Technologies of Self*, ed. Luther H. Martin, Huck Gutman, and Patrick Hutton, pp. 80–98. Amherst: University of Massachusetts Press, 1988.

Rowlands, John. *Holbein*. Oxford: Phaidon Press, 1985.

Rozett, Martha Tuck. *The Doctrine of Election and the Emergence of Elizabethan Tragedy*. Princeton: Princeton University Press, 1984.

Rudnytsky, Peter L. "The Purloined Hankerchief in *Othello*." In *The Psychoanalytic Study of Literature*, ed. Joseph Reppen and Maurice Charney, pp. 169–90. Hillsdale, N.J.: Analytic Press, 1985.

Sachs, Arieh. "The Religious Despair of Doctor Faustus." *Journal of English and German Philology* 63 (1964): 625–47.

Sanders, Wilbur. "Doctor Faustus' Sin." In *Christopher Marlowe's Doctor Faustus*, ed. Harold Bloom, pp. 27–45. New York: Chelsea House, 1988.

Scarisbrick, J. J. *The Reformation and the English People*. Oxford: Basil Blackwell, 1984.

Schade, Werner. *Cranach: A Family of Master Painters*. Trans. Helen Sebba. New York: G. P. Putnam's Sons, 1980.

Scribner, R. W. *For the Sake of Simple Folk: Popular Propaganda for the German Reformation*. Cambridge: Cambridge University Press, 1981.

——. *Popular Culture and Popular Movements in Reformation Germany*. London: Hambledon Press, 1987.

Shuger, Debora. *Habits of Thought in the English Renaissance*. Berkeley: University of California Press, 1990.

Siemon, James R. *Shakespearean Iconoclasm*. Berkeley: University of California Press, 1985.

Snow, Edward A. "Marlowe's *Doctor Faustus* and the Ends of Desire." In *Christopher Marlowe's* Doctor Faustus, ed. Harold Bloom, pp. 47–75. New York: Chelsea House, 1988.

——. "Sexual Anxiety and the Male Order of Things in *Othello*." *English Literary Renaissance* 10 (1980): 384–412.

Stachniewski, John. "Calvinist Psychology in Middleton's Tragedies." In *Three Jacobean Revenge Tragedies: A Selection of Critical Essays*, ed. R. V. Holdsworth, pp. 226–46. Basingstoke, 1990.

——. *The Persecutory Imagination: English Puritanism and the Literature of Religious Despair*. Oxford: Clarendon Press, 1991.

Stallybrass, Peter. "Patriarchal Territories: The Body Enclosed." In *Rewriting the Renaissance*, ed. Margaret W. Ferguson, Maureen Quilligan, and Nancy Vickers, pp. 123–42. Chicago: University of Chicago Press, 1986.

Strauss, Gerald. "How to Read a *Volksbuch*: The *Faust Book* of 1587." In *Faust Through Four Centuries*, ed. Peter Boerner and Sidney Johnson, pp. 27–39. Tübingen: Max Niemeyer Verlag, 1989.

Taylor, Gary. "Forms of Opposition: Shakespeare and Middleton." *English Literary Renaissance* 24 (1994): 283–314.

Tennenhouse, Leonard. "Violence Done to Women on the Renaissance Stage." In *Violence of Representation: Literature and the History of Violence*, ed. Nancy Armstrong and Leonard Tennenhouse, pp. 77–97. London: Routledge, 1989.

Thomas, Keith. *Religion and the Decline of Magic*. New York: Scribners, 1971.

Traister, Barbara. *Heavenly Necromancers: The Magician in English Renaissance Drama*. Columbia: University of Missouri Press, 1984.

Tricomi, Albert H. *Anticourt Drama in England 1603–1642*. Charlottesville: University of Virginia Press, 1989.

Turner, Victor. *The Anthropology of Performance*. New York: PAJ Publishing, 1987.

——. *Drama, Fields, and Metaphors: Symbolic Action in Human Society*. Ithaca: Cornell University Press, 1974,

——. *The Ritual Process*. Chicago: University of Chicago Press, 1969.

Waddington, Raymond B. "Lutheran Hamlet." *English Language Notes* 27 (1989): 27–42.

Watt, Tessa. *Cheap Print and Popular Piety, 1550–1640*. Cambridge: Cambridge University Press, 1991.

Wayne, Valerie. "Historical Differences: Misogyny and *Othello*." In *The Matter of Difference*, ed. Valerie Wayne, pp. 153–79. Ithaca: Cornell University Press, 1991.

Weiner, Andrew D. *Sir Philip Sidney and the Poetics of Protestantism: A Study of Contexts*. Minneapolis: University of Minnesota Press, 1978.

Wheeler, Richard. "Since First We Were Discovered: Trust and Authority in Shakespearean Romance." In *Representing Shakespeare: New Psychoanalytic Essays*, ed. Murray M. Schwartz and Coppelia Kahn, pp. 150–69. Baltimore: Johns Hopkins University Press, 1980.

Whitaker, Virgil K. *The Mirror Up to Nature*. San Marino, Ca.: Huntington Library, 1965.

White, Helen C. *Tudor Books of Saints and Martyrs*. Madison: University of Wisconsin Press, 1963.

White, Paul. *Theatre and Reformation*. Cambridge: Cambridge University Press, 1993.

Wilks, John S. *The Idea of Conscience in Renaissance Tragedy*. New York: Routledge, 1990.

Williams, George Huntson. *The Radical Reformation*. Philadelphia: Westminster Press, 1962.

Woodbridge, Linda. *The Scythe of Saturn: Shakespeare and Magical Thinking*. Urbana: University of Illinois Press, 1994.

Woodman, David. *White Magic and English Renaissance Drama*. Rutherford, N.J.: Fairleigh Dickinson University Press, 1973.

Yates, Frances A. *The Art of Memory*. Chicago: University of Chicago Press, 1966.

——. *Giordano Bruno and the Hermetic Tradition*. Chicago: University of Chicago Press, 1964.

——. *Theatre of the World*. Chicago: University of Chicago Press, 1969.

Index

Accommodation, doctrine of, 102–3
Actes and Monuments (Foxe), 22–52, 100–
102, 114–16; illustrations in, 11–14,
46–53, 63, 185–94; revolutionary
rhetoric of, 43–53; theatricality in, 24–
25, 40–42
Adultery, 166–69, 179
Aesthetics. *See* Protestant aesthetics
Ainsworth, Henry: *An Apologie or Defense of
. . . Brownists*, 159n; *An Arrow against
Idolatrie*, 17, 71n, 152n, 159n
Alexander, Gina, 97
Allin, Edmund, 28–31, 39
Alpers, Svetlana, 86n
Altar, 107
Altarpiece, 54
Ames, William, 202
Andrews, Michael C., 127n
Antitheatricality, 64–66, 173–81, 215–17;
and early modern drama, 64–66, 81–
82, 91, 152–54, 178–81; and
gynophobia, 176–78; and
Protestantism, 5, 65–66, 69–71, 82,
118, 173–76; and racism, 152–54; and
the seductive power of the stage, 70–
71, 76–77, 175–78, 217
Anton, Robert, 176n
Apology for Actors, An (Heywood), 71–72,
84, 89, 205–7
Ardolino, Frank, 112n, 119n
Ash Wednesday, 40–41
Aston, Margaret, 2n, 20n, 68n, 164n,
165, 172n
Atheism, 74, 145
Atheist's Tragedy, The (Tourneur), 145

Baines, Barbara J., 119n
Baker, Steven, 148n
Bale, John, 53, 139, 215
Barber, C. L., 95n, 117
Barish, Jonas, 64, 174–75
Basel, 17, 40–41, 43
Battenhouse, Roy W., 3n
Baxandall, Michael, 9, 170n
Beauty, 156–58, 164–66, 168–69, 179
Belsey, Catherine, 157n
Berger, John, 61n
Berry, Ralph, 195n
Beza, Theodore, 69n
Bible: access to, 29–30, 60; displaced by
image and theater, 16, 70; *The Geneva
Bible*, 132–33, 168; image of, 11, 52;
individual's right to interpret, 29–30,
60; language of, 64; Old Testament
narratives, 54, 58; passages from, 57–
58, 71, 152–53, 161; Protestant
mastery of, 32–33; substituted for
image, 44
Bliss, Lee, 195n, 209n
Bloom, Harold, 73n
Book of Martyrs (Foxe). *See Actes and
Monuments*
Boose, Lynda B., 126n, 148–49
Bouwsma, William J., 67n, 69n, 91, 102,
197n
Bradshaw, William, 165n
Breitenberg, Mark, 23n
Broude, Ronald, 112n
Browne, Thomas, 141n
Bruno, Giordano, 74–76
Bryant, James, 6n

Bucer, Martin, 49, 84n, 102, 103, 121, 134n, 152n
Burke, Kenneth, 43, 163, 182, 193n
Bynum, Caroline Walker, 101n, 161n

Calderwood, James L., 90n, 157n
Calvin, John: on art, 38, 84; *The Catechisme*, 38n, 87n; *Commentary on Hebrews*, 135–36; on conscience, 201; on empathy, 186; on faith, 135–36, 142; *Four godlye sermons*, 103n, 152n, 198n; on images and relics, 16, 129–32, 151–52, 159–60, 163; on imagination, 69–70, 84; on *Imago Dei*, 87–89; *Institutes of the Christian Religion*, 73n, 84–90, 103–8, 122n, 130n, 132n, 142n, 151n, 152n, 159n, 160n, 183–84n, 201; on knowledge, 142, 183, 183–84n; on reflexivity, 91; on sacraments, 99n, 101–11; *Sermons upon the Book of Job*, 186; *Sermons upon Ephesians*, 69–70, 73n, 84n, 87n, 88n, 105n, 142, 164n; *Sermons upon Galathians*, 84n, 89n, 103n; on sinners, 90; on spectacle, 85; on suffering, 197–98n; on *theatrum mundi*, 73, 86–87; *A very profitable treatise*, 16, 130n, 131n, 163n
Calvinism, 67, 72, 75–77, 86, 182–83, 202
Cannon, Charles, 87n
Cardmaker, John, 47
Cardwell, Edward H. J., 83n
Carpenter, Richard, 202n
Changeling, The (Middleton), 143–44, 166–68, 170n, 171–72; and iconophobia, 171–72; and idolatrous love, 166–68; and interpretation, 143–44
Charney, Maurice, 90n
Christensen, Carl C., 15n, 17n, 41, 84n, 134n, 158n
Church, traditional, 1–2, 94–96, 211
Church of England, 77, 97, 99n, 109
Church of Rome, 32–35, 41, 74, 80, 128, 159
Cleaver, Richard, 88n, 161, 165–66n
Coats, Catharine, 46
Cohen, Walter, 82n
Collinson, Patrick, 2n, 63–64, 67n, 68n, 99n
Communion table, 11–13, 107. *See also* Lord's Supper

Conscience, 28, 82, 111, 182, 200–208, 216
Couliano, Ioan, 67–68, 69n, 83, 164n, 180
Council of Trent, 74
Coursen, Herbert R., Jr., 3n
Cranach, Lucas, 53, 58–59, 61–64
Crew, Phyllis Mack, 21n, 162n
Crewe, Jonathan V., 68n, 69n, 174n
Crockett, Bryan, 7, 182n
Cropper, Elizabeth, 159n
Crosse, Henry, 19–20, 70n, 176n
Crucifix, 48–49, 101, 179
Cultural performance, 3n, 97–98, 117

Dance Round the Golden Calf (Van Leyden), 53–55
Daston, Lorraine, 138, 144
Davidson, Clifford, 96
Davies, Horton, 80n, 97, 99n, 100n, 107n, 119n
Davis, Natalie Z., 162n
Dawson, Anthony B., 95n–96n
Debnam, Robert, 26–27
Defense of the stage, 71–73, 83–84, 89–92, 205–8, 213–14
Dekker, Thomas, 6
Despair, 204
Devil(s), 78, 138–41, 179, 204; women as, 168. *See also* Sign: demonic; Theater: demonic
Dickens, A. G., 67n, 99n
Diehl, Huston, 145n, 148n
Doctor Faustus (Marlowe), 72–81, 85, 92, 151; and magic, 75–76; and ritual of desacralization, 79–81; and theatricality, 77–79, 92; and Wittenberg, 72–75
Dod, John, 88n, 161, 165–66n
Dolan, Frances, 152n, 159n
Dollimore, Jonathan, 74n
Donaldson, Ian, 61n
Donne, John, 134
Doubt. *See* Thomas, Doubting
Dowling, Maria, 2n
Du Jon, François the Younger, 85n
Duchess of Malfi, The (Webster), 4, 143, 166, 170n, 182–85, 194–14; and conscience, 203–5; and interpretation, 143; and martyrdom, 197–98; and spectacle, 183–84; and spectatorship, 194–201, 208–10; and theatricality, 183–85, 208

Duffy, Eamon, 2n, 13, 16, 39, 122–23
Dumb show, 83, 111, 196
Dürer, Albrecht, 56–58
Dyke, Jeremiah, 202

Edward VI, king of England, 12, 16, 19
Egan, Robert, 90n
Eire, Carlos M. N., 15n, 16n, 41n, 133n, 172n
Election, doctrine of. *See* Predestination
Elizabeth I, queen of England, 1, 3, 19, 20, 22, 25, 94
Empiricism, 28, 129, 134
Epistemology: crisis of, 136, 143, 147, 171
Erickson, Peter, 157n
Eros, 164–70, 175–76; and images, 147, 158–60, 164, 169–70; and theater, 70–71, 78–79, 154, 177–78
Eucharist. *See* Communion table; Lord's Supper; Mass; Sacrament; Transubstantiation, doctrine of
Eve, 59, 148, 166

Faith, 78, 121, 124, 133–42, 147, 216. *See also* Justification by faith
Faustbuch, 73, 75–76
Finke, Laurie A., 172n
Ford, John, 166
Forker, Charles R., 195n
Four Apostles, The (Dürer), 54, 56–58
Foxe, John: on conscience, 202–3; on iconoclasm, 11–14, 17–18, 26–52; on images, 26–28, 31–39, 139–41, 163n; on martyrdom, 185–94, 197–98, 202–3; on memory of the dead, 122; on sacraments, 28–31, 34, 100–103, 103–7n, 114–17; on signs, 131n, 139–41. *See also Actes and Monuments*
Foxgraver, David, 202
Freedberg, David, 11n, 54n, 162n, 189n
Friedlander, Max J., 59
Frye, Roland Mushat, 82n, 87n

Gallonio, Antonio, 188–90
Garber, Marjorie, 199n
Gardiner, Harold C., 2n
Gardiner, Stephen, bishop of Winchester, 17–18, 24, 140n
Garner, Robert, 26–27

Garner, Shirley Nelson, 159n
Garrard, Mary D., 61n
Garside, Charles, 16n, 84n, 158n, 163
Gasper, Julia, 6
Gatti, Hilary, 74n
Gaze: erotic, 157–59, 180, 216; devotional, 53–54, 57, 100–101, 114–15, 159, 161; idolatrous, 216; male, 59–62; reformation of, 46–63. *See also* Sight
Geertz, Clifford, 3, 4–5n, 95, 97n
Ghost, 143–46, 209
Gibson, Gail McMurray, 101, 128n, 131n, 137n, 161n
Gillies, John, 126n, 152n
Gilman, Ernest B., 7, 68n
Goldberg, Dena, 182n, 195n
Gosson, Stephen, 24, 65–66, 70, 173n, 176–78
Graham, Kenneth J. E., 214n
Grant, Patrick, 70n
Greenblatt, Stephen, 7, 104, 108–9, 157n
Gregerson, Linda, 4n
Guilt, 88–90, 111, 200–205, 209
Gunby, D. C., 204n
Gynophobia, 148, 159–61, 164, 167, 172, 177–79. *See also* Misogyny

Haigh, Christopher, 2n, 13
Haller, William, 67n
Hallstead, R. N., 167n
Hamilton, Donna B., 6, 113n
Hamlet, 4, 67, 81–93; and dramatic theory, 83–87, 111–12, 205; and ghost, 145–46; and interpretation, 149–50; and memory of the dead, 123–24; and the play-within-the-play, 89–91, 110–12, 119–20; and Protestant aesthetics, 82–91, 110–12; and theatricality, 81–83; and Wittenberg, 72, 82
Handkerchief, 130–32, 142; Abragarus', 130; Desdemona's, 125–28, 146–49, 151, 154; Hieronimo's, 113; Paul's, 132–33; Veronica's, 130, 132; Virgin Mary's, 130
Harris, Anthony, 126n
Hattaway, Michael, 113n
Heinemann, Margot, 6
Helgerson, Richard, 22–23

Heywood, Thomas, 6, 71–72, 205–7. *See also Apology for Actors, An*
Holborn, Hajo, 75
Homily Against perill of Idolatrie, 140n, 160, 163n, 171n, 175
Howard, Jean, 174

Iconoclasm, 1–4, 11–28, 35–41, 215–17; at Basel, 17, 40–43; inner, 164–65; and Rood of Dovercourt, 26–28; and Rood of Grace, 21; site of, 210; as symbolic killing of the beloved, 158, 161–63, 172, 180–81, 217
Iconoclastic rhetoric. *See* Rhetoric: iconoclastic
Idol, 40, 133; inner, 67–69, 164–66; theater as, 70–71. *See also* Idolatry; Image
Idolatry: and erotic love, 164–70, 179, 216; and mourning, 121–22; and relics, 131–33; as spiritual whoredom, 160–62; and theater, 69–71, 173–78, 215–16; traditional religion attacked as, 1–2, 16–17, 34–36, 47, 50–52, 54; as the worship of strange gods, 152–54. *See also* Gaze; Idol; Image; Sight
Image: abused and unabused, 36–39, 83–84, 121, 133–34; as artifice, 15, 34–39, 85–87, 160, 169–70, 173, 177–78, 196; of Counter-Reformation, 188–89; efficacious 9–11; erotic, 168–69; fear of, 9–14, 22, 139, 154, 160–61, 164, 167, 172, 178–81; love of, 4, 9–14, 20, 158, 181; royal, 18; sacred, 154, 158, 179; stage, 4, 147–49, 183–84. *See also* Iconoclasm; Idol; Idolatry; Ocular proof; Sign; Spectacle
Imagination, 67–71, 76, 79, 81, 84, 150–55, 163–65, 180. *See also* Eros; Magic
Imago Dei, 87–89
Institutes of the Christian Religion. See Calvin, John
Interiority, 58, 90–91. *See also* Protestant aesethics
Interpretation, 88, 133–34, 143–50
Italy, 74, 166, 175

Jenner, Thomas, 115–16
John, St., 57–58, 106

Johnson, Francis, 159n
Jones, Eldred, 127n
Jud, Leo, 16
Judgment, 202–3, 206. *See also* Conscience; Last Judgment
Judith (Cranach), 58–59, 61
Julius Caesar (Shakespeare), 143
Justice, Steven, 112n
Justification by faith, 76

Karlstadt, 72, 158
Kaula, David, 82n, 127n, 153n
Kay, Carol McGinnis, 113n
Keeble, N. H., 214n
Kemp, Anthony, 24, 42, 44–45
Kendall, R. T., 67n
Kendall, Ritchie D., 5n, 14, 53
Killing, 112–16, 120, 156, 162–63, 172, 180–81, 217. *See also* Sacrifice
King, John, 6n, 23n
King, Robert, 26–28
King Lear, 7, 104, 217
Kirsch, Arthur, 157n, 167n
Kirschbaum, Leo, 73–74n
Kittredge, George Lyman, 167n
Klinck, Dennis R., 182n
Knapp, Jeffrey, 7
Knapp, Robert S., 6n, 95n
Knewstub, John, 161n
Knights, L. C., 74n
Knott, John R., 25n, 198n, 214n
Koch, Robert A., 61n
Kyd, Thomas, 3, 64, 92, 95, 112–14, 117–21, 123, 216. *See also Soliman and Perseda*; *Spanish Tragedy, The*

Lake, Peter, 2n
Last Judgment, 50–52, 204
Lentricchia, Frank, 43
Levine, Laura, 64–65, 174
Lewalski, Barbara, 7
Lichtenstein, Jacqueline, 159n
Loewenstein, David, 216n
Lollards, Lollardy, 74, 80, 174
London, 97
Loomba, Ania, 152n
Lord's Supper, 95–11. *See also* Communion table; Mass; Sacrament; Transubstantiation

Love tragedy, 166–73, 178–81. *See also*
Changeling, The; Duchess of Malfi, The;
Othello; 'Tis Pity She's a Whore; White
Devil, The; Women Beware Women
Luckyj, Christina, 195n
Lucretia (Cranach), 58–63, 180
Luther, Martin, 59, 62, 72, 74–75, 82, 84,
134n, 172n
Lutheranism, 54, 59, 72–75

Macbeth (Shakespeare), 4, 143, 150
MacCabe, Colin, 175
Machyn, Henry, 19
Magic, 70, 75–80, 92, 94, 126–31, 134,
138, 147, 149–55, 164, 215. *See also*
Eros; Imagination; Magician
Magician, 78, 151. *See also* Magic; Priest
Marcus, Leah S., 77
Mark, St., 57–58
Marlowe, Christopher, 6, 64–66, 68–69n,
74–76; and Reformation, 72–74. *See also*
Doctor Faustus
Marsh, Nicholas, 26–28
Martyrdom, 24, 47–49, 52, 182, 203, 208,
210–11, 216; rhetoric of, 185–94, 197–
98. *See also* Actes and Monuments;
Gallonio, Antonio; Witness
Mary, the Virgin 148; image of, 9–11, 35–
38, 159–60, 162n, 172. *See also*
Handkerchief; Schöne Maria of
Regensberg; Virgin
Mary I, queen of England 19, 33
Mary Magdalene, 16, 159–60. *See also*
Whore
Mass, 34, 52, 80, 95–100, 103–9, 112,
115, 117, 119, 184. *See also* Altar;
Lord's Supper; Sacrament;
Transubstantiation
Maus, Katherine Eisaman, 136, 173n
McGee, Arthur, 89n
Mebane, John, 126n
Melancthon, Philip, 72, 130n
Memory, 101–2, 107, 111, 117, 134–36,
209; memory of the dead, 120–24. *See
also* Lord's Supper; Remembrance
Metadrama, 195, 204, 207. *See also* Play-
within-a-play
Middleton, Thomas, 6, 64, 213–16; love
tragedy, 166; and theatricality, 117–18.

*See also Changeling, The; Revenger's
Tragedy, The; Women Beware Women*
Midsummer Night's Dream, A (Shakespeare),
70, 98
Miles, Margaret, 16n, 22n, 100n, 158n,
159n, 163n, 172n
Milton, John, 166, 215–17
Milward, Peter, 3n
Mirror of nature, 82–86, 90. *See also*
Representation
Misogyny, 127, 153, 157, 170. *See also*
Gynophobia
Montrose, Louis Adrian, 94–95
Mullaney, Steven, 96n
Murder of Gonzago, The (Hamlet), 110, 120,
205
Murray, Timothy, 152n, 170n

Nashe, Thomas, 72
Neill, Michael, 148n, 152n
Newman, Karen, 127n, 148n, 152n,
157n
Nicholl, Charles, 75n

O'Connell, Michael, 96
Ocular proof, 125–26, 133–41, 148–49
Orkin, Martin, 152n
Orlin, Lena Cowen, 166
Ostendorfer, Michael, 9–10
Othello (Shakespeare), 4, 125–37, 146–58,
166–72, 180–81; and antitheatricality,
150–55; and Desdemona's
handkerchief, 125–30, 133–35, 146–49;
and faith, 135–37; and iconophobia,
170–71; and idolatrous love, 166–67;
and interpretation, 146–50; and killing
the beloved, 156–58, 172–73, 180–81;
and magic, 147–48, 150–55; and the
stranger, 152–54
Ozment, Steven, 22n

Panofsky, Erwin, 57n
Paradise Lost (Milton), 166
Parker, Robert, 160n, 162, 171n, 211
Patterson, Annabel M., 2, 86n
Paul, St., 57–58, 82, 132–37, 142
Perkins, William: *A Discourse of the Damned
Art of Witchcraft*, 138–39; *A Warning
against the idolatrie of the last times*, 67n,

Perkins, William (*continued*)
69n, 84n, 88n, 102, 111n, 152n, 165n,
175; *The Whole Treatise of the Cases of
Conscience*, 177–78, 201
Peter, St., 57–58, 139
Phagius, Paulus, 49
Phantasm, 67–71; and phantasmic
infection, 164. *See also* Eros;
Imagination
Phillips, John, 2n, 20n, 21n, 38n, 68n,
89n, 134n, 162n, 163n
Piety, popular, 1–4, 10–14, 172
Pilgrimage to the New Church at Regensberg
(Ostendorfer), 9–10
Pity, 185, 193, 195, 197–201, 208, 211–
12, 214
Plainness, 208, 213–14. *See also* Protestant
aesthetics
Player, 81, 199–200
Play-within-a-play, 110–18, 184. *See also*
Metadrama; *Murder of Gonzago, The*;
Representation; *Soliman and Perseda*
Pope, 74, 80, 139
Porder, Richard, 152n
Predestination, 182, 207
Prest's Wife, 31–35, 39, 153
Priest, 131, 139
Priesthood of all believers, 30
Protestant aesthetics, 38, 45, 82, 185,
208, 213–16. *See also* Interiority;
Plainness; Reflexivity; Skepticism
Protestantism. *See* Accommodation,
doctrine of; Calvin, John; Calvinism;
Church of England; Iconoclasm; Lord's
Supper; Predestination; Priesthood of
all believers; Sacrament
Protestant Reformation, 1–4, 82, 97
Puritanism, 6

Race, 127, 152–53
Rainolds, John, 24, 177
Rankins, William, 24, 69n, 70–71, 176,
178n
Reflexivity, 57–58, 89–91, 117–20, 191–
96, 200–3, 212. *See also* Protestant
aesthetics
Relic, 123, 127–31, 211
Remembrance, 83, 127, 134, 147, 149.
See also Memory; Lord's Supper
Repentance, 88

Representation, 38–39, 72, 84, 87–88,
90, 98, 105–16, 120–21, 149, 184. *See
also* Mirror of nature; *Theatrum mundi*;
Sign
Revenger's Tragedy, The (Middleton), 4, 121–
24; and idolatry, 123–24; and memory
of the dead, 121–22
Revenge tragedy. *See* Hamlet; *Revenger's
Tragedy, The*; *Spanish Tragedy, The*;
Women Beware Women
Revolutionary rhetoric. *See* Rhetoric
Reynolds, John, 165n
Rhetoric: iconoclastic, 62; of martyrdom,
185–94, 197–98; revolutionary, 42–45,
47, 50, 53, 61, 65. *See also* Protestant
aesthetics
Ridley, Nicholas: "A Brief Declaration of
the Lord's Supper," 101n, 116n; *A
friendly farewell*, 105n; "A Treatise of Dr.
Nicholas Ridley . . . Concerning
Images," 122n, 131, 152n, 158n, 161–
62.
Ritual, 94–98; of desacralization, 79, 155;
funereal, 122–23; of purification, 162;
Roman Catholic, 49–50
Rochus, 35–39
Roman Catholicism. *See* Church,
traditional; Church of Rome; Mass;
Piety, popular; Pope; Transubstantiation
Romance, 151, 154
Rome, 80
Rood of Grace, 21
Root of Dovercourt, 26–28, 48–49
Rose, Mark, 143n
Rose, Mary Beth, 158n
Rosenberg, Jakob, 61n
Ross, Lawrence J., 148n
Rothwell, Kenneth S., 82n
Rowlands, John, 21n
Rowley, William, 166
Rozett, Martha Tuck, 7, 95–97
Rudnystsky, Peter L., 148n
Ruins, 208–12
Rymer, Thomas, 125–30, 141, 146, 151,
153

Sachs, Arieh, 74n
Sacrament: controversies about, 75, 99,
109, 121; visible elements of, 28–31,
34, 80, 99–108, 115, 119. *See also*

Lord's Supper; Mass; Transubstantiation

Sacrifice, 156, 163, 180, 217. *See also* Killing

Saint, 179; female, 170–172

Saint's tale, 43–44

Samson Agonistes (Milton), 215–16

Sanders, Wilbur, 74n

Satan. *See* Devil(s)

Scarisburck, J. J., 2n

Schade, Werner, 61n

Schöne Maria of Regensberg, 9–11

Scribner, R. W., 11, 79, 154–55

Scripture. *See* Bible

Scultetus, Abraham, 20n, 102, 165n, 168n

Serpent, brass, 133

Shakespeare, William, 6, 7n; and antitheatricality, 150–55, 180–81; and the Protestant Reformation, 63–64, 69n, 217; and the status of signs, 144–46; and *theatrum mundi*, 72–73, 86–88, 92. *See also Hamlet*; *Julius Caesar*; *King Lear*; *Macbeth*; *Midsummer Night's Dream, A*; *Othello*; *Winter's Tale, The*

Shuger, Debora, 7, 129

Sidney, Sir Philip, 83–84

Siemon, James R., 7, 90n

Sight: bodily, 11, 52, 58, 100; and the conscience, 201–7; and erotic love, 164, 168–69; inward, 58, 142, 208–10, 216; modes of, 46, 53, 66, 88, 109, 98–101, 116–20, 149; and the problem of interpretation, 141–50; salvific, 98–100, 103, 119; self-reflexive, 57–58, 61, 118, 195–200; transcendent, 11–13, 52, 103, 208–10. *See also* Gaze; Image; Spectacle; Spectatorship; Vision

Sign, 36–39, 78, 83, 99, 102, 106–9, 115, 121, 150, 155; demonic, 138–39, 144; divine, 132–34, 138–41, 144; preternatural, 138; status of, 137–45, theatrical, 147–49. *See also* Image; Interpretation; Sacrament

Silence, 104, 114

Skepticism, 28–31, 77–78, 120, 143, 151

Snow, Edward A., 74n, 148n, 212

Social drama, 3n

Soliman and Perseda (*The Spanish Tragedy*), 113–17, 120. *See also Spanish Tragedy, The*

Somerset, Edward Seymour, Duke of (Lord Protector), 16, 18, 163

Spain, 25, 36, 112, 118, 166

Spanish Tragedy, The, 4, 112–20, 123–24. *See also Soliman and Perseda*

Spectacle, 216–17; of bodies and blood, 113–16, 119, 183; of the Mass, 99–100, 104–5; of state, 48–49; theatrical, 77–81, 92, 197. *See also* Spectatorship; Theatricality

Spectatorship, 90–91, 185–203, 206

Stachniewski, John, 6, 204n

Stallybrass, Peter, 158n

Stowe, John, 162n

Stranger, 32–33, 150–53

Strauss, Gerald, 73n, 75

Superstition, 27, 126, 130–32, 141, 143–46

Susanna, 61, 148

Taylor, Gary, 6

Taylor, John, 89n

Tennenhouse, Leonard, 172–73n

Theater: demonic, 53, 208, 215–16; divine, 73, 215–16; early Tudor, 5–6; godly, 53, 208; iconoclastic, 43

Theatricality, 72, 82–85, 90–91, 112, 154, 170, 173, 185, 214, 217; Protestant, 5, 14, 24–25, 41; Roman Catholic, 5, 14, 41, 65, 104–5, 119. *See also* Antitheatricality; Spectacle

Theatrum mundi, 73, 87, 91–92, 142, 193, 206–7. *See also* Representation

Thomas, Doubting, 137

Thomas, Keith, 16n, 128–29, 131, 149, 155

'Tis Pity She's a Whore (Ford), 166–69

Tourneur, Cyril, 145

Traister, Barbara, 126n

Transubstantiation, doctrine of, 30–31, 34, 106, 114–17. *See also* Mass

Tricomi, Albert H., 6

Trifle, 125–29, 134, 147, 149, 154. *See also* Handkerchief; Ocular Proof

Turner, Victor, 3, 98, 110n, 117

Tyndale, William, 132–33

Van Leyden, Lucas, 53–55, 63–64

Veron, John, 17, 20n, 86–88n, 101n, 130–31n, 133, 139–40, 151n, 156, 163n

Virgin, 148, 170–71, 180; image of, 170; problem of distinguishing between whore and, 148, 170–72, 180. *See also* Mary, the Virgin

Visions, 140–41, 204, 208–11. *See also* Ghost; Image; Sight; Spectacle; Spectatorship

Waddington, Raymond B., 82n
Warne, John, 47
Watt, Tessa, 22–23
Wayne, Valerie, 158n
Webster, John, 4, 6, 64; and Calvinism, 182–83; and love tragedy, 166; and Protestant aesthetics, 213–15. *See also* *Duchess of Malfi, The*; *White Devil, The*
Weiner, Andrew D., 83n
Wheeler, Richard, 157n
Whitaker, Virgil K., 83n
White, Helen C., 22, 23n
White, Paul, 5–6
White Devil, The (Webster), 4, 166, 170n, 172, 178–80; and iconophobia, 179; and idolatrous love, 166, 179; and theatricality, 178–79
Whore, 31–34, 156–57, 176–81; images as, 31, 33, 156, 160–62, 170–71; problem of distinguishing between

virgin and, 148, 170–72; Protestant association of Roman Church with, 34, 175; theater as, 176–77; Vittoria Corombona as, 178–79
Whore of Babylon, 34
Wilks, John S., 182n, 202n
Wilson, Thomas, 165n
Winter's Tale, A (Shakespeare), 87
Witchcraft, 150, 183
Witness, 187, 191–96, 201, 203, 206–7, 211–12. *See also* Conscience; Martyrdom
Wittenberg, 62, 67, 72, 74–75, 77n, 82
Women Beware Women (Middleton), 4, 117–18, 166–72; and iconophobia, 166–69; and idolatrous love, 166–68; and the play-within-a-play, 117–18
Wood, William, 67–68n, 69n
Woodbridge, Linda, 126n
Woodman, David, 126n
Woolton, John, 202
Word, 98, 103–5, 111, 114. *See also* Bible; Sacrament
Wriothesley, Charles, 19

Yates, Frances, 69n, 74n, 75n, 76, 87n

Zwingli, Ulrich, 16, 84, 158, 163